EMILY GREENE BALCH

To Judy,
I hope you find inspiration
in This life story, as I do.
Enjoy!
Keith

Emily Greene Balch

THE LONG ROAD TO INTERNATIONALISM

KRISTEN E. GWINN

University of Illinois Press

URBANA, CHICAGO, AND SPRINGFIELD

Library of Congress Cataloging-in-Publication Data
Gwinn, Kristen E.
Emily Greene Balch : the long road to internationalism /
Kristen E. Gwinn.
p.   cm. ˙
Includes bibliographical references and index.
ISBN-13: 978-0-252-03578-4 (hardcover : alk. paper)
ISBN-10: 0-252-03578-X (hardcover : alk. paper)
1. Balch, Emily Greene, 1867–1961. 2. Pacifists—United States—
Biography. 3. Women pacifists—United States—Biography.
4. Women and peace—History—20th century.
I. Title.
JZ5540.2.B35G85   2010
303.6'6—dc22 [B]   2010040227

For my mother, Crystal Mayo Gwinn

Contents

Illustrations

Acknowledgments

I extend my deepest thanks to Amy Becker, my partner, my muse, and my dedicated reader; to Louise W. (Lucy) Knight for friendship, mentorship, advice, insight, and support: she has been an invaluable sounding board and critical consultant throughout my revising process; to Sara Berndt for enthusiastic willingness to read countless excerpts and provide crucial feedback even at a minute's notice; to my family, especially Rick Gwinn and Fran Vogt, who have never stopped believing in me; to my mother and father, for everything; to the following friends, who have supported me and advised me through the final stages: Jeff Arena, Adelicia Cliffe, Valerie Gwinn, David Kaplan, Laura Langley, Melissa and Jason Suderman, and Lindsay Wells; to my coterie of friends and colleagues at The George Washington University, including Jennifer Bertolet, Stacy and Matt Bondurant, Andrew Hartman, Chris Hickman, Michael Landis, Bo Peery, Michael Weeks, and Andrew Zimmerman, for helping shape fragmented ideas into coherent historical work; Leo P. Ribuffo, whose mentorship and guidance have shaped and strengthened both this work and my own development as a historian; to the members of my doctoral committee who strengthened my research with their insight and criticism; to Don Pavoni, without whom I would still be writing the index; to Si Balch and his family for opening their home to me, sharing family papers, and confiding their memories; to Wendy Chmielewski, historian and curator at the Swarthmore College Peace Collection, who provided substantial advice throughout the research process: she and the entire staff at the Peace Collection ably assisted my archival research; to Wilma Slaight at Wellesley College's archive and to the staffs at the Radcliffe Institute of Harvard University, the Massachusetts Historical Society, and the Women's

Library in London for their guidance; to Northwestern University's Center for Historical Studies for supporting me with a visiting scholar appointment; to Joan Catapano and the University of Illinois Press for undertaking this project; to Mercedes Randall, without whom the early stages of this work would have been even more formidable: her thorough and loving tribute to Emily Greene Balch will remain a necessary reference for historians of the WILPF and those interested in Balch's life; to Emily Greene Balch for providing inspiration to those of us who wish to make the world a better place; and to the members of the Women's International League for Peace and Freedom who carry forward Balch's vision, work, and legacy.

EMILY GREENE BALCH

Introduction

"A Citizen of the World"

It is not surprising that few people know the name Emily Greene Balch. The stories of countless individuals from the past flit across our history pages, but very few wend their way into the public consciousness. We tend to uphold and preserve the memories of those who pursued grand achievements, those who became leaders of nations or groups, and those who invented revolutionary technologies. It is these individuals who, in one way or another, wield great influence over the masses and capture our attention.

In many ways, Emily Greene Balch was an ordinary citizen. She never ran for or held public office. She never served her government in an official capacity. Neither did she act as the sole founder or promoter of a new ideology. But she did make essential contributions to some of the major social reform movements of her day. She was an active participant in local, national, and international communities and politics. She was pioneering in her ideas and activities, consistently focused on the power of internationalism. The story of her life, as is the case with many others, contains lessons in history and inspiration for the future.

Who was Emily Greene Balch? She was an intellectually driven child who grew into a woman with an avid appetite for knowledge. Balch participated in a spectrum of social reform activities and authored many publications. A member of Bryn Mawr's first graduating class, she undertook two courses of graduate study, one in France and another, later, in Germany. She established herself as a leader of Boston's burgeoning settlement movement during the 1890s. In 1896, she accepted a teaching post at Wellesley College, where she remained for nearly twenty years and became widely published as a recognized scholar on American immigration. With the onset of the First World War, Balch joined her reform-minded colleagues and made great contributions to the international movement to secure an end to the war through neutral mediation. Following the war, the Wellesley College Board of Trustees refused to welcome her back; she then dedicated the remaining four decades of her life to the Women's International League for Peace and Freedom and became the principal organizer of its international office in Geneva. Her leadership culminated with worldwide recognition for her achievements; in 1946, she won the Nobel Peace Prize. Although Balch was a well-known academic and a leading figure in several movements for social reform, she remains an obscure figure in American history.[1]

Balch's forgotten place in our history contrasts with that of her close friend and colleague, the famous social reformer Jane Addams. Both women were active leaders in the settlement movement in the United States, and both were instrumental in the international women's peace movement. Intellectual curiosity and a moral compulsion drove them both; they were individuals of ideas as well as action. Most notably, both received the Nobel Peace Prize for their life achievements. Why, then, did Addams become such an icon in American history, while Emily Greene Balch moved to the periphery?

A difference in their personalities accounts, in part, for their relative degrees of fame. Addams was first and foremost a public figure, an icon. By contrast, Balch preferred organizing behind the scenes. Though certainly not afraid of public attention, Emily Greene Balch truly thrived in private meetings and negotiations. She gave numerous speeches in her life, but she tended toward expression through her published scholarship. In addition, Jane Addams arrived on the scene first. Addams's position as the first American woman to win the Nobel Peace Prize understandably relegates Balch to a position of comparison to the original. Whatever the reasons for Balch's relative historical obscurity, this book represents one important step in bringing her life and work back into the mainstream of progressive, reform, transnational, women's, and peace history.[2]

This work traces Emily Greene Balch's development from a civic-minded child to an avid scholar. It portrays her not as a woman *destined* to be a peace leader but instead as a scholar whose devotion and skills led to multiple careers. Balch's diverse professional experiences honed those talents that made her a successful peace activist in her later life. Her three careers—settlement worker, professor, peace organizer—offer a convenient outline for examining her life, but they also provide a window for understanding her personality and the forces that drove her. At nearly every turn, she was motivated equally by her intellectual curiosity and ambition as by a moral compulsion. This book thus considers what elements and individuals in her life inspired each of Balch's career choices. As the story of her life unfolds, certain threads become apparent. The most obvious is her desire to live a life of service.

Balch's deep and earnest commitment to improving her world, however, is only part of her story. Over these pages we meet a woman who secretly struggled with her ambition. We understand that Balch constantly pushed herself to be a better, more moral person. We empathize with her intense personal insecurity. We discern how she weighed her intellectual curiosity against her devotion to her family, and how she matured into a woman who consistently endeavored to follow her conscience. We are able to identify the trends that dominated her life: networks of women, intellectual demands, service and reform, pacifism, and diplomacy.

The life of Emily Greene Balch spanned from 1867 to 1961, from the Gilded Age to the cold war. She lived through the aftermath of the Civil War. She witnessed the incredible economic, social, and cultural changes that accompanied rapid industrialization and immigration in the United States. She assisted struggling workers to obtain better living and working conditions. She survived two world wars and campaigned to reduce the causes for conflict. In the midst of a rapidly changing world, Balch remained engaged with both her local and the increasingly close global community, and she refused to become discouraged when faced with personal or international upheaval. She witnessed a century of terrific change yet never lost hope (despite almost inconceivable global calamity) that the human community was working toward a new and improved world order. She consistently sought to arrive at fair and just solutions through methodical analysis.

Balch's ideas, in almost every context, shared a common denominator: internationalism. Although she did not originally conceive the term "global citizenship," she doggedly promoted it. Balch saw herself as part of a new generation of women. She and her peers viewed themselves as "citizens of the world, conscious partakers in the sacrament of all human life."[3] Balch's personal and public declarations of global citizenship were the product of a lifetime of learning the necessity of cooperation across national borders and loyalties. Balch continually advanced the concept of global citizenship as the path to peace. Further, in all facets of her life, she emphasized negotiation over conflict. Mediation and the promotion of peace remained constant driving forces in her life and are central elements of her legacy.

The prophetic ideas and interests of Emily Greene Balch continue to be surprising. Her mind was finely tuned to the issues of her day, and she had a knack for discerning and discussing those issues that would become central in the future. Her interest in immigration made her a pioneering scholar in that field. Well before the outbreak of the First World War, she wrote extensively about Pan-Slavism and nationalist movements in the Austro-Hungarian Empire, warning of the potential conflicts that would arise if they were not carefully mediated. Before and during World War I, she argued passionately to bring international attention to the problem of colonialism. She correctly foretold that war reparations would lead to an aggressive Germany. She revered the League of Nations as an attempt at internationalism but accurately pointed to flaws in its structure that would lead to its demise. In 1926, she urged the United States to withdraw from its imperialistic interest in Haiti. Like many of her peers, she campaigned throughout the 1930s against the rising tide of fascism. She urged her own government and, especially, the international community through the League of Nations to take steps to mitigate the economic and political factors that were edging the world close to another war.

Balch embraced pacifism and saw violence, militarism, and war as antithetical to progress. Yet pacifism for her was never an easy choice. She endured public approbation for her beliefs during the First World War. Still, she was not a moral absolutist. During the Second World War, she reconceived her views, determining that violence as a means was less threatening to progress than global fascism as an end. Balch's willingness to reexamine her perspective is telling: the defining characteristic throughout her life was diplomacy. She had many talents, but mediation, without question, was her strongest. She could listen for hours to various viewpoints and then brilliantly synthesize all aspects of the different arguments into a coherent and acceptable solution for all. She demonstrated this skill in numerous and varied capacities: on a daily level, when sitting around a conference table, or as a delegate to the Neutral Conference for Continuous Mediation, in 1916.

This book argues that Balch's professional development was an intellectual journey as well as a moral quest. I aim to uncover why Balch made the choices she did and what factors contributed to her decisions. Specifically, I explore why Balch chose academia over social work in the 1890s and why she chose international peace advocacy in 1919. Balch's leadership in the peace movement, which is the focus of most studies of her life, can only be understood following a survey of the decisions she made and experiences she had when she was younger. How she emerged as a leading figure in the international peace movement is only part of the narrative. This book reveals what led her to that point and how her personality and motivation for her work changed over time. Viewing Balch mainly as a peace leader and interpreting her life as a predetermined journey to that point muddies our understanding of who she was and how her ideas developed over time.

So, who was Emily Greene Balch? Most concisely, she was a progressive reformer turned peace advocate. Throughout this text, we gain an understanding of Balch's complex character. Her relationships and experiences reveal a woman who was at once a scholar, teacher, writer, reformer, diplomat, sister, daughter, friend, and leader.

1. "The Service of Goodness," 1867–85

An ordinary winter evening. A new suburban town on the edge of Boston. A solidly upper-middle-class family, having recently survived the personal and political challenges of the Civil War.[1] Two people deeply in love, and deeply committed to their family, their town, and their church.

This environment surrounded the birth of Emily Greene Balch. At 7:00 PM on January 8, 1867, a child who, seventy-nine years later, would receive the Nobel Peace Prize in recognition of her life of service, came into this world. The second daughter of Francis and Nelly Balch, the child was christened after her mother's dear friend, Emily Greene. She was born with what her maternal aunt called a "nice dark [head of] hair and a tolerable face."[2]

As is true for most individuals, whether or not they grow up to make noteworthy contributions in their world, Emily Greene Balch's character emerged during her childhood. These years held the most important influences: a foundation of family, religion, and education grounded young Emily in her commitment to a love of learning and a life of service. Understanding this is essential to understanding Emily Greene Balch.

Emily grew up in Jamaica Plain, a small, outlying section of Boston, Massachusetts. This town offered Emily and her family a rural environment as well as the many benefits of a neighboring city. Fields and parks dominated the landscape of her childhood; the large Jamaica Pond was just steps from her home. Emily and her siblings flourished in this bucolic environment. Although Boston and all its cultural and social offerings were only a brief train ride away, Jamaica Plain retained its suburban, almost rural character.

While Boston evolved into an industrial city, the Balch family and their town benefited from a wider American movement emphasizing the advantages of suburban living. With advances in transportation, particularly with regard to the local railroads, the suburbs of cities such as Boston expanded. As it became easier to travel into the city, the middle-class commuter community grew. Urban historian Henry Binford has calculated that the population of Boston's suburban communities expanded from 1,500 to 10,800 between 1846 and 1860. Suburban families such as the Balches could enjoy the employment and cultural luxuries of city life, yet they could still retreat to a removed domestic setting, thus avoiding many of the social and economic problems of the city, including ethnic tensions and the growth of slum neighborhoods.[3]

Emily's mother encouraged all her children to take advantage of their semirural setting, promoting vigorous outdoor activities and delighting especially in the winter experience of ice-skating on Jamaica Pond. Emily fondly remembered that she and her siblings devoted most of their early years to playing outdoors. Her Jamaica Plain childhood, being distant from some of the more overt dangers of urban living, allowed Emily a great deal of physical freedom.[4]

With the advent of new technology and expanding industrialization in the region, Emily witnessed firsthand the benefits of industrial society (though she remained more sheltered from its drawbacks). The railroads and telegraphs improved the speed of transport and communication. The changing industrial economy created great wealth (yet it also produced an industrial labor force pushed toward the bottom of the socioeconomic scale). Boston became a center for the wholesale production of foodstuffs and textiles and was well established as a national hub for the production and distribution of wool, boots, shoes, and leather. This booming economy created new fortunes and enhanced the preexisting prosperity of the professional class. It also changed labor, as specialization demanded the establishment of new, white-collar, managerial positions.[5]

Jamaica Plain contained a relatively diverse population, at least in terms of class, from farmers to a growing number of businessmen and professionals who, like Emily's father, commuted into the city for work. Both suburb and city also experienced high levels of population turnover during this period of rapid expansion, with a steadily growing flow of immigrants arriving in the city and then moving outward. During the mid-nineteenth century, Boston's immigrant population swelled with an influx of Irish Catholics. Irish workers provided the bulk of labor in Boston's ironworks, textiles, and shoe industries.[6]

Jamaica Plain itself housed many immigrants, mostly Irish and German. As its diversity increased, the community's classes remained segregated by income. Nearly every section of the town was subdivided into smaller areas, some with tenements and others with working-class dwellings. Close to these communities, but not necessarily abutting them, were the middle- and upper-middle-class neighborhoods. Given the separateness of immigrant communities in her hometown, it is not surprising that Emily was so little exposed to immigrants in her youth. Perhaps the only exception to this would be the Irish domestic servants her family employed. Emily fondly remembered the "Irish girls" who cared for the children, "whether as cook, second girl, or nurse."[7]

The time and place in which Emily grew up shaped her adult perspective on the world. Her childhood was marked by the privileges of living in the suburban setting of Jamaica Plain. Although she was likely sheltered in many ways from the major social debates of mid-nineteenth-century Boston, such as immigration and changing labor conditions, the part these issues played in her adult life shows that she was not entirely removed from them.

The Balch Family

Emily Greene Balch's family constituted the core focus of her young life. Her parents came from a long line of New England families. Francis Vergnies Balch and Ellen Maria Noyes Balch, known as Nelly, had known each other since childhood; in fact, they were first cousins. Emily always marveled at the depth of their love for each other, which they showered on their six children. She once described her mother as "the center of my life" and considered her father the "constant test and standard" by which she measured her own qualities.[8]

Nelly Balch grew up in Newburyport, Massachusetts, forty miles north of Boston. She came from a large family of six daughters and one son. Like her own daughters, Nelly benefited from a family that valued the education of girls. Although she was taught primarily at home, for a time she attended Ipswich Female Seminary. She passed on to her children (especially Emily) a love of languages, particularly Latin, French, and German.

During the Civil War Nelly moved with her family to Mattoon, Illinois, where she had a brief career as a teacher. While living in rural Illinois in wartime conditions, she recorded in her journal her affection for her first cousin, Francis Vergnies Balch, who frequently wrote to her. She felt the distance between them keenly. Revealing the depth of her feelings, she confided to her journal, "God knows how bitterly hard it is to me. God protect my darling wherever he may be, whatever he may do, give me strength to bear what is laid upon me." In the summer of 1862, Francis Balch joined the Union Army. When Nelly received the letter informing her of his enlistment, she reiterated, "May God protect him, my love and give me strength to bear what He may lay upon me. But oh it is hard, bitterly hard."[9]

By the end of 1862, though, both Francis and Nelly had returned to Jamaica

Balch family (Francis Vergnies Balch, standing; sitting from left to right:
Alice, Bessie, Anne, Madie, Emily, Frank). Emily Greene Balch Papers,
Swarthmore College Peace Collection.

Plain. Francis had fallen ill during his service, and Nelly went back home to
be near him. After surviving the painful separation during the early years of
the war, Nelly and Francis married in 1863 and settled into a happy marriage.
Writing in June 1865, Nelly commented that she felt great "content[edness]
in Frank's love and such happiness in our marriage." Emily Greene Balch
admired the depth of affection her parents had for each other. She considered
her mother "deeply loving" and "a fascinating personality." As an adult, Emily
fondly remembered, "[It was] no wonder my father loved her as he did."[10]

Francis Balch was greatly admired and respected in his community. The
son of wealthy Boston merchant Joseph Balch and his wife, Anne Lathrop
Noyes, Francis was born in 1835. His unusual name, Francis Vergnies, derived,
according to family legend, from a French Huguenot missionary in exile in

Massachusetts whom both the Balch and Noyes families held in great esteem (Nelly's own father was named Francis Vergnies Noyes). Though born in Boston, Francis Balch moved with his family at a young age to Jamaica Plain, where he received an elite education and was influenced by a staunch Puritan religious tradition.[11] His father's status as the president of a marine insurance company afforded Francis many opportunities as a young man. Wealth, however, did not protect him from a childhood plagued with sickness.

Chronically ill throughout his life, Francis had a nurse constantly by his side until age thirteen. This hardship of poor health, however, nurtured his love of books. Indeed, he credited much of his scholarly success to being a sickly child. He attended Harvard College and graduated at the top of his class in 1859. Delivering the class oration, Francis related how some boys dreamed of becoming scholars for different reasons, but that "those who love knowledge for its own sake are very few." Undoubtedly referring to himself, he continued: "Such love needs the sickly childhood, the stolen hours of study and of musing, the nervous, sensitive, scholarly temperament."[12] Francis Balch's love of learning continued throughout his life; it was an aspect of his personality he shared with all his children.

Following his college graduation, Francis was admitted to the Massachusetts Bar on April 9, 1861. Despite his physical limitations, he delayed his legal career in order to join the Union Army's Massachusetts Twentieth Regiment Volunteer Infantry; even though his education and social position would have allowed Francis to take a commission in the military, he opted to enlist instead. However, due to his poor health, his time in the service was extremely limited: he fell ill on one of his first marches and was thus forced to resign.[13]

After his recovery, Francis, instead of leaving government service altogether, became a clerk to United States senator Charles Sumner. The senator, one of the leading abolitionists in the nation, shared Francis's devotion to public service and civic duty. In addition to his renowned oratory skills, Sumner, like Francis, was a great scholar. Francis's service with Sumner revealed his political views, as he embraced Sumner's Radical Republicanism. In addition to learning considerably from Sumner, Francis undoubtedly contributed to the senator's legacy. He even drafted Sumner's first bill for the reform of the civil service. After the war, Francis remained close to Sumner, acting as his financial manager, and upon Sumner's death in 1874 he became executor of the senator's will.[14]

Francis did not begin his own law practice until 1868 or 1869. Although it took a few years for him to become established, his career was a success. He set up his own practice in Boston and worked mainly as a conveyancer, specializing in the examination of titles.[15]

Much of Francis Balch's character is reflected in the adult life of his second daughter, Emily. It was from him that she received her love of scholarship. Just as Emily was known as an avid diplomat, it was said of her father that "it was not in his nature to fight." Rather, his position was to "act the part of peacekeeper." His colleagues praised his character; his law partner declared that Francis "broke the Golden Rule only by exceeding it. His rule was, 'Do unto others' *better than* 'ye would that they should do unto you.'" Emily herself described her father as "a combination of Abraham Lincoln, Santa Claus and Jesus" and as "the most selfless person I have ever met." She wished to be just like him but felt she always fell short of such a description. Many disagreed with Emily's harsh self-criticism and praised her for exactly the same qualities that she admired in her father. John H. Randall Jr., historian and friend to Emily, once wrote of her that she "naturally devoted much selfless labour" to work for social justice. Randall also acknowledged Emily's "cool and dispassionate realism," which was another quality she shared with her father. As well, both Emily and Francis were known for being generous with money.[16]

Emily's parents encouraged a home environment that was both playful and intellectually creative. The siblings, consisting of five girls, Anne, Emily, Elizabeth, Alice, and Marion, and one son, Francis Noyes Balch, were a close-knit bunch. They frequently spent their evenings playing charades, acting out scenes, writing poetry, or engaging in some other playful word game. The children kept books of verse, in which they described the role and reputation of each family member; Emily's was that of scholar, organizer, and traveler. As the second child, she was an important role model for her younger siblings, but she was spared the obligation of becoming the female head of household when Nelly Balch died in 1884. That responsibility fell to the eldest daughter, Anne. The Balch children described Anne as the "head of the household" and "queen of us all."[17]

Religion and Social Change

Respectable, upper-middle-class families of late-nineteenth-century New England tended to affiliate with the Unitarian church, and the Balches were no exception. The family was dedicated to Jamaica Plain's First Church, which, during Emily Greene Balch's youth in the 1870s, was a hub of social gospel advocacy. Reform-minded liberal Protestants flocked to the church and others like it.[18] Despite its presence as a bastion of liberal theology, church membership consisted mainly of the town's elite families, including Francis Balch and his wife and children. Young Emily discovered a powerful mentor and salient inspiration through her family's church.

A strong and early church influence for Emily came in the person of Charles

F. Dole, who first arrived in Jamaica Plain in April 1876, when a group invited him to preach at Jamaica Plain's First Church. Dole did not know at the time that the church's minister, Dr. James Thompson, planned to retire, and the congregation was seeking a replacement. The congregation was greatly impressed with Dole and the church leaders extended an offer to him. He accepted, and he and his wife moved to Jamaica Plain in June 1876. Balch's father, a prominent member of the church, attended Dole's initiation on June 18, 1876.[19]

Although he accepted the position, Dole was concerned with the denominational change he was undertaking. Dole was a Congregationalist and disliked many elements of the Unitarian theology. He liked this particular church and its congregation, but he was reluctant to declare himself a Unitarian. The church leaders assured him this was unnecessary, that "Unitarians set no emphasis on denominational names." Dole was particularly intrigued with the church committee's attitude toward a diverse congregation, and prior to accepting the position he wrote to ask if "poor" or "working people" would be welcome in the church. When the committee replied in the affirmative, he could not refuse the position, as he "had always hoped for a church composed of all kinds of people." He felt his church in Jamaica Plain actually had no denominational designation, being rather a "people's church," which did not "sever its connection with other churches."[20]

For Charles Fletcher Dole, spiritual practice was closely associated with responsible living. Social progress and individual responsibility were at the heart of his teachings. He was so devoted to Congregationalism because he felt it wholly democratic and dedicated to the true responsibility of Christians to focus on social betterment and to abide by the Golden Rule, treating others as you would want to be treated. Notably, he believed that religion must "be inclusive of all kinds and conditions of men, on open basis of our common spiritual humanity."[21]

Emily Greene Balch's loyalty to Dole and her commitment to his ethical ideals were immediate. Though only ten years old when she first met the minister, "his noble conception of Right" appealed to her. Dole asked Emily if she was ready to commit herself "without limitations" to a life in "the service of goodness." She was. She later recalled that she considered her pledge to Dole "as genuinely as a nun taking her vows." Dole continued to serve as mentor as well as spiritual leader to Emily, and this strong bond with Dole, established so early in her life, strengthened over time.[22]

Emily's relationship with organized religion transformed as she grew older, yet the influence of Charles Fletcher Dole's theology on her moral development is without question. He challenged her at a young age to take on a lifetime of service to causes larger than herself. His concepts of right and wrong and his ideas about the citizen's responsibility in society profoundly shaped Emily's understanding of the world she lived in. Throughout her life Balch would return to lessons she learned from Dole. She once described him as "the chief . . . of all the influences that have played upon my life."[23] While she utilized this description for two or three other prominent figures in her experience, it was clear that he was among the pivotal characters in her youth.

A Woman's Education

The Balch family valued education, and young Emily thrived in the world of books. Her school days were happy ones; she greatly admired her teachers and established friendships with other young women who remained her confidants and influential friends throughout her life.

Emily first received schooling just down the street from her Jamaica Plain home. A local woman, Mrs. Walker, ran an elementary education school out of her home.[24] Emily attended classes daily, along with Frances Hayward, another girl from her neighborhood. Hayward was the daughter of the local doctor, and the two girls became fast friends and remained so for life. In their nineties, Emily and Hayward would visit, expressing the same enthusiasm to see each other as they had as schoolgirls. Even when Emily started attending school in Boston, she did not neglect her dear friend.

When she was thirteen years old, Emily began attending a small private school for girls in Boston's elite Back Bay neighborhood. On school days she would go by horse to the rail station at Green Street in Jamaica Plain and then catch a train that took her to Boston's Park Street station in fifteen minutes. She would then walk over to Miss Ireland's School at 9 Louisville Square.[25]

The school's head teacher, Catherine Innes Ireland, remained an almost romantic figure in the minds of her students, who, as adults, fondly remembered walking with their teacher at mid-morning recess to purchase sweet buns at a bakery on Charles Street. In addition to this warm memory, many also recalled Ireland's "ardent temperament" and how, as students at her school, they felt "not [merely] a little awe mingled with admiration and affection." For "her girls," she was both a role model and a teacher. As a single woman, Ireland emphasized women's abilities to act as agents of change in their own communities.[26]

Academies like Miss Ireland's were not uncommon in nineteenth-century New England. They were private schools funded by tuition from the students' parents and did not follow any sort of mandated curriculum. The school, as

Emily recalled, "was informal for its time, though less so than the modern progressive school" and took up two floors of a house; Ireland lived on a third level, above. In addition to the classrooms, the school also contained a small gymnasium, reflecting a view of well-rounded intellectual and physical health.[27]

The curriculum at the academy was informal but demanding. As a private school for girls, it had no "standardizing process" in place to influence the curriculum. Such schools were only beginning to educate women toward the goal of attending college. Although lacking a standard, college-preparatory curriculum, Miss Ireland's School, in Emily's opinion, "provided very personal, very inspiring teaching by a group of exceptional men and women." The school offered courses in history, mathematics, literature, Latin, French, and German. Although not all of Ireland's students attended college, the classes at the school did demand vigorous intellectual discipline. Emily once commented that Miss Ireland's had so solidly prepared the young women, many of those who later attended college found that "much of the work there offered seemed immature and mechanical beside some of the work done at school." In the years following Emily's attendance at the school, increasing numbers of female students continued their education.[28]

Emily formed lifelong friendships with many of the girls from school. Without question, the most prominent was with a girl named Helen Cheever. It is likely that the Balches had learned about the school from the Cheevers, as both families spent their summers in the coastal town of Cohasset, Massachusetts. Exactly when the two met is unclear, but the importance of their friendship was monumental. Helen was an upper-middle-class Back Bay socialite. The daughter of a Boston physician, David Cheever, Helen's wealth allowed her a great deal of freedom.[29] Throughout her life she would frequently draw on this power to assist Emily. But even as teenagers, Emily grew to depend on Helen for emotional support. It was Helen who was Emily's constant companion throughout the summer of 1884, when Nelly Balch lay dying after having contracted Bright's disease that summer while the family vacationed in Cohasset. Emily chose to remain with her mother for the course of the illness. Nelly finally succumbed on September 14.

Nelly Balch's early death at age forty-seven devastated her young family. For Emily, who was only seventeen, the event unquestionably had a profound effect on her. Although few letters exist between Emily and her mother, Nelly Balch nonetheless was a key figure in Emily's development. Emily acknowledged the intensity of her love for her mother and how deeply Nelly's early death scarred her. Toward the end of her own life, Emily wrote that her love for her mother "was the only passionate love I have ever felt."[30] It was not surprising that when her mother died, Emily's father, with whom she had always had a close relationship, became the central recipient of her familial devotion.

A few months after Nelly's death, Emily turned eighteen. She was stunted by her overpowering grief. On April 6, 1885, Emily briefly recorded in her diary, "suggested I should go abroad." What could only have been a reaction to her worsening outlook after the family's tragic loss, her father rapidly organized a monumental distraction. In the following day's entry, Emily noted only that the trip had been "decided."[31] A mere four days later she was on her way to Europe. Her first experience with international travel, while not much more than the conventional holiday for upper-class Americans, ignited a curiosity and wonder of other lands and cultures that would remain with Emily for the remainder of her life.

By the time of her first international adventure, Emily already possessed substantial knowledge about the world beyond the United States. Growing up in Boston, she must have been at least tangentially aware of the city's immigrant communities. She had learned German and French as a child, both at school and under her mother's tutorage. At Miss Ireland's School for Girls she added Latin and Greek to her expanding knowledge of languages.[32] Her education certainly included the history and politics of other nations. So before her final year of school, she welcomed this, her father's generous offer to visit foreign lands. The excitement she expressed as she traveled throughout Europe during the spring and summer of 1885 remained with her during numerous excursions overseas later in life. Although it was her first trip to Europe, Emily's focus during those months was less about increased international awareness than about distracting herself from the recent death of her mother.

A European sojourn was not an uncommon experience for those in Emily's peer group. Nineteenth-century Americans of her socioeconomic class embraced opportunities to travel abroad as integral to an individual's education and culture. Europe in particular drew the most visitors from this group. Emily's older sister Anne had visited Europe with their father a few years earlier, during the summer of 1883. Many young women in Emily's position spent a good deal of time planning their European expeditions, but her travels were organized rather suddenly; her father arranged for Emily to join a small group that had already scheduled a tour through Europe (a cousin through marriage, William Allen, was escorting his teenage daughter Katie and her friend, Minnie Spaulding, on their European summer tour). Had Emily dedicated more time to designing the excursion, perhaps she would have been able to travel with closer friends. The hastily made arrangements imply that the family, or at least Francis Balch, felt it necessary for

Emily to escape her grief and figure out what she wanted to do next, and although Emily had not been particularly close with her travel companions, she nevertheless found the situation agreeable. Writing to her sister during the sea voyage, she reported that the group made "a cozy little party and it is very pleasant." She later wrote home how much she enjoyed the company of her Allen cousins. She was more critical of the friend, Minnie Spaulding, but grew fonder of her as time passed.[33]

The group's European tour included the cities and cultural highlights of interest to most tourists. Historian Foster Rhea Dulles, discussing the appeal of European travel for Americans, wrote that "the opportunity to discover for themselves Europe's antiquities—the cathedrals, the castles, the palaces, the accumulated treasures of age-old art" proved particularly attractive to nineteenth-century Americans.[34] After a difficult crossing (Emily was seasick for most of the voyage), the four arrived in Gibraltar on April 24.

Undoubtedly, the most profound episode of the venture occurred early in the trip, and it provided a lesson Emily would never forget. Not long into their tour, the group returned to Gibraltar after visiting Tangier and Algeria. They waited for a steamer to take them to Malta but were delayed by the sudden possibility of war between Great Britain and Russia. Believing that this war would erupt before the next day, Emily excitedly wrote to her brother Frank, "There is a good deal of talk of what would happen if a Russian cruiser (in case of war being declared) should attack or pursue or capture us." While the group awaited word of their departure, their ship "filled with British office[r]s who, back from fighting Zulus and Afghans," had been "hurriedly ordered to rejoin their commands in India and elsewhere." Emily and her companions spent the day wondering what they would do if they were captured and ended up "cooling [their] heels in Moscow."[35]

The threat of war stemmed from a Russian border skirmish with Afghanistan. The British feared Russian encroachment on what they considered their buffer state, protecting India. Without a substantial delay, Emily's party reached Malta, and she later marveled that "the war with Russia that was believed to be immediate in April 1885 has not yet taken place." This knowledge led her to reflect, "Someone should write a history of inevitable wars that have failed to come off and why." The situation and its long-lasting message for Emily were serious; at age eighteen, she learned just how precarious international diplomacy could be. In 1885, however, the teenage girl was less insightful, as she confided to her brother that she saw the whole ordeal as "great fun."[36]

After this exciting introduction, the group spent nearly a month exploring Greece and Italy, stopping in Naples, Pompeii, Rome, Tivoli, Venice, and Milan. They visited amphitheaters, temples, palaces, and cathedrals. Emily was particularly impressed with the architecture, chapels, and works of art that she encountered in Italy. In Naples, the three girls participated in a three-day festival celebrating the "opening of the new water-works." Emily even saw King Francis II in a parade and reported to her sister that the king "is very fine looking, much more so than his portraits." The group also had the good fortune to witness "Vesuvius more or less in action." Emily excitedly described to her sister the experience of seeing the clouds and the hot lava of the great volcano, which was "strong enough to make a faint path of light across the bay."[37]

From Italy, they traveled through Switzerland, Germany, and Holland before spending a final month in Great Britain. There, Emily spent most of her time seeing the sights of London before she sailed home on July 29—returning to Boston with a renewed spirit for her final year at Miss Ireland's. During this period, she decided to enroll in college for the following autumn. Her decision to attend college revealed her deep dedication to scholarship and professional training; although she did not yet know what she would study or how she would apply that education, the decision itself was indicative of the sort of life she wanted to live.

2. "Characteristic of My Generation," 1885–96

In eighteen years Emily Greene Balch had grown into an intelligent woman with a passion for books and a dedication to learning. Yet she still lacked a direction for her life. Her journey through Europe had allowed her a respite from her grief, as well as time to consider her future. It was a time that demanded decisions. With her secondary schooling coming to a close, Balch undoubtedly felt the pressure to choose a path in life. She later insinuated that circumstances, rather than choice, directed her decision making during this period. By her own admission she was a "proud, sensitive and unattractive girl," and these facts left her limited during the critical years for courtship and engagement. She elaborated: "Family circumstances prevented my 'coming out' at the usual time as my sisters did, and the lack of this training, for which my unhappy dancing school hardly made up, still serves me as an excuse to myself for some of my still plentiful lack of social ease and savoir faire."[1] Her humorous, self-deprecating attitude worked to gloss over the possibility that, at age eighteen, Balch *preferred* books to romance.

In fact, more than her situation, it was Balch's character that shaped her decisions. The timing of her mother's death when Balch was just seventeen, certainly the "family circumstances" to which she referred, did affect her early life choices, but not as greatly as she later claimed. Her failure to marry, for example, cannot be solely attributed to her not having a formal "coming out" into society. After all, she had four sisters, all of whom came out, yet only one, Alice, ever married.

Balch was ambitious, but she wished not to seem so. She acknowledged her "pride" but downplayed its importance in her decision making. She enveloped her ambition in humor, writing that she focused on school because she did not want "to be, or appear to be, waiting to [be] courted—a possibility which seemed about as imminent as the judgment day millennium."[2] Perhaps she did wish to be courted. Perhaps she envisioned her wedding and marriage. If she did so, she never indicated such desires as a teenager, only in retrospect. When she was eighteen, Balch was mainly enamored of books and dedicated to the idea of living a life of service.

Balch's financial situation, which was solidly middle class (and certainly not wealthy), dictated that should she not marry, she would most likely have to become a professional. She was far from alone in this situation. Many women of Balch's generation faced a choice between marriage and profession. Both demanded the majority of women's time. The choice of one had a financial impact on the possibility of the other. Perhaps more important than these factors, though, was that Balch and many of her peers were influenced by a strong education. Their minds had been trained and their intellectual curiosity piqued. For many, domestic life held less appeal than pursuing that curiosity. Rather than combine work and family or give up the possibility of a career altogether, many women intentionally chose not to marry. Such was the case with Balch, whose intellectual desires and ambition drove her course of action.[3]

A College Education

Balch's plan to attend college emerged gradually. While in school, she had considered studying law, as her father had, but that idea did not last. During her European tour, she questioned her cousin Katie, who was then a student at the university in Madison where her father, William, taught history. Inspired by what she heard from Katie, she wrote to a friend that she was thinking about moving to Wisconsin to attend college. As Balch's thoughts began to center on her future, she grew anxious. She wrote to her sister that summer, "I wish I could arrive at a decision about my future course; sometimes I can not sleep for thinking about things, and it seems to me I get more and more undecided."[4]

Balch's anxiety and indecision did not result from family pressure or the expectation that she should or should not attend college. Rather, it stemmed from the fact that she had never personally met a woman who had completed a degree. During that era, only 0.24 percent of American women pursued a bachelor's degree. In fact, Balch had only ever heard of one such woman— Elizabeth Van Pelt—and she was a Cornell College graduate who, Balch later revealed, "was regarded as a curiosity."[5]

Even though the concept of college education for women was still uncommon in Balch's social circle in Boston, she grew to embrace the idea with enthusiasm. But she was still wary about undertaking the prospect alone. She discussed the idea with a friend from Miss Ireland's School, Alice Gould. The two corresponded throughout the summer, gradually unfolding a plan. Institutions of higher learning that were open to women were limited. The most sensible option was nearby Harvard College's "annex" for women (the institution that became Radcliffe College in 1893). However, the two could not attend the Harvard affiliate because Alice's father opposed the idea. Balch believed that Alice's father, renowned astronomer Benjamin Apthorp Gould, objected to his daughter's attending the college in Cambridge because he did not wish "to have it known among his Cambridge friends that he was disgraced by having a daughter at college."[6] Of course, Balch could have remained at home and attended the "annex" alone. That she did not consider this an option reveals the depth of her lingering anxiety. Balch and Gould decided that, as an alternative, they would attend the newly opened Bryn Mawr College on the outskirts of Philadelphia.

In August 1886 Balch and her father visited the Bryn Mawr campus. The college, founded by prominent Philadelphia Quaker Joseph Wright Taylor, had only recently opened its doors in 1885. Before his death, Taylor had envisaged that his endowment would create a women's college that would offer its students an academically rigorous education. It was, for example, the first institution of its kind to offer graduate programs to women. When Bryn Mawr opened with James Rhoades as its first president, a young female scholar, M. Carey Thomas, was named the first dean of the faculty. Thomas became the central figure in creating the successful institution that Bryn Mawr would become, and she personally worked to shape the Bryn Mawr women of Balch's generation. Thomas's influence on Balch's undergraduate education was unquestionably significant.[7]

Thomas, who had experienced great struggle with her own family in order to obtain a college education, determined to shape Bryn Mawr into an institution that offered women rare and challenging opportunities. Thomas dedicated most of her life to molding the school according to her own vision. She "believed that she was gaining for women precious resources for education."[8] Indeed she was. The college offered Balch more than a basic liberal arts curriculum.

During her college years, Balch worked exhaustively. She was determined to graduate in three years, to be a part of Bryn Mawr's first graduating class. Although she developed a coterie of friends, she often missed out on important social events in order to study. The friendships she did cultivate at college were mainly with other women of a similar devotion to academic excellence and social service. Women such as Helena Stuart Dudley and Alys Pearsall Smith became lifelong friends.

A notable individual in Balch's social life during her college years was Alice Gould. Though the two were never truly close friends at Miss Ireland's School for Girls, they remained roommates throughout their undergraduate years, even though, according to Balch's sister, Gould made Balch "supremely miserable."[9] Gould's background was similar to Balch's, and the two shared a passion for intellectual advancement. Both women were determined to graduate in only three years, and they succeeded. After Bryn Mawr, Gould continued her studies at both the Massachusetts Institute of Technology and Newham College in England, and she eventually earned a PhD in mathematics from the University of Chicago in 1894. Although Gould resided for most of her life in Spain, she continued a correspondence with Balch throughout their long lives.

While Balch developed a few friendships at Bryn Mawr, she did not neglect her friends and family at home. Particularly notable during these years was her correspondence with Helen Cheever, who remained Balch's stalwart support. After graduation from Miss Ireland's School for Girls, Cheever stayed at her family home in Boston. She attended art school and devoted much of her time to beneficent organizations. Cheever wrote often to her dear friend Balch, sending her regards to Alice Gould but carefully emphasizing that most of her letters were meant only for Balch's eyes. Cheever consistently reassured her friend regarding doubts about her college education, in one instance writing, "I feel sure that you will do something fine with all this knowledge (of which the Greek sounds to me especially hard and advanced)." Cheever continued her encouragement, reminding Balch on one occasion that "wherever you do it, among your sympathizing friends will your 'h. servant' always be found." At many points during her college years, Cheever provided assurances to Balch that she was on the right course and her dear friend back home was thinking of her. During a low point in 1887, Cheever wrote, "I know now just how homesick you must have felt after this winter." She was always quick to ease Balch's doubts about her studies and on one particular assignment she reminded her of her faith in her abilities, writing, "I am sure your essay will go off well. I know I should be proud of you if I could hear it."[10]

Despite Balch's occasional need for encouragement, her studies never suffered greatly from a lack of confidence. By her second year she had impressed Dean Thomas, who in 1887 wrote to her friend Mary Gwinn, describing Balch as "all round the most civilized girl in college." Thomas praised her student's intellect and demeanor, commenting, "Never in any quiz has she said anything but wisdom. She is brilliant and earnest and steady and thoughtful, and a lady, and as wily and wise a Sophomore as I ever expect to see again."[11]

Balch was devoted to her coursework and labored to earn the dean's praise. In the process, her academic interests evolved. When she began her coursework, Balch described her interests as "literary and historical," and so she chose Greek and Latin as a major.[12] But in her third and final year at Bryn Mawr, Balch's academic interests shifted from the classics to the field of study that would become her profession: economics. The influential force in this new intellectual pursuit was the "inspiring and original teacher Franklin Giddings." As a student of Giddings, Balch began to believe that her greater awareness of the social and economic conditions of her day required that she do more than spend her time studying classical languages. This growing consciousness, a common thread among progressive college students in her generation, convinced Balch to alter her path of study to economics and sociology, a decision bolstered in the coming years by the publication of a number of prominent books. Central to Balch's swelling commitment to social concerns was Jacob Riis's monumental study of New York tenements, *How the Other Half Lives,* and, a few years later, Helen Campbell's study, *Women Wage-Earners: Their Past, Their Present, and Their Future.* The emerging Progressive movement, the mentorship of Franklin Giddings, and scholarly emphasis on social conditions "found a repercussion" in Balch. She grew to feel "that this was no time for 'idle singers of an empty day.'"[13]

In the spring of 1889, Balch stood with twenty-three of her classmates for Bryn Mawr's first commencement ceremony.[14] She had reached her goal, but at a cost. Balch later conceded, "It was a disadvantage to everything but my vanity I squeezed so much work into those years." Concentrating so intently on her studies meant that she sacrificed what she later considered important social experiences. Denying herself even vacations, her hours were consumed by her studies. She had worked doggedly in order to graduate in three years but had not paused to determine what she would do next. Her hard work was nevertheless rewarded with an answer. In April 1889, Bryn Mawr announced its very first European Fellowship for graduate study would go to Emily Greene Balch.

The fellowship was M. Carey Thomas's brainchild. Having received her PhD from the University of Zurich, Thomas firmly believed that the opportunity to study at a foreign university would greatly enhance the education of any of her Bryn Mawr women. And Balch was exactly the woman she had in mind. In April, when the award committee announced Balch as the winner, Thomas was elated. The following day, Thomas exclaimed, "I could not sleep from excitement and delight."[15]

Bryn Mawr graduation, 1887. Emily Greene Balch Papers,
Swarthmore College Peace Collection.

Balch responded to her award with mixed feelings. She claimed that it
came as a "surprise," and she even tried not to accept it. Eventually, her father
persuaded her to claim the prize. Balch's response was not due solely to her
modesty; mainly, she was afraid. She felt "inadequacy" when faced with the
possibility of attending graduate school in Europe.[16] In order to calm her
anxiety and better prepare for study, she delayed her fellowship for a year.
During that time, she returned to her family home in Jamaica Plain and
studied under Giddings's direction, and eventually, at Giddings's encour-

agement, Balch decided ultimately to utilize her fellowship in France. The country lacked formal educational opportunities for women, but Balch never balked at a challenge. She welcomed the opportunity to better understand French culture and politics, and to improve her French.

Study in France

Balch's year in France would prove to be a challenging one, and she was grateful not to endure it alone. A schoolmate from Miss Ireland's School, Lena Fabens, accompanied her to Paris. Fabens kept Balch company and undoubtedly tried to comfort her friend as she became increasingly discouraged with attempts to find an appropriate educational path in France. The pair boarded with a French family in order to be immersed in the language and culture. Both women held quaint memories of their time in France, but for Balch the year abroad was "not very fruitful."[17]

Balch's intent when she sailed for Paris in September 1890 was to enhance her understanding of economics, politics, and sociology. Her pursuit of graduate-level education, however, was thwarted by the fact that educational institutions in Paris were unprepared and unwilling to educate women. Balch arrived in Paris to find herself "something of a curiosity."[18] She could not find formal courses that were open to women. At first, she kept busy attending evening lectures, for which she would walk across the city from her apartment in the Étoile quarter. Eventually, she gained permission to attend classes. This was pleasant enough, but not as intellectually demanding as Balch had hoped. Ultimately, she secured an independent study working with the renowned French professor Émile Levasseur.

Levasseur, chair of Geography, Economic History, and Statistics at the Collège de France, appeared to match Balch's diverse intellectual interests. He was an esteemed historian, economist, statistician, and geographer. His willingness to oversee Balch's studies that so initially pleased the young scholar in Paris ultimately led to disappointment, however, and Balch wrote home that that she received "practically no direction" from the eminent professor. She frequently expressed her irritation to her father regarding a seeming inability to develop her studies into something useful, saying that she spent her time attending lectures and reading "stupid books making endless and very pointless notes." Her frustration, in part, resulted from a lack of experience in independent study. To her father she confided, "I really have been and am puzzled about my study here. I don't like to think it is because I am incapable of directing myself at all and need to have my work chosen [and] arranged for me like a child but it looks a little like it." Balch's scholarly pursuits in France were mostly solitary, and she was unfamiliar with working in this way. She informed her father, "Mr. Levasseur is very good and very eminent but so far I have not got anything to speak from him in the way of advice or criticism. He expects me to bring the initiative and I expect him to perhaps."[19]

Balch eventually settled into a satisfactory position as she focused her independent study on an examination of government programs responding to help the poor in France. As her project developed, however, Balch continued to be frustrated by Levasseur's lack of direction. She wished to visit the institutions that were the subject of her research, but Levasseur viewed this "as irrelevant and unnecessary." On one occasion, she embarked on her own initiative to gather research firsthand for her study. She visited the government agency responsible for calculating the taxes involved in public charity work. To her dismay, she discovered that "the receipts were never published and were known only to the minister whose perquisite they appeared to be."[20]

Balch did not complete her work until after her return to Boston. In fact, she spent nearly two years rewriting the text. The resulting study, *Public Assistance of the Poor in France,* was published in 1893. The final work was much improved, but Balch's main complaint lingered: that she had no firsthand experience with her subject. In the most obvious example, Balch complained that she wrote about the conditions of the poor and yet never visited a slum.[21]

Balch opened her study with the statement, "The present constitution of public assistance in France can hardly be well understood without some study of its development." She then surveyed the history of charity laws in France, from the Middle Ages through the French Revolution. She dedicated approximately one-third of her text to a thorough discussion of the historical development of charity law and administration in France. The work then detailed French public assistance programs from the revolution through the early 1890s, when Balch was writing. The study also analyzed and critiqued the effectiveness of the French system.[22]

Although Balch examined all aspects of public assistance, the bulk of the study traced the history of the state's role in public charity. Balch considered both the rationale behind government involvement in charity and the various methods implemented in different locations. Ultimately, according to Balch, the mostly voluntary nature of public assistance in France limited its effectiveness, though at times it was this "voluntary character" that gave the administration more "elasticity."[23]

Balch identified three periods in the development of public assistance in French history prior to the French Revolution. The first, roughly coinciding with the Middle Ages, was marked by its "ecclesiastical character." Public assistance measures during this era were almost entirely voluntary and church driven. In this section, Balch also discussed the establishment and development of hospitals and asylums throughout France. The second era encompassed the second half of the sixteenth century, specifically the reign of Francis I. During this period, according to Balch, public assistance became "largely a secular and even a political function." Specifically, authorities attempted to "establish by law a systematic method of dealing with the poor by requiring the local unit, the parish or the commune, to provide for its own poor." The reforms of this period were continued during the third era, stretching from 1600 until the revolution in 1789. During this phase, Catholicism and "powerful centralization" defined French charity. It was a time of "large and imposing institutions" committed to "indoor-relief." Also, Balch noted the importance of the 1612 law officially outlawing "beggary."[24]

Balch argued that from the reign of Louis XIV (1643–1715) through the French Revolution (1789–99), little changed in either the conception of or laws regarding the treatment of and assistance to the poor. The revolution offered a new outlook on public assistance. Unfortunately, French revolutionaries merely provided promises of change. In fact, Balch asserted, the postrevolution government accomplished "little but destruction and waste." Mainly, the revolutionaries had objected to the previous "inequality" in the distribution of relief and "preferred no relief to relief unjustly distributed."[25]

The second portion of Balch's book explored and analyzed the "modern organization of [public] assistance in France." Balch explained that the two pillars of relief for the poor in France in 1892 were that assistance was both voluntary and local. An essential component of Balch's discussion was the relationship of the state to the people, or the responsibility of the government to care for its poor. What Balch calls the "socialistic view" did not apply to France: the nation recognized no "right on the part of the pauper to demand aid and to recover his claim by legal means."[26] This line would continue to interest Balch. She persisted in studying the ways in which governments related to their citizens, especially in terms of economic relief. Her graduate studies in economics two years after this publication consistently pushed this question.

Balch's survey of the French government and its relationship to the nation's poor showed that, with some very important exceptions, most of the charity in that nation was gathered and administered on a voluntary basis. The state had no obligation to provide relief. The other aspect of modern French assistance that Balch explored was its local nature. Although the administration of relief was increasingly centralizing in France, it was still mainly dealt with at the local level. With the exception of Paris, each area of France maintained essentially similar and completely inefficient (often ineffectual) systems.[27]

In the final section, Balch explored the three levels of relief administration: the communal (or the municipal level); the "department"; and the state. It was in this section that Balch began to assert her judgments about the state of public assistance in 1890. In her discussion of the methods of administration in the communes, she stated that regardless of the condition of the commune, it was "not bound to make any local provision for the poor, the helpless or the sick." In Balch's view, because there was no government obligation to the poor, assistance rarely worked to the great benefit of those in need. A significant development, along with public assistance laws in France, was the growth and expansion of the role of asylums and hospitals.[28]

Balch dedicated the rest of the work, for the most part, to demonstrating how the bureaucratic system of relief fell short of its aims. Of particular significance (for Balch) was the responsibility the government did have to provide for certain groups of needy children and to define the ways in which the limitations of the government's role contributed to generations of impoverished citizens. Following a lengthy analysis of how the French public assistance system dealt with the needs of destitute and abandoned children, Balch concluded that the French system was significantly lacking. She explained how the laws in France fundamentally omitted many children who also needed relief.[29] Balch's particular interest in the relationship between destitute children and the state might have resulted from the fact that she was working with children in need during the time she was editing this work.

Finally, Balch considered the role of the state. The French government viewed children (and only a small segment of children) and the insane as its only obligations in the public relief system. In addition to this noteworthy obligation, Balch saw as another central contribution of the state its "encouragement of thrift." One of her main conclusions in this work was that despite the fact that France failed to implement effective laws regarding the needy, the government's initiatives to implement "thriftiness" among its citizenry had created "fewer French paupers than English." Balch also explored the role of banks and beneficent societies in relation to the state's role in developing systems to mitigate need in the nation. She had a particular interest in the way the French government employed pawn shops as a tool to promote thrift. The French government closely oversaw the workings of pawn shops, as they were central in loan making and "prevented waste." Of Balch's many regrets relating to this work, she bemoaned that she extensively researched French pawn shops yet never actually visited one while in Paris, and she so had only "the vaguest idea" of what they were like.[30]

In her concluding pages, Balch emphasized that, despite much opposition, there was a trend toward "systematized and obligatory" public assistance. In her opinion, public assistance must meet two tests; it must both relieve "exist-ing suffering" and reduce "the volume of preventable suffering." Although Balch's scholarship was mostly objective, she did not hesitate to offer sug-gestions at the end of her piece. She concluded that in both areas essential to public relief, the French system was "not very satisfactory" because the government offered "no guarantee," implying that the legal right to relief and the government's responsibility to provide it were essential to the effective implementation of public assistance laws.[31]

In addition to the generally fair and impartial character of this book, Balch's attention to detail was meticulous. This work truly established Balch as a scholar. One book review praised the study, stating, "The merit of the book lies not merely in its clearness, accuracy and brevity, but especially in the perfect fairness preserved in a field where party spirit and sectarian prejudices have made impartiality difficult." Another reviewer agreed, em-phasizing that Balch provided "insight rather than conclusions" in a field where few remained impartial.[32]

The amount of detail provided in this work is astounding. Although Balch criticized her work for only relying on secondary sources, the historical section was a cogent synthesis of hundreds of primary source documents, almost all of which were in French. In fact, one of the book's reviews praised the work for finally providing an understanding of the French system to English readers.[33]

The publication of *Public Assistance of the Poor in France* in 1893 securely set Balch in the realm of academic social sciences. Although her scholarship in Paris did not result in the formal awarding of a graduate degree (Balch would never formally receive another degree after Bryn Mawr), it did hone her understanding of economics and sociology in an academic sense. How-ever, by the time Balch returned from Paris in 1891 at age twenty-four, she had decided, like many progressives of her generation, that she could not work solely as an academic. She wrote, "I came home determined to see something of things for myself. I had read much of 'ouvriers' [laborers] but I had so to speak never seen one." She arrived in Boston determined to change that.[34]

Boston's First Social Workers

When Balch returned to Boston in 1891, she arrived in a city on the brink of economic recession. Awakened in college to the deplorable conditions in which many people worked and lived, Balch had resolved to focus her energies on mitigating social ills. Her time in Paris, while not entirely the experience she had hoped for, enabled her to more fully develop her skills in economics and sociological analysis. During the 1890s, Balch came to more fully realize what she called "something of the actual life of the poor" as they struggled with the "economic horrors" of that turbulent decade. The economic and social circumstances of the time confirmed her conviction that she "needed to get away from books and have first hand contact with social problems."[35] During the four years after her return from Paris, from 1891 to 1895, she continued to develop her scholarship, but she applied most of her time to social reform work.

Balch's interests and focus during this period were in line with many men and women of her generation and background. The 1890s witnessed the beginning of what has been termed the Progressive Era in American history. This period, broadly defined as spanning from the late nineteenth century through the First World War, was marked by rapid industrialization, urbanization, and a large influx of immigrants, mainly from southeastern Europe, into American cities. These years also saw the rise and consolidation of financial power in corporations. These conditions resulted in numerous and disconcerting side effects. Urban tenements abounded. Struggles between workers and managers dominated many employment settings.

In response to these rapidly escalating conditions, a large reform movement was born. Political, economic, and social reformers aimed, all in their own unique ways, to transform American society. These numerous changes also represented progress, and so could the response to them. Many middle- and upper-class, educated women joined reform groups in droves. Emily Greene Balch, like many of her peers, experienced a call to social reform. She was serving her community, as she had always longed to do, and she was putting her academic skills into action. The reformers who made up Balch's social circle during the last decade of the nineteenth century shared a social consciousness popular among this generation of progressives. Balch recognized that she was part of a greater movement, once commenting that her involvement in social work during this period was not only a significant part of her personal development, but also, as she said, "characteristic of my generation."[36]

The early 1890s presented numerous opportunities for Balch to define her interests and hone her skills in the field of social reform, or what came to be termed "social work." Also, the industrial conditions and labor unrest in Boston during these years introduced Balch to the world of organized labor. She spent this period founding a settlement house in Boston, volunteering time to Boston's growing labor movement, and revising her manuscript on public assistance in France.

As Balch set out on her new career in Boston, she, as in previous times of transition, sought out a mentor. She found one in Charles W. Birtwell and apprenticed herself to him. Birtwell then served as the secretary of the Children's Aid Society. Through her work with this organization, Balch quickly came to witness directly, not just read about, the deplorable conditions in which so many of Boston's residents lived.[37]

Charles W. Birtwell, only seven years Balch's senior, had made a name for himself in Boston as an effective social reformer. Fresh from Harvard in 1885, Birtwell went to work for the Boston Children's Aid Society, becoming its executive officer in 1887. His political networking stretched far beyond the organization, however. Birtwell was seemingly involved in every social reform work in the greater Boston area during these years.[38] He not only gave Balch her first direct experience with service to the underprivileged, but he also introduced her to social reform circles throughout the city. As a result, she was soon busier than she could have imagined.

Birtwell most likely was responsible for introducing Balch to Mary Hemenway, a Boston philanthropist. Hemenway, who was (in Balch's opinion) "a beautiful and sincere patroness of good works," exemplified how wealthy progressive reformers might cultivate a broad range of projects. Balch witnessed how Hemenway was able to assist reform enterprises, carrying "them through the experimental stage and then getting them incorporated in the public school system." Such endeavors included playgrounds, public baths, and classes for cooking and sewing. Hemenway also introduced Balch to the work of vocational schools in Boston. As Balch's social circle expanded, so did her interest and involvement in various causes. She continued to build and maintain her connections with wealthy socialites. But her interests were not solely to work with philanthropists; she also cultivated relationships with working-class Bostonians.[39]

When Balch joined the greater Boston social reform network, she was exposed to a seemingly countless number of causes to work for. Her initial work, under the guidance of Birtwell, focused on children, mainly helping to place orphans with foster families. Balch learned of the many challenges to finding suitable foster care and of the many children in need. This undoubtedly took an emotional toll on her. Sometimes, when she was unable to find placements for her young charges, Balch would temporarily become a guardian. Through this work she was also exposed to the immigrant communities in Boston. She helped run a Home Library in Boston's North End, which was populated mainly with Italian immigrants.[40]

Working with and on behalf of immigrants was central to many progressive reforms, most notably the settlement house movement. Settlement house residents, who were mostly young, well-to-do, and educated, worked to bridge the class divide in cities by living and working in the poorest urban neighborhoods. Residents organized classes, lectures, and artistic and sporting events with the goal of enriching their neighbors' lives. In theory, settlement residents and community members would learn from each other. This system offered an exciting opportunity to those who wished to share their knowledge and improve their communities. Living and working alongside the poor, they could learn from and educate the underprivileged. Settlement houses have been criticized by some as Americanization projects, aimed at efficiently assimilating immigrants into society. To whatever extent settlement workers consciously or unconsciously worked toward such ends, they learned as much, if not more, from their settlement experiences as the immigrants did.[41] The settlement idea traced its roots to the first such house, Toynbee Hall, which opened in London in 1884. Jane Addams established the most famous of the American settlements, Hull House, in Chicago in September 1889.

The initial settlement houses in Massachusetts, like the New York City settlements, resulted from the work of the College Settlements Association (CSA), which four Smith College graduates had formed in 1887. These women admired the work that had been done in England and recognized the need for such work in the United States. According to its first annual report, the organization's mission sought to employ educated young women in the useful and practical application of their educations. The group believed that "a large company of young women, fresh from the privileges of college life, lacked scope for the energy so long trained to definite work." The CSA thus devised a system to direct the interests and needs of women graduates toward work with emerging settlement houses. Central to the conception of the College Settlements Association was the establishment of a network of female college alumnae. In this way, according to settlement movement scholar Mina Carson, the organization "consciously laid the groundwork for a 'movement,' expandable to other cities."[42]

Naturally, Balch was drawn to the movement. She quickly befriended Boston's settlement pioneers and, in the summer of 1892, attended a summer session of the School of Applied Ethics in Plymouth, Massachusetts. This conference, consisting of a series of lectures sponsored by members of the Ethical Cultural Movement, presented many outstanding progressive thinkers in the social sciences. Leading social progressives presented their thoughts on improving social conditions, especially improving the relationship between the individual and the industrialized world. Balch went specifically to hear Jane Addams speak on "the subjective necessity for social settlements." Addams presented the thinking behind the settlement question but then addressed the "objective" side, detailing the development of her Hull House project in Chicago.[43]

Meeting Addams undoubtedly inspired Balch to take up settlement work, but it was CSA founder Vida Scudder who drew Balch into the Boston movement. Scudder, the only daughter of a prominent Boston family, also worked as a professor of English at Wellesley College. Scudder and Balch shared similar backgrounds and devoted their lives to the same causes. Although Scudder taught English, social reform was her central passion. In 1892, Scudder promoted the creation of a new CSA settlement house in Boston and so recruited the enthusiastic Emily Greene Balch.[44]

When Balch began working for the new settlement project, Denison House, in the fall of 1892, one settlement already existed in Boston. Andover Theological Seminary professor W. J. Tucker had founded Andover House in October 1891 (after 1895, this settlement was referred to as South End House). Robert A. Woods, a student of Tucker's, organized the founding and ran the house for the rest of his life. Unlike the residences established by the College Settlements Association, the South End House had a religious origin, although "the method is educational rather than evangelistic." The organizers of the South End House proclaimed two specific goals for the settlement. First, they maintained, the house was "designed to stand for the single idea of resident study and work in the neighborhood where it may be located." Their second objective was "to create a center for those within reach, of social study, discussion, and organization." The settlement's organizers aimed to provide assistance to their impoverished Boston neighbors, but they also hoped to increase their own understanding of how different factors contributed to social conditions. Another important distinction of the South End House was that its residents were only men.[45]

The CSA, then, understood the need for another settlement house in the same area. Their settlement, though similar to the South End House, would consist of female residents only and would not share the religious foundations of its partner settlement. On October 3, 1892, the organizing committee for Denison House met. Balch was one of four who made all of the initial decisions about the new settlement. The others were Vida Scudder, Charles Birtwell, and Katharine Coman. The group voted to lease a house at 93 Tyler Street, in Boston's South End, for $75 per month. They named the settlement house after Edward Denison, a young Oxford graduate who worked to establish a settlement in London's east side but died in 1870 before seeing his idea come to fruition.[46]

The founders worked doggedly, and their labor paid off. Denison House opened on December 27, 1892, only two and half months after planning had begun. When they opened the doors, the young, college-educated women experienced a "sense of refreshing adventure" as they discovered a purpose and learned how to serve their community. Scudder, among others, expressed "gratitude" for the opportunity.[47]

During their first year of activity, Denison House residents came to understand the extent of the poor conditions in which many of their neighbors lived. The communities in Boston's South End, where the settlement houses were established, consisted mostly of Irish immigrants. Poverty was only part of the problem; these people were poorly served by government programs and often were not informed of any rights they might have had. Denison House residents and workers helped where they could. The first annual report of Denison House (although not credited to an author but probably authored by Balch, acting as the headworker) detailed the numerous problems of the neighborhood. It emphasized the problem of alcohol, linking drunkenness to other social ills. The report also noted the lack of services for the area youth. Of particular concern to the social workers that year was the horrific state of sanitation and lack of adequate bath facilities.[48]

Residing in Denison House was a primary component of the settlement house work and philosophy. It was, however, one Balch decided not to follow. Opting instead to live with her family in Jamaica Plain revealed Balch's deep commitment to her family life but also showed the limited way she embraced settlement work from the start. She admitted that her choice of living quarters was "quite contrary to the whole theory and purpose" of settlements. Denison House literature emphasized the central nature of their residency requirement, stating, "It is desirable, for the sake of continuity in the world, that candidates should, whenever possible, plan to remain in the settlement at least one season." Although the settlement made exceptions, the workers considered even short residences "inadequate" because they did not allow a worker to establish lasting and helpful friendships or even to gain thorough insight into neighborhood conditions. Balch's failure to live in the house, even during the first year while she served as headworker, meant that she failed to receive what the settlement leaders believed were essential lessons from the residential component.[49]

Residents at Denison House were expected to contribute to the settlement work and community. The women were required to pay for their board, which varied from $5.50 to $6.50 per week. In lieu of paying rent, the women worked both in the house and in the neighborhood on behalf of the settlement, devoting a minimum of four hours each day to their settlement work. Further, each woman had to allocate half a day every week for any special projects that might be assigned by the headworker. When not engaged in these duties, the residents were encouraged to take on new or enhance existing components of their settlement work, such as visiting community members or preparing lectures.[50]

According to its founders, the general goal of Denison House was "to work in cooperation with the people of the neighborhood for the building of a finer community by sharing in its life, through residence on the part of staff workers and others, and by maintaining a center for social, educational and civic activities." More specifically, Denison House workers outlined seven principles they hoped the settlement would serve in the community. These included efforts to nurture a sense of community between the settlement and neighborhood, articulated by the workers as the importance "to know the neighborhood" and to "develop neighborhood cooperation." Also, the social reformers at Denison House encouraged the community to participate in the settlement, embracing the principle of providing "an opportunity for neighbors to express themselves through activity." As well as neighborhood-focused programs, the settlement sought to inculcate positive values among its residents and provide necessary assistance to those in need. They thus adopted as their purpose to "develop leadership" and initiate "new programs growing out of unmet needs." This included the work "to give counsel and specific service where needed." Its final stated purpose presented its comprehensive effort "to make settlement purpose and aims clear and especially present materials helpful to building a finer community."[51]

Growing from its desire to emphasize the utility of all members in a community, the leaders of Denison House always emphasized the organization's educational component. The workers highlighted the importance of its history as a product of the CSA. It encouraged community members to take the free classes offered at the settlements. Lessons included writing, literature, travel, art, and American history because, the workers believed, "every woman ought to know something of the story of their land." During her first year with the settlement, Balch even taught a class in social work. In addition to these areas, Denison House offered classes on trade unionism, indicating how closely associated the Denison House workers were with the labor movement in late-nineteenth-century Massachusetts.[52]

The link between the settlement and labor movements was not unique to Boston. In Chicago and New York, the settlement houses frequently stood as meeting places for labor organizers, and Boston's Denison House continued the tradition of opening its doors for labor discussions. In 1893, United Garment Workers representatives in Boston met at Denison House to explain their mission to women tailors. This resulted in the formation of a union to organize women. During the settlement's early years, Balch established friendships with key labor organizers, including John O'Sullivan and Mary Kenney, who would eventually draw Balch deeper into labor organizing.[53]

The labor movement represented only one portion of the settlement's relationship to its neighborhood, however, and as the Denison House programs increased, it needed more space to meet the needs of the burgeoning community. By 1895, only two full years after opening, the settlement was already seeking funds to develop further. That year, the CSA purchased both the property at 93 Tyler Street and the adjacent house, number 91. Three years later, Denison House further expanded when it leased yet another house at 95 Tyler Street.[54]

Most Denison House workers resided in the house in order to fully integrate into the community they served. Central to the settlement philosophy was that poor, uneducated individuals live in the houses with privileged, educated workers. Much scholarly debate exists about the extent to which settlement workers, however sympathetic their aims, were simply attempting to speed up the process of assimilation. Some have criticized this as hypocritical, given that many of the workers promoted the cultural diversity within the settlements. While this is at least partially true, it can be looked at from another perspective, particularly in the case of Denison House. The settlement reflected Balch's lifelong philosophy of intercultural cooperation. Women residents, along with men and children, all from diverse ethnic, cultural, and economic backgrounds, studied and socialized together. They pulled together to fulfill needs in their increasingly diverse community. For Balch, the experience added powerful support to her growing understanding of dispute resolution. She learned firsthand the power of interpersonal diplomacy and developed a greater appreciation for differing cultural perspectives. Her years working for Denison House undoubtedly contributed to her identity as a global citizen.

Because Balch was unable to devote as much time and energy as necessary to the position of headworker after the first year, the executive committee asked Helena Stuart Dudley to accept the position. Dudley, Balch's Bryn Mawr classmate, acted as headworker from 1893 until her retirement in 1912. Balch praised Dudley's commitment to the Denison House and community service, crediting her with organizing Denison House into a sort of relief agency during the economic panic of 1893. That effort was crucial to mitigating the suffering in the community. She viewed Dudley as the driving force that carried forward the philosophy and work envisioned by the home's founders.[55] While Balch's own service had unquestionably been integral to the settlement's founding, her ongoing commitment to the house tapered.

Though she had gradually been moving away from full-time involvement, in 1894 Balch officially retired from her regular work with Denison House. Her colleagues asked that she remain on the board and continue to attend meetings whenever possible, and she agreed to do so. Balch occasionally appeared at the meetings and made some suggestions, but she was no longer a constituent part of the organization's work. Although her experience in the settlement movement was relatively brief, it influenced her early understanding of intercultural cooperation and community-level advocacy—lessons that would serve her well later, when she expanded her diplomacy to the international arena. Her resignation from Denison House was part of a more general move away from social work. She had, in her words, "become impatient with the powerlessness of such work."[56] While the work was rewarding, inasmuch as it satisfied her desire to serve, it failed to provide the intellectual stimulation she demanded. In 1894, after being engaged in full-time social work for only three years, Balch turned her mind in a new direction: education.

An American Progressive Abroad

Balch's social reform activities in Boston were in line with those of many American progressive women. The political and social outlook in the 1890s placed her squarely in the tradition of American Progressives. Her scholarly interests and reform mindset also were typical of Progressive intellectuals, who often promoted reform through government programs. Balch's prior study of the French public assistance programs and then her involvement with the American settlement movement perfectly exhibited Progressive interests. When she resigned from full-time social work to prepare for a teaching career, Balch again sought out mentors. She wanted to deepen her understanding of social progress from an academic perspective.

For someone whose educational opportunities were limited on account of her sex, Balch managed to study under the leading figures of her field. In fact, her educational development and career decisions were marked by numerous prominent intellectuals of her day. She studied with leading members from various schools of thought, revealing her strength for approaching a problem from multiple perspectives to arrive at a solution.

Balch spent one semester at Radcliffe College, which had been the Harvard Annex for Women, in nearby Cambridge. This experience offered her the opportunity to work with Sir William Ashley, Harvard University's first economic historian. Although Balch worked with Ashley for only a few months, his presence in her scholastic development is important to note. In 1893, Ashley had recently begun his career at Harvard but was quickly gaining international prominence as a liberal Progressive intellectual who viewed the schools of economics as evolutionary in nature. Ashley understood the deep connections between his own work and social progress; he was a devout admirer of the economic historian Arnold Toynbee, with whom he collaborated for a period. His perspective offered much to Balch, as he was both an historian and economist. A great admirer of Gustav Schmoller, the leader of the German Historical School of Economics who would become Balch's mentor in Berlin, Ashley emphasized the central role of history in understanding economics.[57] The brief connection between Ashley and Balch at Radcliffe affirms that her training as an economist was linked, from the beginning, to an understanding of both historical circumstances and social relevance. As Balch moved forward in her academic career to study with other economists of varying schools of thought, she began to merge strands from each approach to form her own perspective.

After her semester at Radcliffe, Balch ventured to Chicago, where she knew Jane Addams and other settlement leaders. Arriving in time to take in the World's Columbian Exposition, Balch remained in Chicago for eight months. She studied at the University of Chicago under Albion Small, one of the founders of the American field of sociology. The choice to work with Small was interesting, considering his rivalry with Balch's college mentor, Franklin Giddings.[58] She never mentioned this discrepancy, but her choice demonstrated another way in which Balch effectively integrated various schools of thought into her own unique way of thinking, researching, and teaching. Also, her studies in Chicago revealed her attempt to approach her scholarship from two fields: economics *and* sociology. After spending a semester at Radcliffe and another at the University of Chicago, Balch decided to narrow her focus to the study of economics, and Europe was the best place to do so. She selected the University of Berlin, a popular destination for Progressive intellectuals.

The University of Berlin did not actually grant degrees to women during this time. By the mid-1890s, German universities allowed some women to attend courses, but only in a limited capacity. On rare occasions some women, such as Balch, obtained special permission to audit courses. That Balch chose this path revealed that she was mainly interested in increasing her understanding of economics, whether or not it resulted in a graduate degree. Her choice to request the special status necessary to study at a German university was not a common one among women during this time. American women seeking higher education in Europe tended to go to London or Switzerland. Some upper-middle-class, socially conscious women opted to dedicate their time abroad to voluntary work with the international women's suffrage movement or another network within the international women's movement. But such choices were not intellectually rigorous enough for Balch. Still—why Germany? Two aspects of German universities in the late nineteenth century might explain Balch's decision to attend formal lectures and seminars in Berlin: the cost, and the growing number of German-trained American economists.[59]

One consideration in Balch's selection of the University of Berlin might have been its cost relative to similar pursuits in, for example, London. Historian Daniel Rodgers wrote of German institutions, "So cheap were their fees that in 1889 it was estimated that the cost of a year in Germany, transatlantic travel included, was fully a third less than a year's study at Cornell, Harvard, or Johns Hopkins." In 1895, at age twenty-eight, Balch had become increasingly concerned with the financial burden she posed to her father. She frequently voiced this apprehension in her letters. Into her old age Balch was still pained by the memory that she had remained financially dependent on her father until the age of thirty. While in Germany, Balch often wrote home with details about every cent she spent. For example, she wrote to her sister Anne about her accounts and "the idea of Papa worrying about my not spending enough." Although the correspondence indicates that Francis Balch did not impart any of his financial concerns to his daughter, Emily nonetheless worried about how her spending affected him.[60]

Although the question of cost undoubtedly influenced Balch, her main reason for choosing Berlin most likely resulted from the university's prominent position in the field of economics. In the mid- to late-nineteenth century, Germany remained a key location for American students of economics. Throughout the nineteenth century, approximately ten thousand Americans enrolled in graduate study in German universities, and the majority chose the University of Berlin. During Balch's brief stay there, some of her fellow students included Bertrand Russell, *New Republic* cofounder Walter Weyl, Robert Woods (of the South End settlement house in Boston), and future Dartmouth professor Franklin H. Dixon.[61]

She traveled to Europe alone, an uncommon occurrence for a woman of her age and social status in the last decade of the nineteenth century. Though homesick and scared, she remained determined to get the most out of the experience. She informed her father that she had consulted with her college mentor Franklin Giddings and did not expect her studies to keep her abroad for longer than a year. She assured him, "I don't think there is any chance worth speaking of that I should want to stay a second winter."[62] After all, she was not entering any sort of formal program. She felt a year was sufficient time to maximize the potential offered by the University of Berlin.

Rather than go directly to Berlin, she wanted first to practice her German language skills and learn more about the country's social and political landscape. Although she had studied German since she was a young child, Balch remained uncertain about her conversational skill with the language. Revealing a deep insecurity over her abilities, she worried about her comprehension level once she began attending lectures and participating in seminars conducted in German. In an effort to mitigate this concern, she decided to travel to Germany before the semester commenced.

Arriving in Germany at the end of August 1895, Balch traveled to Heildesheim to study with the art curator and historian Dr. William Bode. Her purpose for this excursion was, as she stated, "to brush up my German and for background." On her journey to Heildesheim, located in north-central Germany, Balch paused in the "charming" port city of Bremen, in the northwest. While there, Balch learned that Dr. Bode would not be as available as he had hoped during her time in Heildesheim.[63]

Though disappointed, Balch continued on to Heildesheim, a town steeped in "pure medeaevalism [sic]," where she lodged with "a very lovable" Fraülein Schulzen. When Dr. Bode finally arrived, Balch was pleased that she had taken the extra time abroad. In addition to improving her communication skills, she gained a broader understanding of German culture. She wrote to her father, "Dr. Bode is squeezing out an hour a day for me—telling me about all sorts of things German and answering manifold questions. It is helping to clear up a good many puzzles." Bode answered her questions about the German schools and apprenticeship system, geography, as well as "politics and constitutional arrangements, [and] on distribution of population and its characteristics."[64] This experience perfectly exemplified how Balch assessed the world. In any given country, she wished to thoroughly understand how a nation worked, how a government related to its people and its people to each other.

After only three weeks, Balch left Heildesheim on September 16, 1895, and reached Berlin five days later. She arrived with some time to explore the city and her lodging options before lectures at the university were set to begin. She quickly found a living situation at a girls' day school near the university. The other boarders included two teachers and two art students, all of whom were German. This fact greatly pleased Balch. She wrote to her family, "I want to be where I hear and must speak German."[65]

Balch arrived in Berlin alone but soon met several people who became meaningful figures in her life. Foremost among her Berlin peers was Mary Kingsbury. Balch had known Kingsbury slightly in Boston, but in Berlin the two spent a great deal of time together. Finding themselves with similar educational plans and opportunities in Berlin, Balch and Kingsbury initiated an enduring mutual respect that was both personal and professional. Balch referred to Kingsbury as "the most beautiful person" she had ever met. She praised Kingsbury's beauty not just as her "personal loveliness of face and voice," but her "sympathy and understanding, her active and original intelligence and her humor" were also greatly regarded. Balch most venerated her friend's dedication to social service that mirrored her own. She admired how her friend "enjoyed one of God's greatest gifts, vocation. A sense of purpose, free from any self-consciousness or rigidity, made her living, in all its rich variety, steadily one."[66]

Like Balch, Kingsbury grew up in the outskirts of Boston, in Chestnut Hill, Massachusetts. She also shared with Balch a love of the classics and chose to study Latin and Greek, which she pursued at coeducational Boston University. As a young college graduate, she was increasingly drawn to the plight of the underprivileged in Boston. She became interested in the labor movement, which in many ways in the 1890s connected with Denison House, where she first recalled meeting Balch. After two years of teaching high school in Somerville, Massachusetts, Kingsbury decided she did not care for a life of teaching and returned to graduate studies. She first returned to college, like Balch, by taking courses at nearby Radcliffe, where Kingsbury became a student of the esteemed economic historian, Sir William Ashley. She praised her former teacher, recalling, "I learned more from Ashley than from any teacher before or after that graduate year at Radcliffe." After that year at Radcliffe, the Women's Educational and Industrial Union in Boston awarded Kingsbury a scholarship to study in Berlin.[67]

Kingsbury wrote of her journey abroad, "Mother went with me as I set forth on my first journey abroad. Girls were not free then to make trips by themselves, and, in any case, it was a great adventure for us both, for I was to study in Berlin for a whole year." Although it appears that Balch was "free" to travel abroad alone, she was still grateful for the company provided by Kingsbury and her mother. Balch and Kingsbury spent much of their year abroad together, attending most of the same lectures and seminars and spending "many pleasant hours reading Kant in the park."[68]

Kingsbury also arrived in Berlin prior to the university's opening and stayed with Balch for two weeks while her mother remained in Weimar. The two young women spent much of those two weeks in anxious anticipation of word from the government. Revealing the lack of formality regarding college education for women in Germany during this era, neither Balch nor Kingsbury had obtained formal permission to study at the university prior to their arrival. After her arrival in Berlin, Balch informed her brother that she was struggling with her request for *zuhörer*, or "listener" status, at the university. She and Kingsbury nervously awaited word from the government as the first day of the school year drew near. Balch wrote to her father during this interval, "The prospect of getting what we want here seems to be excellent, only marred by the necessity of a good deal of red tape."[69]

While agonizing over their status, Balch and Kingsbury filled the time before the university opened attending lectures of the *Verein für Sozialpolitik,* or the "Union for Social Politics." The *Verein,* as it was commonly known, was a forum created by leading German economists in 1872, presided over by Gustav Schmoller, with the purpose of discussing prominent economic and social issues of the day. Its lectures tended to advance the perspective of the German Historical School of Economics and thus promoted economic reforms involving greater state participation. As an association for nineteenth century German economists, the *Verein* publicly critiqued laissez-faire economics and the policies that resulted from classical economic logic. Several of Balch's professors at the University of Berlin were prominent members in the *Verein.*

The economics students at the University of Berlin also formed their own association, the *Staatswissenschaftlicter Verein,* which held great debates during this time. Balch found the lectures of the *Verein* and its student counterpart quite fruitful and was thrilled to discover that she was able to understand most of the material (proving herself proficient in conversational German). In one letter to her father, she described the experience of being a woman at the lectures. She exclaimed, "I am afraid your hair would have stood on end if you had seen Miss K[ingsbury] and me Wednesday night at that 'Verein.'" She explained in detail:

> We have been led by gradual degrees to this last venture. There is a "*socialwissenchaftlicher*" [*sic*] association among the student[s] and we were invited very politely to the first meeting. We, with various other ladies, sat in the gallery of a big hall while on the floor the students sat at table[s] and drank beer, and listened to a speech. We *listened* but one could not *hear.* At the second meeting, at wh[ich] Prof. Jastrow was to speak on the unemployed, a paper I really cared about hearing, we found to our dismay a room full of smoke, beer and students, and no gallery, just a plain room. One of the Americans with us went ahead and reported there was a lady there so we went in. We were given seats at the head table opposite the speaker and smoking was stopped, which latter thing Miss K[ingsbury] and I am sorry for.[70]

The series of lectures given by the *Verein* closed one week before classes at the university commenced. Balch and Kingsbury still awaited their official government permission to audit courses. Although others assured Balch not to worry, her experiences with the *Verein* only enhanced her desire to attend lectures and seminars at the university. She expressed this point to her sister: "Hearing these lectures has made me feel more strongly than ever that Berlin is *the* place for me."[71] After her mounting anxiety that she would not be able to benefit from the University of Berlin, Balch finally received the official permission to attend university lectures and participate in the seminar taught by Gustav Schmoller.

To date, no scholar has accurately emphasized the profound influence of Gustav Schmoller on the social and political ideas of Emily Greene Balch. In Berlin, she began to crystallize more clearly her opinions that she had begun to form during her days working on behalf of children's aid and the settlement movement in Boston. Schmoller's ideas and methods were later reflected in nearly every subsequent intellectual endeavor of Balch: her writings, her teachings, her political leanings. Although she claimed an allegiance to a different school of economics than the one Schmoller headed, he nonetheless significantly contributed to the perspective she later brought to the classroom. It is thus important to understand first who Gustav Schmoller was and what the German Historical School posited.

When Schmoller emerged among German historians in the 1870s, he joined a growing coterie of academics in opposition to the then-dominant field of classical, or English, economics. Classical economics derived from Adam Smith's presentation of supply and demand and the idea that a product's value resulted directly from the costs involved in producing that good. A central tenant of classical economics revolved around the argument that governments maintain little to no interference in the economy, which was seen as self-regulating. This school of thought and the widespread support for laissez-faire policies (supporting free markets with limited government interference) throughout the eighteenth and nineteenth centuries dominated academic discussions of economics until the 1870s. In the late nineteenth century, academic revolutions to the English classical model of economics produced new lines of thinking in the field. Two important schools of thought strongly influenced Balch and the era of economics in which she studied and taught.

While followers of Adam Smith continued to present supply and demand as central to economics, others began to question this concept. They formed what became known as the Austrian School. Austrian School economists continued primarily to support laissez-faire policies, but they expanded Smith's conceptions of direct cost and value. The Austrian School, represented in the nineteenth century by such thinkers as Carl Menger, attempted to move away from statistical analysis and advocated a more practical, individual approach to questions. In so doing, this group of economists abandoned the scientific method as a tool of economic analysis. Like classical economists, the Austrian School thinkers highly regarded the right to private property and believed that individual actions were central to economic success. They also agreed that government interference often proved inefficient. Because Austrian School adherents promoted a value-free theory but still maintained that individual choices affected economics, they incorporated a level of relativism into economics. The Austrian School replaced the centrality of supply and demand and advanced the concept of marginal value. Marginalism explained the foundation of a price as including more than a simple ratio between supply and demand; instead, these economists incorporated producers' and consumers' willingness and interest into the creation of a price. Utilizing the rationale behind marginalism also placed the Austrian School thinkers in a relativist approach to social science.

In Germany, a group of scholars offered a new perspective on economics, tying economic success to national history, and snubbed the universal application of economic theories across cultures. This style, termed the German Historical School, looked to Gustav Schmoller as its leader in the last decades of the nineteenth century. Schmoller and his colleagues emphasized the role of the state in influencing economics. As the German state expanded during the mid-nineteenth century, several German academics publicly critiqued laissez-faire policies, pointing to the success of the German state. The German School differed from the Austrian School mainly over questions of method. Although they rejected mathematical theorems, German Historical School thinkers advocated strict adherence to the gathering of empirical evidence and utilization of the scientific method. Many economists from this school sought to apply their discipline to improving social conditions during their time, as did Balch.

The German Historical School economists critiqued Smith's ideas, claiming that the laissez-faire policies they produced were not applicable to the German nation during its industrializing phase. Such German economists argued that laissez-faire economic guiding principles did not help Germany or the United States, both of which needed to protect their industries in order to develop an industrial economy. Schmoller further believed that laissez-faire, in reality, masked a definite dependency on government assistance. He and his colleagues supposed that the unique historic situation of each nation should influence the study of economics as applied to that country.

Without question, Schmoller's impressions resulted from his personal experience in Germany during the mid- to late nineteenth century. He witnessed the rapid industrialization of his native country following a comprehensive unification under Otto von Bismarck in the 1860s and 1870s. He thus observed the economic and social ills that accompanied industrialization. Schmoller came to believe that economists must examine economics in relationship to the multitude of social problems present in a particular country. He believed that part of the economist's role was to offer solutions to the economic, political, and social questions of the day.[72]

Most important, Schmoller and his peers saw economics as containing a moral component, and they rightly believed that laissez-faire policies did not address the social problems of a nation. The necessarily ethical relationship between economics and politics, as Schmoller understood it, led his school of German economists to form the *Kongress für sociale Reform* in 1872. Meetings of his organization, in the form of the *Verein für Sozialpolitik,* were open to everyone. Exploring the relationship between economic theory and political realities, lectures of the *Verein* influenced policy decisions and divulged the link between academics and the government in nineteenth-century Germany.

Much like Balch, Schmoller—once famous in his field—has mostly disappeared from the study of economics. One scholar marveled how Schmoller "literally presided over all that passed for economics in Germany in the last quarter of the nineteenth century," and yet he is so little discussed today. Also, important to both Balch and Schmoller was the idea that economics must be applied outside of the classroom. In addition to a shared outlook as to the purpose of economics, Balch also reflected Schmoller's application of method. Like Schmoller, Balch abhorred broad generalizations, emphasizing exactitude and careful consideration of all factors. Both demanded strict adherence to the rules of scientific method and careful observation.[73] As demonstrated by her considerably detailed scholarship, Balch was always specific and exact in her research as well.

Despite the fact that Balch shared a great deal of Schmoller's outlook and unquestionably embraced his methods, she never claimed to adhere to the German Historical School of Economics. Much later in her life, recalling her studies in Berlin, Balch declared, "I was (and have always been) a disciple of the Austrian School with the theory of marginal value."[74] The fact that Balch later claimed to be a loyal supporter of the Austrian School did not accurately reflect her later teaching and research. It most likely meant she opposed Keynesian economics and the creation of a large government and expansion of the welfare state. Her economic outlook is particularly revealing, given her growing involvement in social activism over the decades following her year of German study. The important aspect to note is that Balch seemed to blend together various schools of thought, taking strands from each to form and support her own outlook.

To an extent, Balch's declared affiliation with the Austrian School is not surprising, given the prevalence of the school's ideology among younger, liberal American economists. In other words, she was part of the broader American movement that adhered to Austrian School economics. In her individual work, however, Balch employed a more diverse perspective. Dorothy Ross, in her study of American social sciences, discussed the dominance of marginalism during the late nineteenth and early twentieth centuries, emphasizing how that concept in economics appealed to Americans (in much the same way Schmoller's Historical School interested Germans). Ross claimed that marginalism was so popular among Americans because it seemed to resonate "with the historical and political aims of American economics." Ross argued that school held such power for this young generation of economists because "marginalism could be put to a variety of political uses, but marginalism had its origins and gained its force not simply as an analytical tool, but as a liberal world view."[75] Balch acknowledged an allegiance to the theory and method that most appropriately related to the historical situation of the United States. Schmoller felt that his historical school best addressed the problems of the newly unified and industrialized German nation. Nonetheless, Balch never boxed herself in to one particular perspective or method, despite her later assertions.

Though she never directly acknowledged Schmoller's influence, in her lectures Balch presented a balanced account of the various schools of economic thought that emerged at this time. In her research, she sometimes adhered to the rules of the German Historical School, in its support of the careful application of scientific method. Amidst the various schools of economics in the 1890s, Balch maneuvered between Schmoller's teaching and the Austrian School's basis of economic thought to create her own understanding of economics that she later imparted to her students.[76]

Balch also learned a great deal outside the lecture hall while in Berlin. She became fascinated with the political atmosphere she witnessed in Germany in the 1890s and understood that the economic concepts she was then studying related directly to Germany's historic as well as current circumstances. After all, it was less than a decade prior to Balch's arriving in Berlin that the new kaiser had dismissed Bismarck and begun to establish his own "tyrannical" rule. Balch recalled that she felt a distinct difference as an American in the classroom during the discussions of government and economy. "As my professors spoke of the State Government as if it were an independent entity, I remembering my American principles would remind myself that it is after all only an instrument to do for the people what the people willed." She later acknowledged that she failed to completely comprehend at the time the model of government being adopted in Germany. She continued, "It was only gradually that I began to understand how far this was from being the case in Germany where the body of expert civil servants were an almost independent more or less self perpetuating body."[77]

Balch's letters home while she was in Germany increasingly discussed the political situation in Germany. She confessed to her father that she was enthralled by the state of international affairs. "I don't know when politics have seemed to one so interesting as now, here, in England and at home and above all internationally," she wrote. Balch was not alone in her interest in the German state. Other scholars have discussed the impact of Americans of Balch's generation witnessing such broad-based movements as were afoot in Germany during the last decade of the nineteenth century. Like many of her compatriots, Balch became fascinated with the role of the expanding German state. In 1896, Balch came to believe that Germany's foreign policy lacked "the moral element that makes America's and England's (in spite of her growing prosperity) interesting." She understood the historical progression of Germany's policies, which were so crucial to its present state. "The unripe and indifferent cosmopolitanism of Goethe's day," she wrote, "has developed, thru the Napoleonic oppression, the excitement and enthusiasm of the war of Liberation and the intoxication of the success of 70–71 into an enthusiasm for the German nationality which has its bad as well as its good side to put it mildly."[78]

The politics and culture of Germany during the last decade of the nineteenth century created an exciting environment for American progressive scholars like Balch. The University of Berlin thrived with stimulating and relevant discussions. Balch's education there began as a student in Schmoller's seminar. She and Kingsbury were the only two women in the "more informal" course. Both women cherished the experience; Schmoller treated them as intellectual equals and demanded that their scholarship be both "very practical and realistic."[79]

Schmoller's seminar required students to write an *arbeit,* or seminar paper. Interested in the German system of public employment, Balch chose to examine state employment offices, including, "labor intelligence, registration, [and] employment agencies." She also realized the ways in which labor was increasingly becoming "a real issue at home" in the United States. It was evident from letters discussing her *arbeit* that Balch intended to continue this study when she returned to the United States and to apply her work toward a graduate degree. Only partially joking, she wrote "I suppose it will be my thesis if I ever 'these.'"[80]

Schmoller's seminar was not the only influential experience in Balch's German year. At the university she also attended lectures delivered by noteworthy German scholars of the day. She particularly admired the sociologist Georg Simmel, describing him as "one of the most interesting of men" she met that year. She did not care much for her professor of moral philosophy, Friedrich Paulsen, confiding to her father that he "does not improve on acquaintance—he can be shallow to an undreamed of extent." Adolph Wagner, another of her economics professors at Berlin, did not seem to make much of an impression on her at first. She considered him "very tiresome at times and given to truisms," but, she added, "one likes the *man*." During her second semester, Balch developed a greater regard for Wagner. She described to her father how she and Kingsbury struggled to get into his seminar and marveled at Wagner's nonchalant acceptance of her studies.[81] Balch wrote:

> We went to see Wagner and asked to be taken into his Seminar—all my German and most of my wits deserted me during the interview but he was very friendly and it is all right. I did not care greatly anyway. Thursday he called his Seminar together to arrange how many would undertake to read papers, etc. I had no intention of doing so. He only wanted some ten or twelve and there are 20 or 30 in the seminar. Just before he came to us he said, "To my surprise instead of being too many, there promise to be too few papers." So I remarked I was "making an Arbeit" on Arbeitsnadeweis but did not know if I could make myself intelligible. Whereupon he wrote me down without further remark.[82]

Balch considered the entire experience of living in Germany part of her education, not just what she learned within the university walls. She insisted on living with German speakers and enjoyed numerous excursions both inside and outside Berlin. She made friends with both native Germans and the many American students in residence at the time. She took advantage of many of the cultural offerings of Berlin, writing home that between "the theatre and opera there is only layers of too much distraction."[83] In her letters, Balch focused mainly on describing interactions with other students and visits with people she knew from home. She spent Christmas 1895 in Dresden with Helen Cheever, who also came to Berlin twice that year. Unlike her collegiate experience at Bryn Mawr, Balch's time in Berlin was as much social as it was about intellectual pursuits.

Despite her great admiration for the culture, university, and friendships formed that year, Balch remained concerned about the militaristic atmosphere in Germany. During this time, Germany seemed militaristic to many of the Americans living there. Kingsbury chronicled one example of how both men and women must get out of the way of any member of the military. In her memoirs she recalled, "We had no hint of how mild this bit of militarism was to seem in comparison with that of these later Nazi years. The period of German life from 1895 on was the time of great industrial upswing, of scientific advance, and yet no less of respect for culture."[84] Although the two women were apprehensive about elements in German culture, Kingsbury and Balch always looked back fondly on their experiences and education there.

Kingsbury and Balch left Germany together in July 1896. Before returning to the United States, they traveled to London, where they attended the International Socialist Workers' and Trade Union Congress, which gathered between eight hundred and twelve hundred delegates in London at the end of July. The meeting resulted from a joint effort between what remained of the International Socialist Organization and the British Trades Union Congress. The purpose was to draw together individuals from both groups that supported, "the necessity of the organisation of the workers *and* of political action."[85] The women's decision to go to the congress resulted in part from the influences of their German professors and an aroused interest in social democracy. The experience also demonstrated to Balch that poor management of such a large-scale conference could lead to disappointing results. Later, when she became an adept organizer of large-scale congresses for the international women's peace movement, she no doubt recalled the chaotic congress in London during the summer of 1896.[86]

Balch was nevertheless awestruck at the spectrum of opinion represented at the meeting, especially the array of what she considered zealous positions. She reported, "Here appeared, as so often, the tendency of extremes to meet." She detailed the various radical groups: "Anarchists and trade unionists, forming in a general sense the Left and Right of the assembly, were the common opponent of the Social Democratic Centre in its effort to get its policy of conquering political power definitely and exclusively endorsed." Within this atmosphere, which one *Times* article described as "distinctly heated," little of substance was effectively addressed.[87]

The great divergence of opinion expressed by the attendees limited the congress's effectiveness and stymied efforts to reach consensus. Noting that "nothing strikingly interesting or new was brought forward," Balch explained, "Outside the questions of party policy, and the constitution of the congress, little was possible beyond a study and comparison of conditions, which was not attempted, and the passing of resolutions." Additional reports from the congress confirmed Balch's assessment. One account that addressed the delegate structure and voting procedures warned, "Such a basis very naturally opened the doors to gross inequalities of representation, and in such an absurd anomaly germs of future trouble were inevitable."[88]

Despite the range of views present at the congress and the overall lack of effective steps to action, Balch noticed that many of the principal figures

there inspired the crowd. She commented, "The individualism of Socialism, as shown in its leading spirits, was more striking than class or national
characteristics." The famous Marxists and Socialists whose presence at the
congress, in part, drew Balch to the gathering included Jean Jaurès of France;
August Bebel of Germany; Enrico Ferri of Italy; and Keir Hardie, Tom Mann,
and Sidney Webb of Great Britain. Balch also noted the presence of Eleanor
Marx Aveling, the youngest daughter of Karl Marx.[89]

Although Balch criticized the general ineffectiveness of the congress, she
praised the participation of these and other notable socialists. She found
certain components of the conference significant, and they formed lasting
impressions in her mind. Of the numerous debates presented at the congress,
Balch followed with great interest the ones concerning the practical application of education. For Balch, the "most interesting debate" concerned Sidney
Webb's report on "Education and Physical Development." To Balch, Webb's
comments represented an aspect of the conference that related to "real experience." She also highlighted the Congress's resolution promoting peace,
which the delegates understood "to be brought about through 'the abolition
of the capitalist and landlord system of society in which wars have their root,'
and, as next means, through a internationally established eight-hour day
and universal suffrage." This meeting was Balch's first experience of large-
scale congresses directed toward a goal but representing a wide spectrum of
personalities and opinions.[90]

When Balch left England for home in August 1896, she had hopes for the
future but no actual plans. Although her memoirs were vague on the details,
her letters from that summer clearly indicated that she intended to pursue a
doctorate. She shared her intentions with her sister, saying, "I guess that now
I had better secure that . . . old PhD somehow or other. I regard it as a kind
of life insurance." While she discussed a few different options, including the
University of Chicago and the Massachusetts Institute of Technology, she
favored studying with Franklin Giddings at Columbia University.[91]

When Balch and Kingsbury boarded their return vessel to the United States,
discussing the possibility of attending graduate school together, they met
with an old friend: Katharine Coman, whom Balch knew from her work with
Denison House, happened to be on the same ship. Coman was at that time
the head of the economics department at Wellesley College, just outside of
Boston. During their journey, Coman listened as Balch pondered her future,
and Coman offered her an alternative. Coman invited Balch to come and
work with her at Wellesley, in a part-time teaching position. Impressed—and
overwhelmed with how to proceed—Balch considered the offer.

3. "Twenty Happy and Busy Years,"
1896–1914

Coman's offer to teach at Wellesley presented Balch with the daunting decision of whether to continue her formal education or undertake a new career path. In trying to decide, Balch focused mainly on how taking the teaching position at Wellesley College would affect her father. If she accepted the offer, she could live at or near home and assist her sisters in caring for their aging father; as well, by accepting the offer she would reduce her financial dependence on him. On the other hand, she still felt driven to continue her education. By opting to undertake a PhD in Boston, she could still live with her family, but she would continue to rely on her father for money. This was unacceptable. She accepted Coman's offer and began at Wellesley as Coman's assistant in the fall semester, 1896. Her later comment that "I gladly gave up my degree" disguised what was actually a difficult decision. When Balch decided to take the instructorship, she consciously set aside her personal ambition. What she obviously could not anticipate was the ways in which her ambition would take new shape during her next "20 happy and busy years" at Wellesley.[1]

A Satisfying Career

Under Coman's mentorship and the intellectually thriving atmosphere at Wellesley College, Balch developed a strong love of teaching. She once exclaimed that her dedication to teaching was so intense that she would even "pay for the privilege."[2] Balch's devotion to her vocation was certainly bolstered by the talented and dedicated students who sat in her classroom. Middle- and upper-class young women of this generation attended institutions of higher education in greater numbers (approximately fifty-six thousand American women attended college in 1890), and Wellesley's admissions process guaranteed that many of Balch's students would be competitive and academically engaged students. It was also an exciting time to be a college professor at an elite women's college. At Wellesley, Balch and her colleagues formed an integral component of shaping the academic and cultural environment. They offered a broader range of elective courses than had previously been available to women.[3] They demanded a great deal from their students and rewarded the most dedicated with their admiration. Balch's affection for her students was certainly reciprocated.

While Balch received the admiration and respect of many of her students, she also gained the reputation of being absentminded. One former student related what she called the "classic legend" of Balch's professorship, explaining, "After requiring a class of students to take down a formidable list of figures, she would frequently pause, and exclaim in a troubled voice, with a look of deep dismay on her kind face: Oh dear! I've given you the wrong statistics." This student confessed that this episode probably only occurred the one time, but "so popular was the legend that every student looked hopefully forward to a recurrence of it." Another student, Ruth Sapin Horowitz, confirmed Balch's distracted nature. In her memoirs, Horowitz remembered Balch's quirky habits, writing, "Often she would forget to return our examination papers, and the required reading in the reference books would also slip her mind." This tendency sometimes resulted in Balch's forgetting entirely to inform her students that she would not be present for a class. Horowtiz wrote of these occasions, "We would sit patiently the required five minutes after last bell, and then learn somehow that our teacher was delivering a lecture in Boston or New York or attending a conference of civic leaders in Chicago."[4]

Balch's absentmindedness was also legendary in her family. A favorite story repeated by her relatives related to what began as a regular morning for Balch. On this morning, as usual, Balch got up and dressed, prepared and ate breakfast, put on her overcoat, rode in the family carriage to the Jamaica Plain train station, boarded the train, and got off at the Wellesley train station. She stood on the platform in sudden dismay, shocked to discover that underneath her overcoat she only had on a slip. The veracity of this story, of course, cannot be confirmed, but so firmly is it planted in family lore that we know both family and friends understood that her head wasn't always on such trivial matters as getting dressed.[5]

Her students so admired Balch, however, that they excused such instances of absentmindedness and even argued that Balch's numerous outside activities only contributed to her teaching. One student listed among her best qualities, "fairness, intellectual honesty, a deep respect for facts and a shining faith in the perfectability of mankind." She was more than just kind and honest; she was a brilliant scholar. And her students noticed. The same student commented that Balch was "guided by accurate statistical data and a wise use of economic theory."[6] She was a highly disciplined intellectual whose conclusions were reached after a thorough analysis and were grounded in a keen understanding of economic theories. Teaching offered Balch the opportunity to influence other minds and also to satisfy her mind, which demanded methodical rigor.

Balch found it intellectually satisfying to be a scholar and to teach young scholars, but she also utilized her teaching for a broader purpose. She encouraged her students to participate in solving social problems, with a thorough knowledge of economic theory. In this way, she fulfilled a central yearning: to live a life of service to her community. What Balch found at Wellesley College was more than a vocation—it was a purpose.

In the middle of her second year at Wellesley, Balch faced a tragedy that shook her to her core. Her father died suddenly in February 1898. The emotional impact of that event manifested a depressed outlook and, according her to own admission, poor teaching performance. Although this was in relation to her high standards, Balch nonetheless felt the loss grievously. In her journal she plead to God for strength and comfort. Her dear friend Helen Cheever "simply kindly and strongly" assisted in any decisions related to her father's death and estate. Despite her grief, Balch endeavored not to be morose, and for the most part she succeeded. But she continued to feel her father's presence in her life, carrying his letters with her throughout her travels and frequently turning to them for wisdom and inspiration. She longed to shape her own values and decisions after his. The year after his death, her prayers expanded beyond asking for relief from her grief. She prayed that God assist her in her endeavors to be more like her father, that is, "not slothful, duty loving, serviceable, considerate, generous and loving in thought and speech of others," adding at the end of her prayer, "as he was."[7]

Balch's desire to live a life of service, modeled on her father's, may have contributed to her decision to continue her teaching career after his death. After all, she had accepted the offer to teach mainly in order to be near her father and to relieve him of her financial dependence. Both points now seemed moot. Yet she did not even contemplate returning to her doctoral pursuits. Was she too devastated to consider altering the course she was on? Was she so in love with teaching after a year that she consciously chose to continue? Perhaps a bit of both. She also had close friends on the Wellesley faculty who were at her side during this difficult time. So she remained at the college and engaged in her teaching with a renewed commitment to achieve a life of service.

Balch's service to her community through her continued work with social reformers flourished at Wellesley College in part because the culture
supported her convictions as well as her scholarship. Historian Patricia
Palmieri described the community of professors during Balch's time as "a
hothouse for reformers." Central to this grouping of progressive reformers were Katharine Coman and Vida Scudder, both founders of Denison
House. During the 1890s and the early twentieth century, women faculty at
Wellesley discussed and supported many causes in addition to the settlement
movement, including women's suffrage, the rights of Native Americans,
consumer leagues, and the labor movement. Scudder's partner, American
author Florence Converse, described the faculty of this era as mainly "identified with modern movements toward better citizenship." Balch found this
environment suited her interests of teaching, writing, and serving as a leader
in social reform circles.[8]

Balch's teaching transformed during her two decades with the college,
revealing the ways her interests and ideas developed and adapted. Descriptions of programs in the college course catalogs over the years testify to this.
Although the trustees of the college held considerable power, Wellesley
tradition allowed the faculty great autonomy in organizing their courses.
By closely considering the ways in which economics courses at Wellesley
changed over the twenty years of Balch's teaching there, we gain insight into
how Balch adjusted her scholarly thoughts over time. The evolution of the
Economics Department, for example, reflects Balch's social reform experiences and the progression of her scholarship.

Balch witnessed and participated in the development of the Department
of Economics into a substantial presence in the college. When she began
teaching her own courses in the fall of 1897, she did so in the History Department. Economics did not even exist then as a separate discipline. Katharine
Coman taught classes in both history and economics within the History
Department. In 1900, recognizing the high demand for courses in economics,
the board of trustees approved the formation of an independent "Political
Economy" Department under Coman's leadership. The college named the
new department "Economics and Sociology." The addition of Sociology as a
main heading revealed Wellesley's view that the emerging social science was
related to the field of economics. The changing purview of the Economics
Department during Balch's tenure also mirrored the evolution of education
in the social sciences in the United States during this era.[9]

Balch's frequent increases in salary reflected her professional development
over the course of her teaching. When she began as an assistant in 1896, the
board approved a salary of $500 ($12,774.50 in 2008) for the year. The follow-

ing year she was made instructor, a post she held for six years. While Balch taught in the position of instructor, her salary was never exactly certain, due in large part to the fact that at the end of the nineteenth century, Wellesley College experienced significant financial hardship. When the board hired her as an instructor, she received a salary of $900 ($22,994.09 in 2008). After several salary fluctuations, the trustees finally settled on a salary system, and by 1902 Balch was earning $1,100 ($27,022.97 in 2008) annually. During the academic year 1902–03, Coman took a leave of absence, and though Balch still only held the rank of instructor, Coman entrusted her to act as head of the department, a privilege that included an additional $100 ($2,456.63 in 2008) per year. The following year, the college promoted Balch to the level of associate professor of economics, and she received a steady annual salary of $1,200 ($28,400.39 in 2008). In 1907, her title changed to recognize her expertise and scholarship in the field of sociology, and she became associate professor of economics and sociology. Finally, in 1912, the trustees bestowed the position of full professor of political economy and political and social science, a five-year appointment with a salary of $1,800 ($39,666.26 in 2008) per year and an annual increase of $100 until the salary reached $2000 ($44,073.62 in 2008).[10]

While the rapid progression of Balch's professional status indicated her success at the college, the courses Balch chose to teach throughout her twenty-one-year career exhibited her own changing interests (see table 1). During her early years at Wellesley, she taught introductory courses, such as Elements of Economics. In her memoirs, she recalled how she felt about the field of economics as a young instructor: "As a beginner I had been captured by those essential harmonies which Adam Smith set forth." With time, however, Balch learned that Smith's classic model of economics and a system of laissez-faire politics were incomplete. Specifically, they failed to take into account "the economic-social workings of the time—descriptive, historical, on the streets of reform and of complete social renovation." That is, Balch increasingly incorporated social considerations, such as questions of labor equity and factors resulting from industrialization and urbanization, into her teachings of economic theory. She also began to incorporate more specialized subjects into her curriculum, revealing the direction of her personal interests as well as the popularity of certain subjects.[11]

Of the many courses Balch taught during her tenure, she vividly recalled one particular lecture course in socialism, which the college asked her to teach in the fall of 1898. As the catalog described it, the course was a "study of socialist theories, 'Utopian' and 'Scientific,' in their historical development, with some consideration of modern socialist parties, and especially of Ger-

TABLE 1. The Teaching Schedule of Emily Greene Balch during Her Career at Wellesley College

FALL 1897
Social Economics I
Elements of Economics
    (with Katharine Coman)
The Evolution and Present
    Conditions of Wage-labor

SPRING 1898
Social Economics II

FALL 1898
Elements of Economics
The Evolution and Present
    Conditions of Wage-labor

SPRING 1899
Socialism
Social Economics II

FALL 1899
Social Economics I
Elements of Economics

SPRING 1900
Social Economics II
Labor Problems in the
    Nineteenth Century

FALL 1900
Social Economics I
Elements of Economics
Socialism

SPRING 1901
Social Economics II
Labor Problems in the
    Nineteenth Century
Introduction to General Sociology

FALL 1901
Introduction to General Sociology
Social Economics I
Industrial History of England

SPRING 1902
Social Economics II
The Modern Labor Problem

FALL 1902
Introduction to General Sociology
Social Economics I
Industrial History of England

SPRING 1903
Social Economics II
The Modern Labor Problem

FALL 1903
Introduction to General Sociology
Social Economics I
The Modern Labor Problem

SPRING 1904
Social Economics II
Practical Problems in Economics
    (with Coman)

FALL 1904
* Absent on leave

SPRING 1905
* Absent on leave

Information for this table was compiled from the Calendars of Wellesley *(Boston: Frank Wood, Printer), for all the years between 1895 and 1917.*

man Social Democracy." The course description demonstrated that professors shaped courses to their specific interests and expertise. Since Balch had recently returned from Germany, it made sense that she would tailor the course around German socialism. Two years earlier, when Coman taught socialism, her course description centered on socialism in France. After Balch returned from sabbatical in 1906, she altered her course description to focus on a discussion of Marx's *Das Kapital* and broadened the focus from German socialism to "the consideration of modern socialist propaganda" in several nations. Balch taught this course intermittently throughout her career, though she offered it less often as she initiated courses that emphasized her other interests.[12]

Wellesley's course in socialism gained some notoriety when, in 1907, H. G. Wells mentioned it in his book, *The Future in America*. This work considered the many problems and opportunities in the United States at the turn of the century, and Wells presented many criticisms of American institutions. Although Wells detested Boston, he felt that its universities (Harvard in particular) held great potential for the future. He was unsure, however, what to make of Wellesley College, writing, "How far, I wonder still, are these girls thinking and feeding mentally for themselves?" Although, in his opinion, the college offered too many arts and language courses, he was slightly consoled by the socialism class in the Economics Department, but he even criticized that prospect. Wells complained that "the text-book is still *Das Kapital* of Marx." Balch reviewed Wells's book, generally approving of his thoughts. Although she considered him "a man drunk with the future," she still felt the book was useful. His snide remark about her choice of textbook, however, remained with her for a long time. She was amused by the criticism of using Marx as a textbook, remarking, "As if one could discuss that history without doing so." She considered the subject of socialism valuable not just for the specific knowledge it imparted but also as "valuable training for the study of thinking for oneself in the face of conflicting [ideas] and arguments." So objective was her teaching of socialism that the students did not know her own political stance on the subject. She recalled that at the close of a semester, "a student came to me and asked what my own conclusion was."[13]

Balch's socialism course revealed her broader approach to teaching. She believed that a thorough understanding of economics could be applied toward social betterment. That is, the field of economics could be "both intellectually disinterested and ethically and practically interested." Balch wanted her students to excel academically, to gain a full understanding of the concepts and methods in her field. But she also felt it was important that the young women comprehend the applicability of sociology and economics to real life situations. In this way, she designed her courses to be "practically interested";

they focused on applying an understanding of economics to people's everyday lives. To this end, she frequently brought her students into Boston's working-class and poor communities. She wanted her students to grasp the ways in which the industrialized world affected workers as well as to comprehend how production related to modern economics. She also wanted, perhaps, to encourage students to take up the call to social action. She hoped that field trips to poor houses, prisons, and reform schools would give her students the opportunity "to check their impressions derived from books" with the "reality" of actual individuals' lives.[14]

Balch often employed this teaching method in her two-semester course on social economics. This was the only subject that Balch taught consistently, nearly every year, throughout her career at Wellesley (see table 1). The first half of the course offered a "study of the defective, dependent, and delin-quent classes, accompanied by discussion of methods of dealing with each." The content specifically examined the roles of crime, prison reform, and alcohol in relation to those classes. During the second semester, students engaged in a "discussion of methods of meeting certain normal social needs, such as sanitation, housing, household economy, education, recreation, and thrift." Gradually, Balch added to the course description such components as investigating Boston neighborhoods as case studies and considering "the boundaries of self-help and collective assistance" in relation to the poor.[15]

The content of Balch's classes revealed the importance she placed on inter-action with the community. She later recalled of one course, "We visited the North End of Boston as one subject. Each student handed in a 'final paper' describing it, together with a map showing centers of social [gatherings], . . . fire houses, schools, hospitals, saloons, churches, settlement houses, and so forth." Balch wanted to impart her experiences with immigrant communities to her students, but not through her lecturing. She explained, "For some years I had had home library groups of Italians and their children in the past and consequently knew something of this rather isolated [and] largely foreign quarter, and I did my best to give some real sense of it [to] those . . . young women, having like most young people to understand reality first hand." Balch's approach also introduced her students to the world of reform. Her method of incorporating neighborhood visits into her lessons supported her philosophy that students benefit from trying to understand social problems firsthand. It also allowed her the opportunity to recruit students into reform work. Balch was often successful in this endeavor, which she once described as the "most fruitful side of my teaching." Many of her students entered social work professionally or participated in reform work. One student, Mary Wy-man, attributed Balch's approach to awakening in her "a sense of responsibil-ity for meeting social problems in our contemporary world."[16]

The college, as well as the students, recognized Balch's innovative teaching strategies. The department even entrusted her to design and implement new courses. In 1901, for example, the newly independent Department of Economics and Sociology requested that Balch institute a course in sociology. She later modestly claimed that she was in no way prepared to teach such a course but did so because "the Trustees had come to feel that Wellesley was behind the times in having no course in sociology." Thus, as she related the story, "Considerably against my conscience I undertook . . . [the] task. I think I feel that if I did not know what a course Sociology should cover, neither did anyone else." Her apprehension that she did not possess the necessary understanding to teach the course displayed an aspect of her general insecurity and was unjustified. After all, she did study with two of the premier American sociologists of the nineteenth century, Franklin Giddings and Albion Small. Balch's course offered "a study of facts and theories of social development, and more especially of the growth of institutions such as the family, the State, law and property" and required that students possess the ability to read in both German and French.[17]

Although Balch pioneered the field of sociology at Wellesley, the subject either did not greatly interest her or else held little appeal for Wellesley students. She first taught the course during the spring semester of 1901, when, according to Balch's recollection, she only had three students. She then offered it as a two-semester course for the following three years. However, after she returned from her two-year leave of absence in 1906, she never taught the course again. It remained on the course calendar, but no regular professor took it over until 1913, and then only for that one year. This was not an unusual trend for Balch, who often immersed herself in new projects and moved previous interests, such as teaching a course in sociology, out of her line of vision. Most often, she became distracted by her increasing interest to publish. Her commitment to chronicle her many interests in print made many demands on her time over the course of her teaching career.

Published Works

Balch was an intellectually curious person who held an almost insatiable desire to master newly emerging disciplines. Over the course of her teaching career, her expanding scholarly interests were reflected in her vast and varied published works. Her earlier writings, mainly in the fields of sociology and economics, beginning with her 1893 publication on public assistance in France, continued to hold an interest for her. But over the course of her first decade of teaching, her interests expanded to incorporate other disciplines. The vast amount of work she published during her teaching career not only reflected her evolving academic interests, but these pursuits also prepared her for her future work as a peace advocate, which would demand volumes of written work.

The first significant publication Balch produced after beginning at Wellesley College was an *Outline of Economics,* first issued in 1899. In this detailed and efficient little book, Balch provided her students with her perspective on the field. Totaling merely thirty-one pages, the text quite literally was an outline. She summarized the terms, principles, scope, and methods in the field to date. Writing her own text, however, allowed her to interpret all of the components and present them in her own way. For example, Balch claimed to adhere strictly to the Austrian School of Economics, but her textbook judiciously presented the contributions of various schools of thought.[18]

The first section of her outline dealt with the "preliminary" components of economics, including production, consumption, exchange, and distribution. Balch remarked that these constituted "convenient headings, but an imperfect analysis." Providing her students with the vocabulary necessary to discuss economics was primary. Another important definition in this section was Balch's careful presentation of "utility" as the "power to satisfy a want." Utility, she noted, decreases in relation to an individual's want being satisfied. Balch succinctly defined marginal utility as the "utility of last unit supplied." After setting out the central concepts in the field, Balch's text then examined the principles of economics.[19]

Balch diplomatically set up for discussion the varying views of the principles discussed in the first section—production, consumption, exchange, and distribution. Another central component to Balch's school of economics was marginalism, which she consistently emphasized in her text. Marginalism declared that an individual's consumption was only profitable up to a point. So a marginalist analysis seeks to determine the point at which benefit becomes cost.[20] On the other side of marginalist thinking was the role of consumers.

Balch reminded her students of the "responsibility of consumers"—in other words, themselves—"for conditions of production," and she asked them, "How far is purchase equivalent to an order to produce?" She also considered the "economic function of the housewife" in her discussion of consumer power. The example of a housewife's economic power continued to interest Balch; more than a decade later she published an article analyzing the economic contributions of homemakers. Balch argued that although housewives had lost their status as producers with the industrial revolution, they retained economic importance as consumers. Further, she demanded that economists examine housewives' role as producers of not easily quantifiable goods, namely, "the intimate conditions of human life."[21] Balch's decision to publish her own text allowed her to include such examples she believed were important to impart to her students.

In the final section of *Outline of Economics,* Balch acquainted her students with an understanding of the "scope and method of political economy." This began with a historical overview of the field of economics. She traced the development from the classical period but highlighted the unquestionably important role of Adam Smith and the English classicists, though she was careful to note their "capitalistic bias." She then presented the "critical period," from approximately 1850 to 1900, as a reaction to classical economics. Notably, she acknowledged the German Historical movement, the Socialist perspective, and the "ethical movement" of Arnold Toynbee. She placed her own Austrian School under the "theoretical work" heading, commenting on its tendency toward "psychological analysis and mathematical expression." Balch's outline included the development of economic schools of thought as well as the progression of the field's scope and method.[22]

Outline of Economics was useful for economics teachers and elevated Balch to a position of serious scholar. Several professors at the turn of the twentieth century produced such outlines, including the prominent American economist Richard Ely in 1893 (though Ely's text was considerably longer). A few years later, in 1908, another Boston professor, John Daniels, produced his own brief *Outline of Economics,* which offered similar information, though it was considered more biased.[23] Balch's book demonstrated her desire to have her particular formulation displayed to students rather than use another teacher's outline. It revealed her originality of thought as well as her status in the profession.

Balch also liked to examine case studies. She was interested in how cities affected individuals. One example of this interest resulted with the publication of *A Study of Conditions of City Life, with Special Reference to Boston,* in 1903. She produced this text as part of a lecture series held at Wellesley College and Denison House. She hoped the bibliography would be utilized as a tool for studying localities. Most of her direct experience related to Boston, but her study of France, for example, had affirmed her belief in the necessity of investigating municipal developments. By centralizing the informative studies of city conditions into one bibliography, Balch worked to heighten interest in local conditions and the role of civic commissions.[24] She contributed to the public discussions of city conditions and to the field of economics through her publications. She also used her pen on behalf of other subjects in which she took great interest. Particularly notable during this era was her ongoing involvement in the settlement and labor movements.

Balch's commitment to the labor movement generated a considerable amount of scholarly research. In 1899, for example, Boston's Twentieth Century Club chose Balch to serve on a three-member panel to investigate the shoe workers strike in Marlboro, Massachusetts, that had occurred dur-

ing the previous year. Balch's service on this committee demonstrated her
interest in and understanding of labor disputes. Her work on the report,
which was published later, reflected her commitment to a thorough investigation of all circumstances surrounding an issue and portrayed how such
an endeavor could be stymied. Despite her efforts to have a thorough and
objective investigation, Balch and the committee met with difficulties. One
obstacle Balch faced in her attempt to write a fair report was the employers'
refusal to speak with the investigators. The strikers happily complied, but
without "equal access to information from both sides," Balch admitted that
she had trouble producing an accurate assessment.[25] Although the process
was no doubt a frustrating one, Balch demonstrated her diplomatic skill
throughout the investigation and also revealed her proclivity for participating in committee-driven investigations. Work in these types of environments
would continue throughout her life.

Balch's investigative studies, articles, and academic textbooks certainly
provided an outlet for her scholarly interests. But when, in the early twentieth century, she turned her attention to the newly emerging field of immigration, she began to work on her largest study yet. Balch's immigration
study combined her knowledge of fields within the social sciences. History,
economics, and sociology were still defining their boundaries during this
era, and social scientists like Balch worked across disciplines. She applied
her experience in economics and sociology to a research project, becoming
a pioneer in the new field of immigration studies.

In 1906, Balch requested a paid sabbatical year, which Wellesley College
at that time awarded to professors after seven years of teaching. The board
approved, and she decided to take an additional year off without pay (one of
the few times in which she took advantage of the inheritance left to her by
her father).[26] This allowed her the time from the summer of 1906 through
the fall of 1908 to pursue her independent research on immigration.

Balch's findings took multiple published forms. Having originally released
the work as a series of articles for the journal *Charities and the Commons* (the
predecessor to *The Survey*) in 1906 and 1907, Balch revised the individual essays over the next three years, increasing the volume of material in the book
by adding several new chapters and incorporating more biographical and
statistical information. The Charities Publication Committee published her
study in book form, titled *Our Slavic Fellow Citizens,* in 1910. She hoped that
her work would be of interest to the general public, but she geared it especially "to busy social workers" and students.[27] She was right on both counts:
the extraordinarily focused study and the novel subject matter generated
considerable interest.

Balch's research focused on the immigration of Slavic peoples from various parts of the Austro-Hungarian Empire to the United States. She examined eight of the thirty-nine groups acknowledged by the U.S. Immigration Department as "Slav." So, her subject body was composed of "(1) Polish, (2) Slovak, (3) Croatian and Slovenian, (4) Ruthenian or Russniak, (5) Bohemian and Moravian, (6) Bulgarian, Servian, and Montenegrin, (7) Russian, (8) Dalmatian, Bosnian, and Herzegovinian" individuals and communities. Balch necessarily had to limit her study; to examine all thirty-nine groups would take a lifetime. She reasoned that those eight groups would be an interesting focus because they were the populations that lived mainly in the areas immediately surrounding Austria-Hungary, an area containing significant intercultural turmoil at that time.[28]

Balch's topic was innovative, and the resulting book was one of the first published works on the subject of Slavic immigration to the United States. So groundbreaking was this research that in 1976 a review of Slovak historiography described Balch as "so far ahead of her time that to this day no American historian has written a book of comparable depth and scope about the various Slavic ethnic groups in this country." Balch's masterpiece indeed presented an unprecedented immigration study, especially given that she

Balch in Hungary, 1905. Emily Greene Balch Papers, Swarthmore College Peace Collection.

chose to examine the effects of immigration in both the home country and in the United States. Balch even acknowledged that her study had "not yet been done for any other immigrant group equally thoroughly and systematically."[29] This was an uncharacteristically direct statement, revealing the depth of her pride in the study. Balch's work was groundbreaking in the social sciences. Most interesting, it provided insight into an area of the world that became the birthplace of war.

Published less than four years before World War I broke out in Europe, Balch's book contained observations of the conflict-entangled region of the Austro-Hungarian Empire that demonstrated the author's foresight into some of the problems that erupted into war. Specifically, Balch directly addressed the tensions among various national identities as well as the economic difficulties for many groups in the area. Balch's concern about growing nationalism in the region is particularly noteworthy, given the role of nationalism in the war. She keenly observed, for example, how temporary emigration frequently intensified nationalistic loyalties.

An anti-immigrant political and social outlook, known as nativism, grew increasingly popular among Americans in the early twentieth century, and Balch brilliantly attempted to refute such anti-immigrant attitudes in this work. She employed a diplomatic style that did not directly attack nativist assumptions; rather, she reframed the immigration question to test the validity of nativist claims, thus neutrally asking Americans to consider a clear presentation of the facts. She asked her readers first to acknowledge that immigration, regardless of one's feelings toward it, was "of transcendent importance" in their age and, given that fact, she reasoned, "It behooves us to understand as far as we can."[30]

Balch's presentation of information in *Our Slavic Fellow Citizens* was particularly powerful because she combined both qualitative and quantitative information to support her assertions. While she discussed cultural factors at length, she also pointed to voluminous data to support her assertions about particular immigrant groups. The book contained a fifty-page appendix, which by itself offered an abundance of data on immigrant populations. Throughout the text as well, she provided charts and maps to augment the quantitative side of her study. She also offered an equal number of photographs, demonstrating a clear interest in the individuals in her study. For example, in her extensive consideration of the conditions of Slovakian peasants, she included photographs depicting the homes they lived in and the clothing they wore.

Balch approached her study with her customary interest in presenting a balanced view. She was interested in both the individuals and the trends. In

the same manner, she wished to understand the Slavic immigrant experience from both sides of the ocean. That is, she wanted to learn where the
immigrants came from and what factors contributed to their immigration;
she also wished to show how those immigrants interacted with and affected
the communities to which they immigrated in the United States. Further,
Balch worked to understand exactly how the experience of immigration affected the home country, economically and culturally, "by the drawing off
of workers by the money sent home and by the immigrants returning with
or without savings."[31]

To do this, she organized her study into two parts. For the first she traveled throughout southeastern Europe to examine the causes and effects of
emigration on various groups of people. She carefully noted the distinctions
between the groups in her study, such as Bohemians, Slovaks, and Croatians.
In the second part, Balch discussed her investigations of the immigrants once
they arrived in the United States. For this section, she rarely was able to make
national or ethnic distinctions between immigrants, as the U.S. Immigration Department did not organize information with the same attention to
ethnic differences. Balch focused on the effect of emigration on the people
and economy a person left behind and, on the other side, she considered the
ways in which the immigration experience changed the people who came
to the United States and affected the American economy. In her words, the
"interest" of the study was "in the social character and consequences of the
emigration in question."[32]

Balch began by discussing the role of nationality among Slavic cultures. By
defining what constituted a "people," she justified the boundaries she drew
between the groups she studied. She argued that an individual's nationality
is dependent on a "physical kinship" (shared physical attributes with others),
a common language, and a "community of culture." She brilliantly presented
the complicated nature of nationalism among Slavic groups. Although she
was careful not to generalize among the groups, she maintained that the
Slavs constituted a large group that maintained a kinship through a shared
speech. This fact assisted the Pan-Slavic movement that emerged as early
as the eighteenth century and was particularly strong at the close of the
nineteenth. This movement continued to unite Slavic groups and agitate
for independent Slavic states.[33]

In her book, Balch differentiated among the multitude of groups that constituted "Slavs." She began with "the stream that comes to us" from various
regions within Austria-Hungary, which provided "a fair basis for the discussion of the Slavic movement to America." She then considered, in this order,
Bohemian and Slovak emigration, immigrants from Galicia (Austrian Poles

and Ruthenians), and Slovenian and Croatian migration; she ended the section with a look at emigration from the Adriatic coast of Austria-Hungary.[34]

In each section, Balch methodically examined a series of questions, beginning with a consideration of the historical factors that catalyzed emigration. The histories of individual lands and groups explained much about the reasons for emigration. For example, in the case of the Slovenians, Balch detailed how the transitions of lands and incorporation of languages among the peoples produced a long history of "radical friction" with the Germans. This buildup of animosity among cultures was one element leading to the desire to emigrate. For the Austrian Poles and Ruethenians from Galicia (also known as "Austrian Poland"), emigration related to the wretched climate and even worse poverty-stricken economies, as well as to problems of clashing nationalities.[35]

Economics and politics also contributed to patterns of emigration. Many Slavic peoples had experienced a relatively rapid transition from feudalism to semi-industrialized economies. Others remained in semi-feudal conditions. Balch remembered, from her time in the region, that "it was surprising to see how much of the feudal middle ages still survived." While some Slavic groups emigrated for political reasons, other emigration stemmed from severe economic conditions. Not surprisingly, in some cases, a combination produced large-scale emigration. Political and economic conditions resulted from the historical circumstances in the area, and Balch closely examined such historical factors. With regard to Bohemia, for example, Balch cited economic factors as the central reasons for emigration. People began to leave Bohemia in the middle of the nineteenth century as the area suffered the economic consequences of "making the fateful transition from a mainly agricultural to a mainly industrial economy." For Croatia, as well as for Galicia and upper Hungary, emigration usually resulted from the economic circumstances inherited from the end of feudal serfdom in those regions in 1848.[36]

Balch peppered the text with interesting stories about the traditions of individuals she encountered while traveling throughout the Slavic lands. Her interest in Croatian traditions was particularly extensive. She detailed the courting and marriage customs, writing that the ceremony was always "extremely elaborate" and contained "a wedding speech which is handed down by verbal memory [and] takes up eight or ten printed pages." She also showed a particular fondness for the folk legends and songs of the Slovaks of Hungary. She marveled at the effect folklore left on both the people and the country itself. She wrote, "On almost every crag in some districts stands a ruined castle, all that the most romantic could desire in site and story." This led to a multitude of legends, some containing historical truths.[37]

After examining the histories and cultures of each group, she considered at length those characteristics that defined each group's emigration pattern. She considered whether emigrants sought employment in urban or agricultural areas. She also pointed to the ways in which American culture changed the Slavic immigrants. She discussed, for example, the Slovaks' "proneness to drink" and how the American work system only enhanced such a quality. Balch also examined which groups were more likely to settle in the United States than return home, the settlement patterns (where they existed), and the transfer of funds back to home countries. In one example, she noted that unlike their Bohemian counterparts, Slovak men tended not to settle in the United States but to earn enough money to support their families at home until they could return. However, Balch noticed that the Slovaks' emigration pattern was changing to one of increased permanence. As this sequence evolved, the husband usually journeyed to the United States first and then decided to remain. After saving enough money, his wife and children would join him. Balch noted that this system did not always please other family members, especially wives who feared traveling alone with small children. Balch related one such story: "One woman we met just starting out, waiting at the home railroad station with baby and bundles. Her husband, after vainly urging her to come to him, had finally cut off supplies and sent a prepaid ticket, and willy-nilly she was going."[38]

Balch's careful detailing of these trends and her subtle commentary on them reveal what was essentially her outlook on an early phase of globalization. While she related the many advances made by groups of people through the experience of becoming immigrants in the United States, she bemoaned the many losses, particularly the cultural ones. As more immigrants became "Americanized," significant cultural distinctions and traditions disappeared. Unlike many American progressive reformers, Balch found this to be sad. In her discussion of Bohemians, she addressed the "cultural effects" of American immigration, stating, "It probably goes to enhance the tendency of the civilization of our times to wipe out all distinctive traits." In another instance she argued even more explicitly that immigration's consequences included the elimination of important cultural traditions. She described immigration as "a part of that great leveling and fusing activity which is one side of the historical process." She then concluded, "Civilization of the prevailing type is becoming planetary." The concept of planetary civilization held many prospects for peace, as Balch would write about in the future. Yet Balch did not fail to recognize that such an achievement would sacrifice cultural distinctions.[39]

In the second part of her book, Balch explored the lives of Slavic immigrants in the United States. She conducted her research for this section first, as it allowed her the opportunity to study languages that would assist her with her investigations in Europe. She visited immigrant Slavic workers across the United States, including communities in Massachusetts, Pennsylvania, Nebraska, Texas, Minnesota, and Wisconsin. She spent much of the summer living in "nursing villages" around Pennsylvania. She then moved to New York, where she boarded with a working family on the Upper East Side, which "was no 'settlement' experience but something far more intimate." From the coalmines of Pennsylvania and Texas to the farmlands of the upper Midwest, Balch meticulously recorded the conditions in which people lived and worked.[40]

The portion of Balch's study that focused on the United States contained significantly more quantitative information, despite the fact that this information was, at times, problematic. She argued that American census data was unreliable because the government could "supply no precise information as to nationalities." Also, the United States did not gather the kinds of information she sought, such as urban versus rural settlement patterns. Utilizing a variety of sources, Balch estimated that four million Slavs were living in the United States in 1910. She acknowledged, however, that this was merely an estimate, and the actual total could be anywhere between 3,700,000 and 6,420,000.[41]

Balch introduced the second section of her study with a historical review of Slavic immigrants to the United States prior to 1880. In this, as with the rest of the chapters, Balch found it more useful to review common trends and then specify the differences among national groups where possible. Generally, this group of immigrants consisted of farmers who went to the American Midwest to establish their own farms. She was careful to remind her readers, and most likely those nativist-thinking Americans, that state governments as well as federal bodies had actively solicited the agricultural labor of these immigrants.[42]

For the remainder of the work, Balch examined Slavic immigration after 1880 and considered the circumstances of immigrants during the time in which Balch conducted her research. Whereas most of the Slavic immigrants prior to 1880 had consisted of Bohemians and Poles, the Slavic immigrant population became much more diverse during this later period. Also, far fewer of the more recent immigrants journeyed to the United States with the ability and intention to start their own farms. Balch noted that fewer of the new immigrants intended to settle permanently. Slavic immigrants during this period were widely known for their work in the mining industry, especially in the anthracite mines of Pennsylvania.[43]

Balch's analysis of the "economic situation of Slavs in the United States" as of 1906 revealed that the Slavic immigrant worked mainly in "mining, metal work, common labor and agriculture." She concluded that Slavic immigrant labor did not depress the American wage standard, again rebuking nativist notions. She categorized their work as "the rough, manly labor of the country." This type of labor abounded, she argued, and immigrants did not affect the wages of others.[44]

Toward the end of the book, Balch returned to her interest in the cultural transformations among the immigrants. Utilizing more of a qualitative approach, Balch analyzed the "household life" of these immigrants. She explored in detail the consequences of having so few women in the Slavic colonies. Approximately one third of Slavic immigrants in 1906 were women, and thus those women had a greater social value, as wives and as overseers for boarders. Balch also considered the ways in which American work increased the standards of living for many Slavic immigrants, but she did not ignore the darker aspects. For example, she cited the problems with tenement housing and overcrowding, conditions which frequently led to "disease and immorality." While American life affected immigrant groups in both positive and negative ways, many Slavs labored to maintain a cultural identity. Balch's interest in this aspect of immigrant life ranged from clothing, homes, music, and immigrants' involvement in social groups. She devoted one chapter to the study of Slavic "organized life," particularly national societies and church groups.[45]

Our Slavic Fellow Citizens concluded with an exploration of "the question of assimilation." Here, Balch made her most overt arguments against nativist claims. Keenly examining the "Americanizing pressure" and its influence on different Slavic groups, Balch concluded that often this burden led to heightened nationalism and thus greater intercultural conflict. Finally, Balch asserted that, in spite of nativist influences in the United States, immigration policy would always be determined by economic interests, regardless of whether or not increased immigration would be of any benefit or detriment to American culture or immigrant workers.[46]

Finally, it is important to consider Balch's choice of a title for her magnum opus. *Our Slavic Fellow Citizens* issued a call for Americans to understand the lives of a group of people who were their *fellows,* their equals. Further, they were indeed citizens, in Balch's definition, not temporary workers, despite the fact that many returned to their home countries. This could be considered an early declaration of Balch's global citizenship idea. Our "fellow citizens" implied equality.

Although Balch's book was not popularly distributed, it received superb reviews in the academic press. The annals of the *American Academy of Politi-*

cal and Social Science considered it "excellently done" and "one of the most sympathetic and interesting studies of the immigrant." The *American Journal of Sociology* praised Balch's work for being "both scientific and popular." Her peers recognized Balch's skill in synthesizing so much quantitative and qualitative data while still producing an engaging book. The same review declared, "Miss Balch is thoroughly in line with the best thought in social science when she traces the line of continuity of life and development by following the immigrant to his native land and thence to the home beyond the waters."[47] Balch's comprehensive treatment of Slavic immigrants in the United States and Europe constituted a significant contribution to the fields of sociology, history, economics, and immigration studies.

Balch believed so deeply in the importance of her immigration research that she uncharacteristically financed the project herself. With regard to her financial compensation, she later recalled, "I think I received for this work of 2½ years $17 in royalties besides a generous number of gift copies. I spent some thousands of dollars preparing it." Balch claimed to not resent this fact, stating, "It was well worth it if only in the pleasure it gave me and I hope it has also been of some use."[48] Whether or not Balch felt so generous at the time she doled out her own money is unknown, yet she did receive widespread acknowledgement for the work, and *Our Slavic Fellow Citizens* remained prominent as the published work for which she received the most accolades prior to her career in the peace movement.

Why did Balch choose to study Slavic peoples in the early twentieth century? Certainly, immigration as an academic discipline offered her the opportunity to combine her talents in quantitative analysis and qualitative synthesis. But the specific choice to study Slavic immigration is noteworthy. What this group ultimately provided for Balch the scholar was an opportunity to show the effects, both positive and negative, of immigration. Obviously, the assimilation issue was of constant concern to her. She could have chosen any immigrant group to demonstrate the complicated nature of that issue. Examining the labor contributions of any pool of immigrants might also have been fine to make her arguments to debunk nativist claims. What remains fascinating about Balch's choice of the Slavs is her interest in the part of the world from which the groups emigrated.

Without question, Balch's immigration scholarship stood as the masterpiece of her Wellesley years. She did not neglect her other interests, however; as well as pursuing professional studies in print, Balch became an advocate through her publications. Her interests were diverse, though mostly interrelated. Throughout her years as a professor, Balch's social reform work, as a volunteer and as a scholar, remained significant.

Social Reform

During Balch's two decades at Wellesley College, she became increasingly involved with social reform activities then popular among Boston progressives. Her interests, often reflected in her teaching and writing, ranged from the settlement movement to women's suffrage, from the Consumer's League to organized labor, and, eventually, to peace activism. Understanding the development of Balch's involvement with reform is key to seeing her path from college professor to international peace leader.

Balch and other like-minded professors at Wellesley believed they could utilize the settlement movement to impart a real-life understanding of classroom topics. Such professors at Wellesley remained personally involved with settlement houses in Boston and often encouraged their students to participate in the movement. After all, a central "object" of the College Settlements Association (CSA), which founded Denison House, focused on "extend[ing] the educating power of the Settlement" by continuing to recruit female college graduates to work for the movement. Balch and some of her colleagues successfully generated support for the settlement ideology among their students. In the year 1897–98, for example, seven graduates of Wellesley College were full- or part-time residents at the Boston settlement.[49]

Several of Balch's friends on the Wellesley faculty were women she met while founding Denison House. Although these women did not establish full-time careers in the settlement movement, they continued to volunteer at the house and urged their students to become involved in these activities that they considered vital to social change. In December 1915, Vida Scudder wrote an article for the *Wellesley College News* magazine on the subject of college settlements, with the explicit purpose of recruiting college women into the CSA. Her article was the first of a series that intended to place "the work of the Association and the opportunities it offers before undergraduates of the different women's colleges who nominally support it." Scudder emphasized that educated women had a responsibility to apply their privilege toward the advancement of their fellow citizens. She called settlement work a "responsibility" of educated women, "voluntary, of course, but sanctioned by the loyalty of a quarter century, by a record of productive and noble work, by devotion and sacrifice which can never be narrated, on the part of college women."[50] Scudder's vigorous efforts to recruit CSA members reflected the unyielding commitment of professors such as herself to the settlement cause.

Balch also remained loyal to the settlement movement, and to Denison House in particular, throughout her academic career. In her classroom, she integrated her experiences as an activist into her teaching. Like Scudder,

Balch penned articles aimed at increasing CSA membership. In one such essay, she discussed the shared education experience of a settlement house and how it offered elite young women the opportunity to learn about different cultures and countries, without ever leaving the city of Boston. Balch, ever the social scientist, also emphasized that the settlement allowed students to study the social conditions of the underprivileged more thoroughly. She appealed to her students as budding social scientists and emphasized the ways in which they could help "the immigrant who is looking for a way to 'break into America,' the victims of the loan shark and the grafter."[51]

Although Balch never joined a political party, in 1906 circumstances convinced her that it was time to claim a political affiliation, and she publicly declared herself a socialist. Prior to that year she had supported certain socialist ideas and maintained many close friendships with socialists, but she had avoided identifying herself as such. In her memoirs, she recorded that she "had long struggled" with the question of calling herself a socialist. As a student in Berlin she was exposed to "democratic socialism," then popular among German students, as well as "national socialism," favored by her professors. Balch wrote of her understanding of socialism, "I was influenced by [the] Fabians, by [Charles] Kingsley and the Christian socialists, [and] by revisionist and reformist tendencies in the socialist movement."[52]

Balch's eventual acceptance of a socialist identity resulted from events she witnessed the previous year. She traced her decision to one particularly powerful experience she had while conducting research in Prague. Her thoughts on the subject were so vivid, they are worth reproducing in full. She recalled:

One unbearably bleak morning I saw a man fumbling with his bare fingers in an ash barrel to try to find something to eat. Heaven knows I had seen enough misery and actual starvation in Boston in 1893, when Denison House was new, seen sweating of the old dreadful sort that prevailed before the garment trades were unionized, when in the Rivington Street Settlement the rattle of foot power sewing machines ran from earliest morning till late at night during a period of hideous overwork, to be followed by a period of unrelievable lack of work. I had lived for weeks in an old-time New York tenement, where the bedroom depended for light and air on a narrow shaft ending in a well into which garbage was dropped. I had lived in Allegheny at a time when social-political corruption was incredibly bad, with plenty of unpunished murder. I had seen the impersonal cruelty of our immigrant laws. I had had the sickening experience of being publicly prayed for by the poor outraged little delinquent boys in an institution of which I was one of the trustees, and "enjoyed" a fine dinner waited on by the prisoners in a penal institution on Deer Island that was a disgrace to my native city of Boston. The Prague experience was merely the final drop too much which led me to call myself a socialist.[53]

While Balch declined to join Eugene Debs's Socialist Party in the United States, so completely did she embrace her ideological position as a socialist that in 1906 she informed Wellesley College of her declared outlook and demanded that the trustees know this when considering her contract.

As a professor, Balch continued to teach classes and speak at events at Denison House, especially those involving women and organized labor. In addition to its settlement mission, Denison House was the center of activity for Boston's labor movement, and so it was through Denison House that Balch became a dedicated leader in the trade-union movement. The house's position as a hub for labor activists and intellectuals in Boston was highlighted when, in 1894, the women's labor leader Mary Kenney married the labor organizer and reporter for the *Boston Globe,* Jack O'Sullivan. Shortly after the ceremony in New York, Denison House in Boston hosted a celebratory dinner for the couple, and numerous social reformers, including Balch, attended this dinner. That both settlement reform workers and labor organizers attended the celebration indicated the closeness of the two movements in turn-of-the-century Boston. Denison House's central standing in Boston's turn-of-the-century labor movement was also revealed by the fact that it hosted numerous meetings of labor unions and organizers of labor campaigns. The settlement assisted such groups as the Massachusetts Association of Working Girls Clubs, the Massachusetts Consumers' League, and the Women's Educational and Industrial Union.[54]

Balch worked closely with Mary Kenney O'Sullivan, who had become a central figure in Boston labor. The two women first met through Jane Addams at Hull House but became close colleagues when Kenney moved to Boston in 1894. Balch felt that both Mary and Jack O'Sullivan shared her own outlook on social reform work. The couple "understood trade unionism not as a struggle for material advantage." This resonated with Balch. She also believed that the trade union movement was "part of a wide-spread and many-sided effort for juster and more humane social relations everywhere."[55]

Balch's passion for organized labor was also shared by another friend, Mary Morton Kehew, who had been responsible for bringing Mary Kenney from Chicago to organize Boston women trade workers in 1894. At that time, Kehew served as president of the Women's Educational and Industrial Union (WEIU) in Boston, which endeavored to improve the education of all classes of women by holding lectures and discussions open to working women. Balch greatly respected Kehew and saw her as "a leader and initiator" in the effort to bring together different classes of women. Balch deeply admired Kehew, commenting that "when unionism was still an economic heresy she saw the need for organization and for organization of women as well as of men." In fact, Balch credited Kehew with the success of Boston's settlement house during its early years, praising her as "essentially the statesman." Balch marveled at Kehew's talent to examine a social situation and determine "where was a thing that needed to be done and what old or new organization might effect it." Kehew then brilliantly organized actions to meet problems. Balch admired and mimicked this quality.[56]

Balch's involvement with Boston's organized labor movement increased over the course of the first decade of the twentieth century. She volunteered much of her time to supporting the establishment of trade unions. Balch later recorded her thoughts concerning her early involvement with labor in Boston, revealing both her hopes at the time and her subsequent disappointment: "There was a great deal of idealism in the trade-union movement of the time and as we saw it and it has been one of the [saddest] experiences of [my] life that it has done so relatively little for the . . . most unskilled and those that found the greatest difficulty in forming effective means."[57]

Balch became involved in the formation of a national Women's Trade Union League (WTUL) in 1903. The WTUL aimed to confront those issues by organizing national campaigns and lobbying for protective legislation on behalf of the women who worked in the industries. This differed from previous incarnations of women's auxiliary units of male labor organizations in that the primary focus of the group's efforts related to the problems faced by wage-earning women across the trades. It joined together women of middle- and upper-class backgrounds, such as Balch, with working-class women. Balch's understanding of the new group's purpose was to join "women with more leisure and means than working girls" with those in the trade union movement to work toward "trade union protection." Originating in England in the 1870s, the movement arrived in the United States in 1903, when Boston hosted the American Federation of Labor (AFL) convention. At that time, Kehew met with William English Walling to discuss his desire to create an American version of the British Women's Trade Union League. Balch was one of three women who attended this founding meeting.[58]

In the following year, 1904, Balch, Kehew, and Kenney O'Sullivan worked together along with other labor figures to found Boston's own branch of the national WTUL. At this time, Kehew acted as president, Jane Addams as vice president, and Mary Kenney O'Sullivan served as secretary of the national organization. The Boston branch named Balch as chair of its executive committee. Balch remained dedicated to the organization but did not seek to occupy any national leadership position during those early years, as much of her energy during that time was also devoted to preparing for her research sabbatical.

Amazingly, Balch did not struggle with balancing both her professorial and labor duties. In fact, with time she became even more involved with her volunteer activities, though she did not give less to her teaching and scholarship. In 1908, the WTUL elected her president of its Boston branch. Notably, Balch's memoirs refer only briefly to this position, which she falsely indicated was more of an honorary one. Perhaps she downplayed her involvement with the league out of modesty; more likely, however, she did not wish to highlight a period of public controversy.

Not long into her presidency Balch found herself in the middle of an internal labor dispute, one that disclosed much about Balch's reform outlook. Two opposing positions emerged within the women's trade union movement. One held that the organization's purpose must be to advocate directly for protective legislation. The other wished to focus on allying with the men's labor movement. Balch stood firmly on the side of supporting efforts to create change through passing legislation. This fundamental divide over how to make gains for labor plagued the Boston branch of the League, and Balch's election to the presidency in 1908 emphasized a direction for their work that stirred much disagreement among its members.

In her history of the WTUL's Boston branch, Kathleen Nutter specifically blamed Balch for the Boston organization's many problems. Balch had always supported change through legislative means and thus believed more strongly in legislation than organization. Mary Crawford, the branch's secretary who disagreed with Balch's position, resigned when Balch became president in 1908. At the time, Crawford remained ambiguous about her decision, but Nutter argued, "Crawford was a staunch advocate of organization, claiming that 'women in industry will receive just treatment and fair wages only if they ally themselves with the Trade Union Movement.'" Pointing also to Balch's involvement with various state commissions, Nutter demonstrated that Balch's clear preference for labor reform through legislation over labor organization for women upset many. The situation continued to worsen until June 1908 when the branch faced disbanding. In that month, the national office sent organizers, as well as the national president, to try to sort out the Boston situation. When relations continued to deteriorate, the League leadership cited Balch as the problem. The situation remained unresolved until January 1911, when the branch elected a new president, Sue Ainslie Clark, who had been Balch's student eight years before.[59]

The controversial years of Balch's presidency do present an important struggle in the women's labor movement, and the event opens a window to Balch's ideology. Usually a consummate mediator, Balch remained adamant in her position. Refusing to compromise, she enhanced a political divide within the organization. She later downplayed her role in the WTUL, perhaps embarrassed from her lack of diplomatic tact that she was so typically associated with. Her behavior had revealed a strict stubbornness that she rarely exhibited. The debate between those who supported labor organizing versus legislative measures to gain labor advantages continued within the labor movement and also foreshadowed the breakdown in the woman's rights movement after the passage of the federal suffrage amendment.

In 1911, Balch left the presidency of the WTUL, but her commitment to the labor movement never waned. In addition to her labor community, some of the radical professors at Wellesley College shared her political views. Vida Scudder, professor of English and Balch's friend since the days of founding Denison House, was also a staunch socialist. The two women planned a conference in Boston in 1909, "Socialism as a World Movement." Balch said of the symposium that it "proved both very enjoyable and I believe useful." Scudder and Balch successfully recruited popular speakers and organized a well-attended forum. The two main speakers the first day of the conference were John Spargo, the British muckraker, and Victor Berger, the Austrian-born socialist politician from the American Midwest. Berger traced the historical development of the socialist movement and claimed that in 1909 approximately 8.8 million voting socialists existed. He believed that socialist transformation would occur without revolution. Spargo spoke on the natural development of socialism, associating the movement with the American abolitionists. The conference drew a large crowd that first evening in Boston's Chickering Hall. One newspaper report amusingly noted that the audience "displayed more outward evidences of prosperity than are commonly seen at a meeting of the kind." On the final evening of the well-attended conference, Scudder delivered a powerful speech on the necessity of Christian Socialism. She emphasized the natural kinship between Christian civilization and a socialist society, and she argued that the two in fact were interdependent in order to deliver their common vision of community. Scudder and Balch acted as the main organizers of the conference, though Balch worried that other socialists might not have considered her a true socialist because she was not a party member. She remarked of the conference, "One of its by-products was the personal contact with men like Maurice [*sic*] Hillquit and Victor Berger, both of whom were generously friendly to a half-way ally like myself."[60]

Balch thrived when busy and so, not surprisingly, found time to dedicate to other causes. A sampling of the numerous organizations to which she belonged during this period—Boston Equal Suffrage Association for Good Government, the Woman's Education Association, the American Political Science Association, the American Statistical Association, and the Fabian Club—shows the range of issues she endorsed or remained informed of. Clearly, she balanced her reform commitments with professional associations. She also became increasingly drawn into the antiwar movement.[61]

One organization that received a good deal of Balch's time was the local Consumer's League. The Consumer movement, a vital element of Progressive Era reform, spawned Consumer's Leagues beginning around the turn of the twentieth century. These groups focused on educating consumers about their power and about the conditions in which products were made. Consumer's Leagues ran a multitude of campaigns relating both to consumers' rights legislation and to the education of shoppers. The ultimate goal was to assist the working class by promoting the purchase of those goods that were produced under fair working conditions only. Balch explained the league's efforts to protest the rampant "sweating" conditions during that period, writing, "The idea of the Consumer's League was to induce conscientious buyers to use their purchasing power to strengthen employers who offered good wages and good conditions of work, safety against accidents." The ideals and methods of the Consumer's Leagues fit perfectly with Balch's personal beliefs and professional development. She even incorporated a class on consumerism into her teaching schedule and worked with Consumer's Leagues in both Boston and New York.[62]

Balch combined her extensive involvement in Boston's reform activities with her teaching during her years at Wellesley, especially prior to 1914. After August 1914, her broad interest in social reform began to focus exclusively on war mediation and prevention, American neutrality, and ongoing campaigns for international peace. Her work with the international peace movement continued to infringe on her teaching responsibilities and ultimately threatened her professorial career at Wellesley College.

4. "Tragic Interruption," 1914–18

When war broke out in Europe in the summer of 1914, American Progressives overwhelmingly responded with shock and dismay. Many were horrified by actions that seemed a reversal of the great social progress of the time. After nearly a century of peace (or at least an absence of war on a large scale among the major nations of Europe), a return to widespread warfare disturbed many. Jane Addams described the American response to the war in Europe as an "almost instantaneous" feeling throughout the country of "astonishment that such an archaic institution should be revived in modern Europe.[1] While Americans, in large part removed from the immediate dangers of war, were perhaps less concerned with European affairs, Progressive reformers were particularly alarmed.

The war altered the fabric of Progressive reform. The American peace movement prior to 1914 was, not surprisingly, dominated by men and focused on instituting international methods of arbitration should war occur. Most female social reformers focused on domestic issues, including immigration and labor. With the onset of war, most of these women turned their energies toward the peace movement. Through their work with immigrant populations, settlement workers such as Jane Addams and Emily Greene Balch had developed deep convictions that all differences, even those based in class and racial tensions, could be resolved without resorting to violence. The experience of war was antithetical to that view. Further, war diverted national attention away from the work of domestic social reform. As Jane Addams asked, "What are a few children suffering under bad conditions in the factories" compared with men dying in the trenches throughout Europe?[2]

Such social reformers rightly feared that the experience of war would set back their advancements in social progress. Addams believed that at the war's end, "the long march of civilization would have to be taken up again much nearer to the crude beginnings of human progress." Balch agreed. She further saw the war as an imperialistic conquest, a return to barbaric modes of conflict resolution. Most important, she viewed the onset of the war as a "tragic interruption" of "the real business" of their era: "the realization of a more satisfactory economic order."[3]

The new peace movement that blossomed in 1914 joined the subject of international peace with local issues of social justice. Women from social reform movements not surprisingly became leaders in newly formed peace organizations. Jane Addams, Emily Greene Balch, Florence Kelley, Fanny Garrison Villard, Lillian Wald, and many others, expanded the ranks and scope of American peace activism. Many of these women also transformed the peace movement by incorporating feminist goals into peace work. After all, women working to expand their national power by campaigning for federal suffrage saw also that their participation could transform international policy as well.[4]

Through her friends and colleagues in the settlement and labor movements, Balch became involved with many of the modern peace organizations that formed in response to the war. Her professional relationship with Jane Addams was an important link to the burgeoning peace movement, but it was far from her only connection. Given her history of involvement with Progressive reform, it made sense that Balch would join organized efforts to improve a specific condition. As an economist, Balch adopted a method of examining concrete problems from multiple perspectives. In 1914, the problem was the reliance on warfare rather than diplomacy, and Balch approached the question of war in her characteristic way of appraising the international situation from the point of view of all invested parties. Furthermore, an organized response, founded in the spirit of social improvement and advanced through democratically run meetings, reflected Balch's fundamental beliefs in how to analyze and confront a problem. With the onset of war in 1914, her interest in questions of war and peace changed from the theoretical and scholarly to the practical and immediate. She thus transferred her classroom considerations to the question of war and how to respond to it. She came to believe that "there is no half-way house" in one's attitude toward the war in Europe and that "war can and must come to an end."[5] As her convictions against the war solidified, she bolstered her understanding that a dilemma is best confronted first through careful scrutiny and investigation.

As with all of the other issues in her life, Balch approached the question of peace in Europe with her characteristic passion balanced with methodical analysis. Her training as an economist and sociologist, as well as her extensive knowledge of languages, enhanced her usefulness to the peace movement. She ultimately joined several organizations throughout the course of the war, but she and her like-minded colleagues focused their support on one specific strategy: negotiated peace through continuous mediation. To this end, she and her fellow pacifists promoted that the United States remain neutral in order to act as the main arbiter toward a peace settlement.

Balch never lost hope that individual people, working together across national boundaries, could produce change. This idea stemmed in part from her experiences abroad and her work with the settlement houses. It also provided the basis of her work with the women's international peace movement, which would dominate the rest of her life. As Balch made the transition from professional academic to international activist, she never surrendered her position as an educator. She simply refocused her subject matter and vastly expanded her audience.

Balch and the Modern Peace Movement

In the early weeks of the war, Balch did not yet view the European conflict as a "tragic interruption" of progress. She had yet to comprehend the magnitude of the situation. She was also secluded from the immediate activities and discussions that dominated in urban settings. Balch spent the summer of 1914 vacationing in Maine with Katharine Coman. Less than six months later, Coman would succumb to cancer, so most of Balch's attention that summer focused on her friend's health, not the war. She did write to her sister in August expressing a general concern regarding the war, remarking, "Isn't this war too terrible for words? We can only trust it will be both short and *final*."[6] Balch's hopes for a swift end to the conflict gradually gave way to a more complete understanding of the seemingly endless scope of the war and growing importance of neutral nations in bringing the war to a close.

Balch's initial response to the war also revealed her diplomatic character. She felt deeply conflicted regarding the responsibility of Germany, unlike many of her compatriots. She was "surprised" to discover that most Americans "were condemning Germany." Although she detested German militarism, Balch retained a deep connection to that nation since her Berlin days and despaired at its position in the war. She denounced the chauvinistic nationalism of Germany, but she never lost faith in the nation's potential. Nor did she believe that blame lay entirely with one side. In November 1914, Balch wrote to the editor of a German magazine in the United States, criticizing the publication's assumption of Slavic inferiority. In her letter, she referred to herself as "a lover of Germany" and revealed that she felt "most Americans are unfair to the German position in the present war."[7] This letter demonstrated Balch's complicated feelings toward Germany, but it also showed her dedication to a negotiated peace. She did not wish merely to reproach one side in the war and celebrate the other as the victor. She endeavored throughout the war to try to remain neutral toward all belligerent nations.

The first organized meeting of American Progressives in response to the war occurred in the fall of 1914. Balch had returned from Maine to Wellesley College. She received a letter from Lillian Wald, a well-known social reformer who ran the Henry Street Settlement in New York City. Wald and Addams were organizing a meeting of social workers and others who "deal with the social fabric." The purpose of the meeting was to "clarify" their position on the war and, "if it seems wise, to act in concert."[8] Addams and Wald both wanted Balch to join their group because they knew that her background in social work and her reputation for intelligent and diplomatic observation would be an asset. Balch, eager to participate in discussions of how Progressives should proceed, traveled to New York for the September 29 meeting.

In New York, Balch joined approximately twenty colleagues and friends, many of whom, like Balch, were (or at one point had been) social workers or other professionals dedicated to improving conditions in their communities. Florence Kelley, a friend and the head of the Consumer movement, was there. So were George Kirchwey, prison reformer and dean of Columbia Law School, and Felix Adler, founder of the New York Society for Ethical Culture. Paul Kellogg, editor of the leftist journal *Survey*, also joined the group and became the author of its manifesto.[9]

The participants discussed possible campaigns and organizational plans should the war continue. Although those present shared a common goal, division was already evident at the first meeting. The group debated creating a new organization with the purpose of setting up committees throughout the United States working to "consolidate public opinion" in support of American involvement in a negotiated peace. After substantial discussion, this suggestion was eventually withdrawn. Despite its failure to form a new, nationwide organization at this meeting, the gathering was significant in that it demonstrated the link between the settlement workers, academics, and progressive social reformers in the creation of the modern peace movement. Jane Addams emphasized that those in attendance at the earliest wartime peace meetings were "trying to formulate the reaction to war on the part of those who for many years had devoted their energies to the reduction of devastating poverty."[10] What they had in common was a vision of the future, a vision that the war might destroy.

Although the Henry Street meeting did not result with the formation of a national association, its members continued to meet, frequently adopting new names. Initially, they convened under the auspices of the Peace Committee or the Henry Street Committee. Balch continued to maintain a close association with this group throughout the war, but she dedicated most of her time to another newly formed organization, the Woman's Peace Party.

The Formation of the Woman's Peace Party

Although multiple peace organizations were in existence in the United States at the time, the Woman's Peace Party (WPP) brought women from peace, suffrage, and reform work together in an association solely for women. The organization formed at the encouragement of two international suffrage speakers, Emmeline Pethick-Lawrence and Rosika Schwimmer, who happened to be on a speaking tour of the United States in the summer of 1914. Pethick-Lawrence, a world-renowned British suffragist, shifted the focus of her lectures that summer from voting rights for women to international peace. Schwimmer, a Hungarian suffragist, similarly altered the subject of her speeches at the same time and, in August 1914, began to campaign for neutral nations to work as mediators between the belligerent countries in order to end the war. Lecturing during the late fall of 1914, the two women urged the establishment of a new women's peace organization, one that, like its international counterparts, would work for both suffrage and peace. They called upon Jane Addams and the American suffrage leader Carrie Chapman Catt to pilot the new movement.

Despite their reservations about creating yet another peace association and the potential difficulties that might (and did) arise from combining the goals of the suffrage and peace movements, Addams and Catt organized the formation meeting for January 1915 in Washington, D.C., with Addams presiding. More than three thousand women attended. The organizers even had to turn back several hundred others because of space limitations. Among the participants were eighty-six delegates who represented thousands of other women not in attendance.[11]

Balch was not present at the meeting in Washington, nor did she attend the early meetings of the Massachusetts state branch, which was the first state group to form. Her involvement with the WPP began in the late spring of 1915, when international suffrage leaders invited American women reformers to attend an international conference of women in The Hague. This city had hosted peace conferences in 1899 and 1907, which produced discussions of diplomatic solutions to international disputes and resulted with the signing of international treaties.

Jane Addams, on behalf of the Woman's Peace Party, invited Balch to the meeting, asserting, "We feel that American women, having more freedom than those of most other countries, should especially respond to such a call, issued by European women, at this very critical moment in world affairs." Addams urged her friend to persuade Wellesley College to grant her a leave of absence, arguing that the college must understand that "nothing could be better for the college in which you are teaching economics than the experience which the conference at The Hague would give you." She tried to persuade Balch of her particular value to such a mission by writing, "I am especially anxious that we should have delegates conversant with the racial and nationality situation, and I know of no one who would meet these requirements better than you would."[12]

Addams's letters successfully convinced Balch to lobby for a leave of absence. She even forwarded Addams's letters to the college president, Ellen Pendleton. After convincing Pendleton that she would carefully arrange for the management of her classes and grading of papers should her absence be extended, Balch received permission to leave. Pendleton conceded to the request only two weeks before Balch departed for the Netherlands. While the college permitted the leave of absence, it refused to assist Balch in financing the expedition. Pendleton informed Balch, "I can well understand that the expense involved in such an arrangement might make it impossible, but I do not feel justified in asking the Trustees for any appropriation to make such an absence possible." Although Pendleton refused to lobby for funding, she processed Balch's appeal under a very tight deadline (Addams first invited Balch on March 13, and the women sailed on April 13). Pendleton's support for Balch's mission extended beyond her practical assistance; she related to Balch that she remained "entirely sympathetic" to Balch's desire to attend the conference, indicating an agreement that participation in the international peace movement would be an asset both to Balch and to the college.[13]

In the few days she had before sailing for Europe, Balch patiently dealt with her family's struggles over her new position. Her oldest sister, Anne, worried about travel across the Atlantic during wartime. Her brother, Frank, however, wrote to his older sister, "I don't believe the actual risk to your life is great and it seems to me perfectly legitimate in so vastly important a matter to disregard it." Frank's concern was not for his sister's welfare but about her participation in the congress. He warned against the methods and motives of the "feminist politicians" backing the conference. He abhorred the

relationship between the women's peace movement and the suffrage movement, believing it "a very ill-judged thing and . . . an intensely selfish thing,
to inject the woman-suffrage issue into the peace question." Although he
fully supported efforts toward establishing peace, Frank seriously doubted
the abilities and effectiveness of the international convention of women. He
asked, "What are those quite as single-mindedly in favor of peace, but who
oppose woman suffrage, now to do?"[14] Balch's brother was not alone in his
trepidation over the connection between suffrage and peace.

Balch did not seem overly concerned about the connection between
the International Woman's Suffrage Association and the Woman's Peace
Party. She did, however, reproach her brother for his vehement opposition to women's suffrage. So intense was Frank's hostility toward women's
voting that he found the concept "inexplicably repulsive." He equated it
as offensive as women "swearing" or "drinking." He openly admitted the
hypocrisy of his perspective, stating, "I don't know why, theoretically, they
haven't as much right as men. In fact I know that, as far as *right* goes, they
have. But the fact remains that it is repulsive when they do." Balch's efforts
to convince her brother of the merits of women's suffrage proved unsuccessful. He continued to liken the campaign for women's franchise to "a
passionate enthusiasm to demonstrate their equal rights to alcohol." Since
Frank objected to suffrage, but supported peace, he admonished his sister
and believed that the international meeting at The Hague would only harm
the cause of peace by associating the cause with such an unpopular and
"repulsive" movement. Frank concluded by saying that he would support
his sister's efforts, but he continued to feel that "the course the organization
is pursuing is selfish—thoroughly selfish."[15]

Many Woman's Peace Party members shared Frank Balch's concerns about
the close relationship between the women's peace and suffrage movements.
From the founding meeting through the conference in The Hague and subsequent annual meetings, the issue of suffrage continued to trouble the organization, deeply dividing its members in irreconcilable ways. Although the
American WPP body owed its existence to the call of international suffrage
leaders seeking an American women's peace organization, its constituents did
not uniformly support suffrage, nor did the WPP demand they do so. While
suffrage organizations in other countries more easily evolved into larger
organizations espousing peace, the American peace movement continued
to struggle with the question of suffrage.

However controversial, the fact remained that the international women's
movement was a product of the suffrage movement. Furthermore, most of
the international leaders in the congress believed that the issues of peace

and suffrage were intricately related. Since the international group, and not the WPP, established the requirements for delegates, it determined that in order to attend the congress in The Hague as a delegate, an individual had to agree with two convictions: that "international disputes should be settled by pacific means, [and] that the parliamentary franchise should be extended to women."[16] Most Americans within the international leadership, including Balch, embraced these tenets and dismissed remarks that the relationship would harm the effectiveness of the congress.

The American delegation sailed from New York for Rotterdam on April 13, 1915, aboard the *Noordam*, carrying a peace flag at its mast. The evening before embarking, Balch attended a farewell dinner for the American delegates in New York, sponsored by the New York Woman's Peace Party. More than four hundred women—told to "check their husbands at the door," as the *New York Times* put it—attended the event to support the delegates. The speeches delivered at the dinner by WPP leaders both celebrated the delegates and inspired them as they set out on their mission. In addition to the forty-two American women delegates aboard the ship, some men from the peace movement journeyed to Europe to see what might be gained from such an international gathering. One prominent figure was Louis Lochner, the head of the American Peace Society in Chicago. Jane Addams asked Lochner to join the women on their sea voyage and to give lectures on peace and international relations, as he had been lecturing at the University of Wisconsin for several months. Lochner also took minutes aboard the ship, since he was also acting, in his words, "as a sort of ghost writer for the daily story she [Addams] had agreed to cable to the *New York Times*."[17]

Balch found the speeches presented on their voyage enlightening and inspiring. She was especially compelled by Lochner's presentations and noted that they sparked fierce debates among the ship's passengers. In particular, the delegates argued over the issue of whether war could ever be a just means for resolving international conflict. British leader Pethick-Lawrence supported the idea that some wars could be just, while Addams argued the case for "Tolstoyan non-resistance." Intrigued by the discussions this dispute ignited, Balch carefully noted that unanimity of opinion was not necessary, stating, "It was agreed that it is no disadvantage if we do not all agree on these theoretical points." Lochner also recalled the debate between Pethick-Lawrence and Addams as a "highlight" of the crossing. He recorded, "Here were two highly educated, outstandingly intellectual women, each believing fervently in the viewpoint she defended, each logical and persuasive in her presentation, alert and clever in rebuttal, with a vast practical knowledge of human nature to support and illustrate her arguments, yet both of them unwaveringly courteous, equable, even-tempered, and blessed with a charming sense of humor. It was debating at its best."[18]

Among the impressive figures in the delegation was a young teacher from the University of Wisconsin, Julia Grace Wales. Wales had recently authored a plan for continuous mediation, commonly referred to as the Wisconsin Plan, because the Wisconsin state legislature had passed a resolution urging President Wilson to adopt it. The plan centered on establishing a government-sponsored Neutral Conference for Continuous Mediation. The tradition of diplomatic relations required that neutral nations not interfere in negotiations until called upon to act as mediators after one side had been established as the victor. Wales's plan argued that the present war would prove catastrophic for all nations and thus demanded a new role for neutral nations. Lochner summarized the core approach by asking, "Why should not a group of neutral powers delegate its best diplomats to sit in continuous conference for the duration, with the task of offering concrete proposals of mediation again and again until, finally, before complete exhaustion of one or all of the belligerents, an acceptable basis for an armistice and peace negotiations could be found?"[19] The congress in The Hague, along with several other peace associations, adopted many of the tenets of this plan. Balch, who first became aware of the plan on board the *Noordam,* fully endorsed the idea.

Although primarily occupied with attending lectures and participating in discussions with her fellow passengers during the sea voyage, Balch found some leisure time during her journey. She devoted her spare hours during the first few days of the voyage almost exclusively to reading. Far from narrow in her intellectual or leisure-time pursuits, Balch read books in French, German, and Dutch. The availability of free time on board the *Noordam,* however, did not last long. After several days of lectures, women turned their attention toward preparing for the congress. The group named Balch as secretary, and the delegates proceeded to meet three times a day. One day, Balch was made so frantic by attending the meetings and organizing the minutes that she noted, "I was busy all the time from breakfast up to five o'clock and had not even discovered that the day was misty and a little wet."[20]

Balch and the forty-one other American delegates maintained an intense schedule during their voyage but received an unexpected extension of time when they were delayed for four days off the coast of Dover. She and her fellow delegates received a firsthand education in the difficulties of traveling during wartime as well as in the ways in which peace efforts could be hindered by opposing forces. It remains unclear who or what exactly prevented the ship from docking in Rotterdam as scheduled. While the ship was held indefinitely, the delegates had difficulty sending and receiving messages. What little news the delegates did receive via telegram suggested that a great many people were "bitterly opposed to the conference." As the women continued to wait, Balch became angry, asking, "By what right even in wartime can they refuse neutrals passage to another neutral country?" Balch's declaration reveals a stubbornness and arrogance rarely visible in her recorded thoughts. Her outrage at the infringement of a neutral nation's rights exposed her sense of exceptionalism even as it enhanced her devotion to end wartime conditions and to the importance of neutral waterways. While awaiting passage, Balch confided to her journal, "Our desire to see the seas neutralized increases as is readily intelligible as it comes home to us that it means for a single irresponsible power, however well intentioned, to exert its own will unchallenged over all shipping."[21] Balch remained devoted to internationalizing all waterways for the remainder of her life.

The ship was finally allowed to pass just in time for the American delegates to arrive in Rotterdam for the beginning of the congress. They were lucky. Government policies or military restrictions prevented many women from attending. Those from nations at war met with restrictions on overseas travel. England granted passports to only twenty members of its delegation but subsequently barred all travel, thus preventing the delegates from attending the congress. The government cited wartime dangers in crossing the channel, but the delegates remained skeptical; three members, however, were not in England when these measures were implemented and so were able to participate in the congress. Pethick-Lawrence had traveled with most of the American delegation. Two British delegates, Chrystal Macmillan and Kathleen Courtney, had left for The Hague prior to the British restrictions. The three women thus represented all their peers in the United Kingdom.

When the Americans finally arrived, they joined approximately fifteen hundred other delegates. In addition to the United States and United Kingdom, other nations represented included Germany, Belgium, and, of course, Holland. The meetings, held between April 28 and May 1, 1915, resulted in the democratic passage of twenty resolutions and the formation of a transnational union of women peace advocates, the International Committee of Women for Permanent Peace (ICWPP). The ICWPP became the umbrella group for all of the national women's peace associations. The resolutions produced by the congress established the group's mission and outlined the agenda for the women peace activists for the duration of, and the years following, the war.

Numerous differences in the delegates' outlooks created dissention from the beginning of the congress. The issue of integrating suffrage and peace activism into a single movement (about which Balch and her brother had disagreed) quickly rose to the surface. In her first published account of her experiences in The Hague congress, Balch stated that several of the Americans remained concerned by the emphasis placed on suffrage, a subject that dominated many of the delegates' discussions. Women who objected to combining the issues urged that doing so would exclude anti-suffrage people from the international peace campaign. Balch argued that this strategy also held the potential to convert peace advocates to the suffrage cause, writing, "I hear that many Dutch ladies went opposed to suffrage and came away convinced that if women are to do anything effective for peace they must have a voice in public questions." In addition to the ideological divisions over suffrage, the congress organizers feared conflicts between nationalities. In their effort to confront this possibility, they resolved to "shut out all discussions of relative national responsibility for the present war or the conduct of it or of methods of conducting future wars."[22] In their effort to reduce tensions over the war in Europe, the delegates broadened their discussion to include methods toward establishing a permanent peace.

The congress was centrally concerned with establishing an opposition to all war and promoting a quick and just conclusion to the present conflict. Throughout the four-day congress, delegates met continuously, conducting meetings in the mornings, working in committees during the days, and attending public addresses to the entire body in the evenings. Some highlights for Balch included the welcoming speech given by the Dutch physician and suffrage leader Dr. Aletta Jacobs. This address was important because it made clear the long-term objectives of the meeting. The decision to hold a meeting during the course of the war rather than delay it until the treaty negotiations caused numerous difficulties with those delegates who believed little of value could be achieved until official government positions were adopted. Despite any discord, the congress (its delegates believed) constituted a powerful symbol before the world. The meeting of women from countries at war with each other, gathering in friendship and the spirit of peace, would have what Jacobs termed a "moral effect" on the world.[23] Despite public scoffing at their efforts to stop the present war, finding a path to peace was not their only goal. This international group emphasized staging a long-term protest against war as a method of conduct in international relations.

The congress produced a list of resolutions, which Balch viewed as "the best peace platform that has yet been drawn up."[24] The twenty-point program reflected the conclusion of four days of intense, intellectual debate about the mission of the new international women's organization. Central to the resolutions and to the ongoing work of the international women's peace movement was the demand to establish peace through continuous mediation. Before organizing and instituting a forum for this mediation, the women understood that they first needed to raise awareness of the concept. Toward that end, the congress resolved, after a good deal of debate, to send delegates from the congress to each of the European capitals. These women were to carry the message of the congress as well as gauge each government's openness to the plan for continuous mediation. The delegates selected Balch to serve as one of its envoys, and so began her long career as a messenger of peace.

The ICWPP Envoys

After the congress concluded on May 1, 1915, Balch and other delegates who were chosen to serve as envoys remained in The Hague to plan for the next phase of action. The women's decision to present the ICWPP resolutions to the governments of both belligerent and neutral nations exhibited their desire to mediate. That the delegates correctly assumed that they would be able to gain access to government officials during wartime demonstrated their confidence as diplomats. The congress sent two delegations, composed of women from both belligerent and neutral nations. Each delegation departed for a five-week tour immediately following the close of the conference. Addams and Balch represented the United States in separate delegations. Addams led the first, which included Dr. Aletta Jacobs and Frau Palthe from Holland, and Alice Hamilton from Chicago. Charged with visiting belligerent nations, this group visited heads of government in London, Berlin, Vienna, Budapest, Berne, Rome, Paris, Le Havre, and The Hague. Balch's delegation included Rosika Schwimmer of Hungary, Chrystal Macmillan from Scotland, and Mrs. Ramondt-Hirschmann of Holland. This group visited the Scandinavian countries, and all the delegates but Schwimmer also visited Russia. Julia Grace Wales accompanied the delegation on their Scandinavian tour, acting as secretary.

Balch's delegation to neutral nations faced tremendous difficulties in traveling through war-torn Europe. After the delegates presented the ICWPP resolutions to the government in The Hague, Balch's deputation ventured toward Denmark. The women were unable to secure transportation across the Baltic, and so Balch, Schwimmer, and Ramondt-Hirschman braved traveling by train through Germany from Amsterdam to Copenhagen (Macmillan [British] and Wales [Canadian] could not travel through enemy territory and thus had to secure water passage separately). After their two-day, nonstop voyage, Balch and her peers met with Danish Prime Minister Carl Theodor Zahle and Foreign Minister Erik Scavenius. Pleased with their discussions, Balch and her colleagues then continued on to Norway, where they spoke first with King Haakon VII. Balch remarked, "The King appeared to be deeply interested in

Balch with ICWPP Envoys Delegation to Petrograd, 1915. Women's International League for Peace and Freedom Papers, Swarthmore College Peace Collection.

our mediation plan." In Norway they also met with Prime Minister Aanon Knudsen and Foreign Minister Nils Claus Ihlen, as well as various members of parliament. After they met with Swedish Foreign Minister Wallenberg in Stockholm, Balch wrote, "He is not only a statesman but a man of affairs and a great banker, and appears to be throwing all his weight on the side of peace." After two weeks in Stockholm, the group began their journey to Russia on June 7. Rosika Schwimmer, however, could accompany the delegates no farther, "being technically an enemy." The ICWPP chose the Swedish feminist Baroness Ellen Palmstierna to take her place. It took the delegation three days to reach the capital city of Petrograd, where they met with Sergei Sazonov, the minister of foreign affairs. Sazonov left a "memorable" impression on Balch. She never forgot the weighty experience of talking "for nearly an hour in conference with one who has so large a part in the making of history in this tragic crisis." The women were excited to learn that the foreign minister "appeared to be already familiar with the resolutions passed at The Hague, and interested to consider them with us." Although Sazonov had read the women's resolutions, he remained skeptical about the effectiveness of a conference of neutrals. In her report about the meeting, Balch described Sazonov as "reserved in substance more than in manner." Most important, the minister emphatically claimed that the "war could not be brought to an end till it was fought out." Nonetheless, the women secured his vague concession that he would find a conference "not unacceptable" and returned with his signed statement to that effect.[25]

The women did not formally secure backing of the mediation plan from any of the statesmen, but this was not their intention. In every city, they raised awareness among government officials and the general population about the possibility of mediating a peace. They also ascertained that among the neutral nations in Europe there was substantial support for the idea. Even Russia, a belligerent country, conceded the possibility. Although the travels proved arduous, Balch's delegation ended its journey confident the women had advanced the cause of peace.

Before returning to the United States via London, Balch and her delegation met with other leading members of the ICWPP in Stockholm, where they voted to reaffirm The Hague resolutions and to campaign for mediation. Originally skeptical of the proposal to appeal to statesmen, both Addams and Balch afterward commented that the receptions the ICWPP received greatly benefited their cause. Balch later wrote that she had originally only "agreed to go out of loyalty to a collective decision," but after learning of widespread support for the mediation idea, she changed her mind, stating, "I am wholly a convert to the plan." Addams also recalled the power of their conversations with the leaders of the fourteen nations they visited. Impressed by the over-whelming feeling of willingness to establish an immediate peace, Addams wrote that in the warring countries all officials (except one Frenchman) as-serted that their "country would be ready to stop the war immediately if some honorable method of securing peace were provided." Further, Addams noted that the delegates were able, "as women," to carry on an exchange between capitals that could not officially discuss peace issues. Balch observed this fact as well, reporting to her brother about women's power to negotiate during times of war. She likened it to labor disputes: "The situation is really much like a strike where neither party can admit that it is ready to let go. Women being outsiders have a peculiar *locus standi* which is proving to have con-siderable strategic value."[26] The ICWPP women had established their value as peace delegates in their meetings with European heads of state.

Envoys in the United States

Balch returned to Wellesley College with a heightened understanding of her importance to the women's peace network. Her work with international women instilled in her a greater sense of purpose, and she believed that the delegations offered hope for peace. Balch felt assured that a profound change in the international social reform movement had occurred. Most important, she learned the vital role that citizens in her own country must play in peace efforts. Balch revealed this in a summary of her experiences as an envoy on behalf of the congress, wherein she reminded American citizens of their particular responsibility in international affairs: "Money and workers are needed and America, unstricken by war, must do more than its share. Its fair share, even, is a large one. The work already done has cost considerable sums, although many of the delegates, including all of those from the United States, paid all their own travelling expenses and contributed as well to the general expenses of the Congress. The future offers opportunity for still larger investments."[27]

In Balch's view, Americans were central to any possible success of an international peace movement. They remained physically distant from the war but not free from responsibility. Their very distance provided Americans with a greater freedom to advocate that their government mediate between the belligerent European nations and negotiate a peaceful settlement.

Balch learned a powerful lesson during her time as an envoy. At age forty-eight, she reconceived her notion of political power, particularly the political power of women. She understood more clearly that American women must play a central role in the international peace movement, and in so doing they could carry political clout. "Never again," she argued, "must women dare to believe that they are without responsibility because they are without power." They were responsible in what they decided to condone. Although American women did not yet have national suffrage, Balch emphasized their role as opinion shapers, exclaiming, "Public opinion is power."[28]

Balch's own political prominence was growing. After her return she held a series of meetings with President Woodrow Wilson, during which she outlined the ICWPP's interest in having him call an official mediation conference of the neutral nations. In the late summer of 1915, Balch presented the delegates' findings to President Wilson. The next day, she confided her insecurities to Addams, "I feel such a babe in judgment in all these things." Despite her anxiety, it appears she held a productive conversation with the president. As Balch's meetings with Wilson and White House officials increased, she exuded more certainty in her abilities. She secured meetings between officials and Aletta Jacobs, the feminist physician and an organizer of The Hague congress. Jacobs and Balch first held meetings with Wilson's secretary of state, Robert Lansing, and then with another top presidential advisor, Colonel Edward House. In response to the Secretary Lansing's ambivalent responses to the women's proposals, Balch described her meeting with him as a "disheartening experience."[29] House, while appearing sympathetic, secretly had his own plans to advance a peaceful settlement and thus never seriously entertained the women's platform. Although Wilson was reluctant to meet with a foreign peace advocate, the president, influenced by Balch's advocacy on her behalf, finally granted Jacobs a meeting on September 15, 1915. Wilson seemed responsive but did not commit his support to sponsor a conference of neutrals.

In early November, Louis Lochner, along with David Starr Jordan, the head of the American Peace Society and president of Stanford University, secured another meeting with the president. On November 12, 1915, the two men again presented Julia Grace Wales's plan for continuous mediation to President Wilson. Jordan informed the president that the neutral nations in Europe were prepared to send delegates to a Neutral Conference for Continuous Mediation (as Balch's delegation had confirmed). Wilson's response was both politically vague and enlightening as to the president's worries. He responded, "I have been revolving this proposal in my mind dozens of times. I wish I might see my way clear to it. But there are these objections: (1) the neutrals in Europe in several cases have governments out of sympathy with their peoples; (2) one side (the Allies) might object to mediation as a partisan measure; (3) therefore America might be outvoted by the other neutrals, and more harm than good be done."[30] Lochner and Jordan began to accept, as did other peace activists, that the president would not actively support an official conference.

On November 26, Rosika Schwimmer met with President Wilson and issued a final plea for support. For this meeting, the Woman's Peace Party organized a large-scale campaign to lobby for the president's backing. Mrs. Henry Ford donated $10,000 to fund telegrams from all over the United States demanding the establishment of an official Conference of Continuous Mediation; the telegrams flooded the White House on the day of Schwimmer's visit. The campaign aimed not only to draw the president's attention but also to raise public awareness of the conference. The effort was so successful that, as the WPP happily noted, the president received two thousand more telegrams than Ford had funded, meaning that individuals had paid to make their own statements. Despite such popular support, Schwimmer also failed to convince Wilson of the need for an immediate and official conference.[31]

By December 1915, it was obvious to all in the peace movement that the president was not going to sanction an official meeting. In addition to the reasons he stated to Lochner and Jordan, Wilson set forth at least two other concerns. The United States, in backing a conference of neutrals, would have to include South American nations, which might have made the conference size unwieldy. Also, and perhaps most important, at that particular time in the war the Central Powers had a considerable advantage, and Wilson did not want to give one side (or perhaps just that side) a strong position in the peace negotiations. Another consideration was that Colonel House had his own plans for mediation and therefore continued to advise the president against the conference. This plan failed, however, when the British delayed their response to House's proposal. The United States waited too long for House's plan to be effective.

Wilson's explanations all contain some element of truth. His intentions, however, were far more illicit. Some historians have correctly argued that Wilson's greatest ambition by that stage of the war focused exclusively on being a part of the postwar diplomacy. The president realized that the nation's global position, and his own legacy, would be advanced only when he established himself as a major power at the peace table. While Wilson undoubtedly valued the peacemakers' attempts to establish neutral mediation, his long-term vision did not include the United States in such a role.[32]

Americans who promoted a Neutral Conference for Continuous Mediation were being stymied by their government. But they did not give up their belief that mediation was critical to ending the war and establishing a just peace. They gained an ally in another prominent American, Henry Ford.

Ford's Peace Ship and the Conference for Continuous Mediation

Rosika Schwimmer, David Starr Jordan, and Louis Lochner, all discouraged by their meetings with the president, turned their attention to Henry Ford. The American automobile tycoon had been voicing his opposition to the war, and peace groups wanted him to back an *unofficial* conference, which would be attended by citizen delegates rather than governmental diplomats. After meeting with Schwimmer, Ford agreed to underwrite the unofficial conference and employed Lochner to head the project. Before beginning the endeavor, however, Ford wanted to offer Wilson one last chance to lead an official, government-backed conference. Ford expressed to the president his approval of the Wisconsin Plan. Wilson responded in a vague, noncommittal way to Ford's suggestion of holding an official, American-sponsored conference. Ford asserted in response, "I have today chartered a steamship. I offer it to you to send delegates to Europe. If you feel you can't act, I will." Wilson refused, and Ford upheld his promise.[33]

Wanting to create a grand public image of his endeavor, Ford chartered a steamship, the *Oscar II*, dubbed the Ford Peace Ship, and made a media spectacle of the peace process. The response was far from positive, disappointing numerous American peace activists. Fueling a media spectacle, Henry Ford made the outrageous claim on November 23, 1915, that his scheme aimed "to get the boys out of the trenches by Christmas." Such a far-fetched, untenable notion laid the entire mission open to endless public derision. The purpose and objectives of the conference itself, in the words of Louis Lochner, ended up "lost in the shuffle." The peace ship concept was a gimmick and one that alarmed Jane Addams, who felt the delegates could get themselves to Europe easily enough and that transportation should not be the focus of the public's attention. Addams and others further objected to Ford's decision to invite a wide array of individuals, including college students, to participate as delegates. Despite her concerns, Addams agreed to participate in the media extravaganza, since the end result would be the much-hoped-for mediation conference. Defending her position, she later stated, "It became clearer every day that whoever became associated with the ship would be in for much ridicule and social opprobrium, but that of course seemed a small price to pay for a protest against war."[34] She still fervently believed in the power of the conference and trusted that the delegates could overcome the ridicule of the American press once in Europe. Although she had decided to suffer ridicule and board the ship, Addams fell ill at the last minute and was unable to participate.

Despite Ford's blunders and the gimmicky peace ship, the neutral conference itself, which began in Stockholm in 1916 and later moved to The Hague, included several prominent European figures. Notable participants were Kristoffer Markward Klausen, vice president of the Danish parliament; Jan van Wolterbeek-Mueller, professor of international law at the University of Rotterdam; Nikolaus Gjelsvik, professor of international law at the University of Kristiania, Norway; Carl Lindhagen, burgomaster of Stockholm; Professor Ernst Wigforss, who later became the Swedish minister of finance; and Fritz Studer, chairman of the Social Democratic party of Switzerland. That the conference contained a combination of government figures and European intellectuals revealed the level of interest from those in Europe's neutral nations. Beginning in 1916, these people held continuous meetings to debate possible solutions for ending the war. They discussed their ideas with each other and published important suggestions for bringing the war to a close and establishing postwar conditions that would better ensure lasting peace. They forwarded their propositions to both neutral and belligerent governments.

Balch did not join other pacifists on the Ford Peace Ship in 1915. Instead, she returned to Wellesley to prepare for the spring term of 1916. During the fall of 1915, Balch had offered only two courses. Most of her focus remained on her international peace work. At this stage, before the United States entered the war, Balch's colleagues at Wellesley encouraged her peace work. Most saw it as a valuable contribution to the intellectual atmosphere of the college. Not far into the semester, Balch convinced the trustees to grant her another leave of absence so that she could go to Stockholm to join the Neutral Conference for Continuous Mediation. According to Lochner, Balch became the only "internationally known member" of the American delegation.[35]

In the fall of 1916, Balch published an article in the *New Republic,* hoping to clarify popular American misconceptions of the conference. First, she asserted that the "character and work" of the delegates at the conference were better understood in Europe than among Americans. The ridicule attached to the Ford Peace Ship obscured the public's understanding of the mission. Most Americans, Balch felt, believed that the conference was just a publicity stunt and that the organizers had no definite course of action in mind. "On the contrary," Balch argued: the participants "had a well defined plan, and executed it."[36] The plan was to hold continuous mediation discussions, though in a nongovernmental capacity.

Balch clearly explained the proceedings of the conference in Stockholm and outlined the phases that had occurred up to that point. The first meetings involved thirty delegates, five from each of six neutral nations—Denmark, the United States, Norway, Holland, Sweden, and Switzerland. The first phase of meetings was held between February and April 1916. During these months, the delegates concentrated on "formulating two appeals, one to neutrals asking for the calling of an official conference, the other to the belligerents proposing specific peace terms for a just and reasonable settlement."[37] Both of these appeals showed the central mission of the conference to be not only sorting out a peace negotiation but also working to involve neutral governments, and with the hope of transforming their efforts into an *official* mediation congress.

After widely distributing these two important appeals, the delegates reorganized the conference and created a twelve-member committee. This smaller group focused on contacting representatives of the belligerent governments to determine both the common and conflicting purposes of the warring nations. Balch wrote of this daunting work, "The difficulties are enormous and often it has been like fighting a fog, yet the wonder is not that so little but that so much recognition should be given to a purely unofficial group."[38]

The conference delegates also addressed the question of how to ensure a stable postwar Europe. Balch asserted that a central problem would be the ongoing struggle with colonialism. She firmly maintained the view that the war could best be understood as an "effort to possess and exploit the backward parts of the world." Understanding the global conflict as a war of imperialism,

Balch demanded that government leaders think critically about the future administration of colonies in order to avoid further conflict. Balch conceded that, often, definite improvements resulted from colonist involvement with native lands and economies. "Yet the man who believes that every population has a right to settle its own affairs, to enjoy the territory that it inhabits and to be respected in these rights," she wrote, "must face the facts, however unpleasant." The fact remained that "some sort of domination" resulted from colonial involvement, and if not handled properly, the eventual outcome would always be conflict. Balch admitted that many colonial nations still needed assistance, and she emphasized that the international community must direct its efforts toward the betterment of colonial peoples and lands, not their exploitation. To this end, she proposed the idea of establishing an international commission to oversee assisting developing nations. Balch's ideas on colonial administration anticipated the League of Nations' mandate system.[39]

Balch also wrote on another subject that foreshadowed the substantial rifts that would take place during the postwar peace negotiations: war reparations, which she proposed be paid from a specially created international fund. In 1916, Balch argued that the question of the neutral nations negotiating a peace should "hinge" on settling the problem of war indemnities. The payment of reparations to the victors of war, though an ancient tradition, demanded that the war be fought to the bitter end, with a clear victor and loser. This contrasted the idea of a negotiated peace, which would attempt to balance the interests of both sides and not produce a winner-loser dynamic. Balch conceded that payments would be necessary in a devastated, postwar Europe, but punishing one particular nation by demanding reparations, she wrote, provided "no guarantee that such indemnities will be either just or in the interests of permanent peace." Specifically, reparations would economically devastate that nation and hurt the economies of neighboring nations as well. Moreover, reparations "carry with them a bitter and lasting desire for *revanche.*" As an alternative, Balch supported the proposition that neutral nations take the lead in establishing an international fund to pay for restitution to both sides. The idea that no individual nation would pay reparations reflected Wilson's "peace without victory" perspective, which was subsequently rejected during the treaty negotiations.[40] Many of Balch's fears about war reparations proved valid when the German economy suffered greatly under its postwar strain, pushing Europe again toward war.

Balch left the Neutral Conference in the summer of 1916, but the delegates continued to produce significant work until January 1917. By that point the United States was well on the road to joining the war, and Ford knew he would back the president. Therefore, early in 1917, Ford called Lochner and his associates home. Lochner recalled a meeting with President Wilson upon Germany's announcement of resuming unrestricted submarine warfare in January. He realized at that moment that, for the United States, "entry into the war was now only a matter of time." Ford then volunteered his automobile plants for defense work and ended his financial support of the neutral conference.[41]

The Neutral Conference for Continuous Mediation was short lived, though not without its successes. Emphasizing the conference's achievements, Lochner and others pointed out that the peace proposals produced there were reflected in President Wilson's Peace Note of December 1916, in his address to the Senate on January 18, 1917, and, most important, in his Fourteen Points, presented in January 1918.[42] In addition to its published recommendations, the conference proved useful just by its existence. The idea of the conference—that neutral nations could mediate a peace—might have changed the more disastrous effects of a prolonged war.

Anti-preparedness in the United States

When Balch returned to the United States from Stockholm in the summer of 1916, she encountered "a powerful Preparedness Movement in full swing and a steady pull toward war." The war fever in the United States produced obvious concern in peace circles, many of which implemented broader and more intense campaigns to counter the voices for war preparedness. Balch was eligible for a sabbatical year in 1916–17 and decided to devote all of her attention to the peace movement. On leave of absence from Wellesley College, she went to New York City, the heart of American peace activities. Although she was away from the college and focused on the peace campaigns, she remained committed to scholarship. She attended lectures at Columbia University and, perhaps most significant, began to edit her next book, *Approaches to the Great Settlement.* This work compiled and discussed many of the proposals for peace then in circulation. Her attention in the fall of 1916, however, like that of many other peace advocates, was fixed on the reelection of President Wilson and on confronting the rapidly expanding campaigns for war preparedness.[43]

Throughout 1916, most progressive peace leaders, believing that President Wilson would help establish peace, still admired and supported him. When Balch returned from the Neutral Conference, the president asked her to report on the group's progress.[44] Balch, like other peace advocates, continued the effort to persuade Wilson to initiate an official conference, but by the end of 1916, it was too late for him to do so. Colonel House's negotiation efforts had failed, and Wilson's relationship with the Entente forces had only strengthened. However hopeless the outlook, peace advocates continued efforts to keep the United States out of the war and promoted that the government should utilize its power in mediations.

New York City was the hub of the anti-preparedness movement. The Woman's Peace Party (WPP) in that city, under the leadership of Crystal Eastman, headed many of the campaigns against war preparedness. The pacifists, not without reason, worried about those industries that would profit from war. The WPP mission statement held as a core component to promote the limitation and nationalization of armaments.[45] The New York City members lobbied this issue in Congress and promoted such ideas in local communities.

The local WPP campaigns provided important touchstones for antiwar sentiment prior to April 1917. While national leaders struggled to persuade officials to oppose American intervention in the war, local leaders developed public interest in the causes of war and the possibilities for peace. At their first annual meeting in January 1916, representatives from local WPP branches proudly related the "social" accomplishments of 1915, which nurtured peace sentiment in their communities. The Little Theatre Company in Chicago, for example, received a $5,000 grant from the Carnegie Foundation and was used to mount a production of *The Trojan Women*, which toured for four months, with performances in several western states. The Washington chapter sponsored a successful run of *War Brides*, another play aimed at raising awareness of peace. Volunteers from the Philadelphia branch ran a "peace shop," at which, according to their annual report, they displayed numerous "posters in its windows [which] always brought a crowd of men around their doors, and the newspapers were forced to take notice." New England branches, such as the one in Boston, established a network of reading groups and knitting circles to discuss peace literature. Kentucky, Maryland, and Colorado women reported carrying out very successful campaigns to flood state offices with peace literature. New York City's branch, which had more than fifteen hundred members, held well-attended forums, while Chicago's smaller group held fortnightly meetings.[46]

Balch did not limit her participation to the New York WPP. In fact, she joined several organizations. She attended meetings held by a number of different groups, representing both middle and leftist viewpoints. She preferred leftist organizations that focused on achieving realistic and practical results. One example of the "left-to-middle" groups in which Balch played a prominent role during the early years of the war was the Anti-Preparedness Committee, which had been the Henry Street Committee and remained under the leadership of

Lillian Wald. Other prominent figures in this group included Paul Kellogg, Rabbi Stephen Wise, Max Eastman, Charles Hallinan, and Louis Lochner. The Anti-Preparedness Committee evolved into a national organization and became the American Union Against Militarism (AUAM). In early 1916, the AUAM officially adopted its new name and elected the energetic Crystal Eastman as its executive secretary. Although Balch was still serving as a delegate in Stockholm at that point, Eastman wrote to her that her "name was among the first suggested" to serve on the organization's new executive committee.[47] Balch accepted the position and, as a leader in yet another large peace organization, recommitted herself (and a substantial amount of her time) to direct lobbying against American intervention in the war.

In late 1916 and early 1917, Balch's activism became more daring. She became, as she wrote, "especially identified, as the situation developed, with a younger and more adventurous group which was doing what it could toward preventing the United States entering the war."[48] This group was the Emergency Peace Federation (EPF), which formed from the ashes of the American Neutral Conference Committee (the central organizing committee that had promoted an official mediation conference). Balch believed that this group was "more adventurous" than others because it sponsored numerous and daring public meetings in the face of growing public opposition to the peace movement. The organization did its best to fuel antiwar sentiment right up until Wilson requested that Congress declare war on April 2, 1917.

One of the EPF's impressive acts was to place advertisements in the *New York Times* condemning preparedness and asking supporters to submit a $1 donation to be used to fund more advertisements. The response produced an overwhelming $35,000 in contributions. When Balch got to the Fifth Avenue office that morning, she saw "long queues down the corridor." Women brought their dollar bills in person. So many contributions flooded the office, between visitors and the mail, that they "had to borrow waste-paper baskets" to hold all of the bills.[49]

The EPF held a broad appeal to American pacifists. The organization encompassed both liberal and conservative wings of the American peace movement, and its decisions and actions reflected the problems involved in doing so. The more conservative side of the movement, dominated by the American Peace Society, opposed the campaign for a national vote in order to declare war. Its members believed in fully supporting the president and the government should they agree to join the war (and they did so). The American Union Against Militarism and the Woman's Peace Party, on the other hand, fully supported the campaign for referendum to determine whether or not to join the war. During this period, as Balch's prominence within the AUAM and WPP grew, she increasingly placed herself on the left side of American peace politics.

In December 1916, all factions of the peace movement joined together for a momentary glimmer of hope. President Wilson's "Peace Note" to the belligerent nations demanded that the governments outline their objectives in the war. This was interpreted by some pacifists as an effort to conceptualize an official mediation process. The request, however, was not successful, and the following month Germany began unrestricted submarine warfare. On February 3, 1917, Wilson officially ended diplomatic relations with Germany. Clearly understanding that the nation was now on a direct path toward war, members of the WPP, AUAM, and other peace organizations vaulted into action. The WPP telegrammed Wilson again to request an immediate, American-backed conference of neutral nations. Peace advocates also demanded a referendum vote to allow American citizens to decide whether or not to participate in the European conflict.

In early March 1917, Addams and Balch visited Wilson in a last attempt to stave off intervention. The two women, as well as the numerous other peace leaders who lobbied Wilson that spring, were unsuccessful. Nonetheless, Balch stayed in Washington along with other colleagues to petition against the war vote in Congress until the very second it passed. Another activist, Frances Witherspoon, recalled the atmosphere in the capitol as Balch and her colleagues paced "those long stone corridors of the House and Senate office buildings" and awaited the looming vote on the war. Congress convened a joint session, which began on April 4, 1917, to vote for the war. According to Witherspoon, when the vote began and the hall was cleared, Balch and about twenty of her friends in the Emergency Peace Federation, including Louis Lochner and David Starr Jordan, "crept up into the Gallery and stood well back against the wall in the shadows so as not to have one's presence noted. Hardly breathing and whispering to one another, we heard the vote cast, heard Jeanette Rankin's 'I love my country, but I cannot vote for war.'"[50]

Balch carefully reminded the American public that the nation, and even Congress, had not unanimously backed the war. She worried that this fact would soon be forgotten in the fever to win the war. After examining all of the reports of peace workers who had lobbied their members of Congress, Balch wrote a letter to Representative Isaac Sherwood of Ohio, which he placed in the March 1917 *Congressional Record.* In it, Balch remarked that many congressmen had voted "against their own judgment, against their conscience, and against what they have reason to believe to be the will of their constituents." Balch emphasized that a substantial number of Americans opposed the war and that Congress had supported it not because its members believed in the war, but because they wanted to back the president. She wrote, "The early days of April 1917 may appear in history as more fateful than the early days of August 1914. A war urged by the President on a reluctant Congress upon the grounds of the most disinterested idealism will apparently be 'wished upon' the country against its will by the votes of men who fear the press more than they fear their constituents, who fear the party whip more than they fear their consciences." In the letter Balch went on to emphasize the need for the country to retain its democratic spirit, which she felt was dying even as the country turned toward voting for war.[51]

Wartime Peace Advocates

After the United States entered the war in April 1917, Balch's efforts took a new direction. On the heels of Wilson's war declaration, Congress passed the Espionage Act and the Selective Service Act. In response, the American peace movement, or what remained of it, in addition to advocating an immediate and just peace, expanded its mission to face the issues presented by those laws. Protecting the civil liberties under assault across the country and providing assistance to conscientious objectors emerged as crucial aspects of many peace groups' platforms.

Despite the expanded mission of many peace organizations, and in some cases because of it, when the United States entered the war, membership in American peace societies dwindled. In addition to the significant drop in membership, the central organizations with which Balch had been involved were plagued with internal conflicts and clashes with other organizations. As each association gradually determined its stance toward the government and relief operations, Balch worked to mediate disputes within the peace movement but also moved toward more radical groups.

In the spring of 1917 Balch's sabbatical year was about to end, but she could not fathom returning to college when the movement so desperately needed her. Having devoted her sabbatical year to preventing the United States from entering the war, she did not wish to give up on peace advocacy now that war had been declared. She requested that her sabbatical be extended to an additional year of absence without pay, and Wellesley College granted it. She later explained this decision by stating that she did not want to "embarrass" Wellesley by her work in the peace movement.[52] Whether she remained in New York that year in order to fulfill her own desires to work in the peace movement or in order to spare Wellesley the embarrassment of her presence,

Emily Greene Balch, 1917.
Emily Greene Balch Papers,
Swarthmore College Peace
Collection.

or because of a combination of these motives, she clearly felt compelled to continue her work.

Balch dedicated much of her time and energy in 1917 and 1918 to the Woman's Peace Party. The group's membership plummeted after the United States joined the war. The majority of WPP members chose to leave the organization immediately when it did not disband. Others gradually dropped away as it became clear that the work of the WPP might conflict with their sense of patriotism. By the end of 1917, the membership list contained fewer than one hundred members, compared to the more than 25,000 on the eve of the United States' entry into the war. The vehemence with which former WPP members began to condemn their former peace leaders revealed how bitterly the war issue divided the organization.[53] In the face of great opposition from former WPP members and the general public, the handful of women who continued to maintain their loyalty to the national WPP worked to support its mission.

While many peace organizations in the United States during wartime faced internal struggles, particularly in relation to civil liberties and conscientious objectors, no association confronted the sort of intense internal feuding that the Woman's Peace Party did. The national WPP had always allowed local branches great autonomy, and this policy proved especially problematic during wartime. Some branches, such as the one in Massachusetts, turned themselves into relief organizations, fully supporting Wilson and the war. That branch nearly broke with the national organization. Under the leadership of Lucia Ames Mead, who also held the position of national secretary of the WPP, these women publicly backed the president and devoted their time and energy to numerous war relief efforts. Although the branch's autonomy enabled it to retain more of its members than it would have had it been tied to the national agenda, the membership levels still fell. What remained of the Massachusetts branch focused on promoting Wilson's League of Nations. Like Wilson, several WPP members concentrated on how American involvement in the war would enable the United States to take to a strong position in the postwar peace talks.[54]

Balch worked primarily with the New York City branch, which was known to be the most liberal within the organization. This office continued its vehement opposition to American involvement in the war, even after Congress's declaration. The small force of dedicated peace workers in the New York City WPP thrived under the leadership of Crystal Eastman. They even established their own publication, *Four Lights*, in which they published thoughtful (though often controversial) insights about the war and home front.

Eastman also headed up another organization, the American Union Against Militarism (AUAM), which was the descendant of the first peace committee meeting at Henry Street Settlement in September 1914. The AUAM embodied the mainstream, antiwar liberals in the United States prior to American intervention. Its agenda shifted with Wilson's declaration of war.

In the summer of 1917, the AUAM introduced its "wartime program," which addressed ongoing efforts to end the war and promote a just peace, but it also set out a program for responding specifically to new wartime legislation. The Selective Service Act, passed on May 18, 1917, raised a question in the peace movement about how much emphasis should be placed on defending those who objected to participation in the war on moral grounds. Less than a month after the passage of the Selective Service Act, Congress passed the Espionage Act (on June 15), which offered only a vague definition of treasonous speech and allowed broad freedom for citizens themselves to determine what actions could be interpreted as obstructing the country's war effort. Pacifists and others feared, perhaps rightly, that the legislation gave the federal government sweeping powers to limit free speech and assembly. The AUAM committed itself to defending both these civil liberties and conscientious objection.

The AUAM's wartime program reflected the challenges posed by the new wartime legislation. The organization's six-point agenda included opposition to any legislation that might "fasten upon the United States in war time any permanent military policy based on compulsory military training and service." In addition, the AUAM emphasized the defense of constitutional rights, especially free speech, freedom of the press and assembly, and further promised to provide "legal advice and aid" for conscientious objectors. The organization also demanded that the government publish "all agreements or understandings with other nations" in order to promote greater transparency in international relations. Finally, the AUAM worked to establish itself as the central organization for promoting "international fellowship" and fostering internationalism within the United States' borders.[55]

The AUAM executive committee quickly became bitterly divided over support for, or opposition to, the organization's work to defend conscientious objectors and protect civil liberties. While some peace workers shied away from campaigns defending conscientious objection and the Espionage Act, others focused on them as central to maintaining the principles for which the United States claimed to fight. A young associate director of the AUAM, Roger Baldwin, created a branch dedicated to defending conscientious objectors. The short-lived Bureau for Conscientious Objectors (BCO) provided legal assistance to men who maintained a moral objection to fighting. The organization's leader, Crystal Eastman, fiercely defended the AUAM's campaigns for conscientious objection, while its founders, Lillian Wald and Paul Kellogg, staunchly opposed the BCO, and later the Civil Liberties Bureau, both of which were under the auspices of the AUAM. Wald and Kellogg advocated severing the BCO from the greater AUAM and therefore separating the issues AUAM members were encouraged to support.

Leaders in the AUAM continuously debated whether or not to maintain the organization's work on behalf of conscientious objectors. As early as June 1917, top members of the AUAM discussed the potential future of the bureau's work under their heading. Some members objected to the AUAM's support of legal aid to conscientious objectors in addition to the incorporation of the BCO into the AUAM. Those individuals wanted to work only for a democratic peace and not campaign so explicitly against government policy. Although many had fiercely opposed the Selective Service Act (Balch had even proposed legislation to authorize alternative service should the nation vote for conscription), they declined to encourage breaking the law once the act was passed.

In June 1917, the AUAM voted to continue its relationship with the Bureau for Conscientious Objectors. Opponents on the board, especially Lillian Wald, were enraged. Writing to Eastman, Wald stated that although she had originally opposed the Selective Service legislation, she did not agree with opposing it now that it had passed. Wald clearly stated the problem that would plague the AUAM for the remainder of the year when she confessed, "I believe that . . . we are not all agreed as to the fundamental policy and progress of the American Union." Eastman, however, believed that the pacifists' obligation lay with such actions even when the country was at war. She stated, "We should not have much hold on this country without that work in war-time."[56]

Thus, in the summer of 1917, Eastman faced a crisis in her organization. After the decision to keep Baldwin's work within the AUAM, Wald and others threatened to resign. Eastman temporarily avoided a slew of resignations by convincing Baldwin to rename his branch the Civil Liberties Bureau, since it provided legal advice to those who were being deprived of their constitutional rights as well as to conscientious objectors. Many within the AUAM, however, continued to push for the Civil Liberties Bureau to become an independent organization. During the months of debate over these issues, Balch asserted that the AUAM should remain an umbrella peace organization. She explained to Eastman her belief that "there is need of an organized group to study and propagate the practical lines of a democratic peace settlement—a group acceptable to persons who are not in sympathy with opposition to conscription nor to any other incidents of carrying on the war and who will not collaborate with a group connected as such with those views." While this version of the AUAM would embrace those who did not oppose the draft, Balch assured Eastman that it must also "welcome those who are radical on these points also."[57]

Eastman had been able to stave off a great exodus during the summer, but by the fall of 1917, the leadership of the AUAM again divided over Baldwin's committee. The board began to fall apart as key figures left the organization. Rarely were the resignation letters bitter. They either mentioned that the aims of the organization had changed, or the authors claimed to have too many other commitments. Oswald Garrison Villiard resigned, as did Jane Addams. Ironically, the bureau severed itself from the AUAM shortly after the slew of resignations and, in 1920, reestablished itself as the American Civil Liberties Union.

Balch also resigned in September 1917.[58] Between the controversy and increased demands on her time from other peace factions, she could not sustain her involvement. She wrote to Eastman that serving on the AUAM was a great "privilege and pleasure," but she had too many other commitments. Whether or not Balch's resignation had anything to do with the dispute over the Civil Liberties Bureau, she left that unsaid.

What Balch's resignation from the AUAM did make clear was her shifting allegiance to a radical peace camp. Despite its internal conflicts, the AUAM still embodied a more moderate form of liberal peace politics. Balch did not frame her transition as a move toward more radical politics, but instead emphasized that her first priority was establishing a democratic peace. Though not immune to concerns about protecting civil liberties and supporting conscientious objectors, she was most interested in the methods for establishing peace and the terms of the peace agreement.

The most radical contingent of the pacifist movement during the war evolved from the Emergency Peace Federation, the group with which Balch had traveled to Washington, D.C., the previous winter and witnessed the declaration of war. Almost immediately after the war declaration, leaders from the EPF, including Lochner and Balch, met to decide what stand they would take for the duration of the war. They quickly reorganized to form a new entity. They planned a public event to advertise the new group's opposition to the war and hopes for a swift peace. The First American Conference for Democracy and Terms of Peace was held in Madison Square Garden in New York City on May 2, 1917. Balch, along with Louis Lochner and Rebecca Shelley, spearheaded this conference. In her speech, Balch stressed that pacifists must look beyond the present war and work to minimize the causes of war, which she argued were rooted in social and economic problems.[59]

From that conference the People's Council of America (PCA) emerged (and the EPF officially dissolved). Its leaders formulated its program immediately after the conference. Seeing the Espionage Act as a direct threat to the productivity of peace organizations, they worked to protect civil liberties and especially to defend freedom of speech. The PCA went further than other organizations regarding conscription by demanding a repeal of the law. The PCA leaders stated in their program that they would "seek to preserve labor standards." In fact, the organization established strong ties with American socialists. Rebecca Shelley, perhaps the most radical of the PCA leaders, outlined in her address to the conference how Americans should look toward the Russian model when creating a peace plan. Although the PCA never seemed to be radical enough for Shelley, it did admit delegates of the radical International Workers of the World.[60]

The PCA drew a great deal of attention. The organization planned to hold its national convention in Minneapolis on September 1, 1917, but as the date approached, the reaction in Minnesota against the assembly was so great that the governor refused to allow any tents to be erected for the meetings. The leaders scrambled to find an alternative location. Finally, the mayor of Chicago, William Thompson, invited the peace activists to hold their conference in Chicago. However, Illinois governor Frank Lowden did not believe that the government should allow the PCA to hold its meeting even though the mayor supported it. The delegates began their meeting, but, shortly after establishing their constitution and electing their executive committee, Chicago police, under orders from the Governor, broke up the convention. The delegates reconvened the following day, under the mayor's assurance of police protection. Worried that state troops might arrive soon, however, the conference was brief. The executive committee then met in private to formalize the organization's platform. Such a prominent, public display of government opposition to the PCA discouraged other peace societies from participating in its campaigns. Despite the staunch opposition, Balch remained committed to the PCA's mission and thus continued to participate in the organization.[61]

Other factions of the peace movement refused to ally with the PCA, believing it to be too radical. Jane Addams could not publicly give her backing, though she secretly supported its activities. At certain points, Balch even worried about how far left the organization might move. However, she never condemned the PCA or its members and continued to devote the majority of her time during the war to its work.

Despite her apprehensions about the PCA, Balch's political identity shifted from liberal centrist to securely radical during the course of the war. Whether or not Balch anticipated the extent of public reaction against radicalism during that era, she never hesitated to defend her position against the war. Balch's family continued to support her, but they still condemned her political position. Her younger sister Marion expressed the mutual understanding between Balch and her family, claiming, "She must have known that the family did not share her views. I certainly did not and do not to this day."[62] Marion's blatant disapproval of her sister's opposition to the war and her claim that the rest of the family shared this view indicate the personal obstacles Balch faced when choosing to ally herself with the peace activists and identify with radical campaigners.

Although Balch's relationships with her family members may have been strained, many of her school friends maintained their connections with her, regardless of their views on the war. At a meeting held in 1917 by the *Erin Go Bragh*, the alumni organization from Miss Ireland's School, members discussed Balch's work in New York peace societies. Balch was too busy to attend the meeting, but the minutes indicated that she would have been welcome. The group declared, "In the crisis brought upon our country by the world war, our members have used the independence of thought always encouraged by our dear teachers, and various shades of opinion are represented among us."[63]

The experience of war challenged the small but intensely dedicated group of individuals who remained in its opposition. Balch admitted that it was "a hard thing to stand against the surge" of public pressure to back the war. At every turn, citizens were faced with "the endlessly reiterated suggestion of every printed word, of the carefully edited news, of posters, parades, songs, speeches, [and] sermons."[64] Although she found it incredibly difficult, Balch steadfastly held to her conviction that war was neither the best nor the only method of resolving international conflict.

5. "A Basis for a New Human Civilisation," 1918–29

In early 1918, Emily Greene Balch elected to return to college teaching, being only one year shy of eligibility to receive her pension. Having taken two years off to work with the American peace movement, she could not afford—professionally or financially—to stay away longer. When she arrived at Wellesley College, however, she met an unexpected challenge.

When Balch had requested a leave of absence the previous autumn, she had done so with the support of Wellesley College's president, Ellen Pendleton. The two women had agreed that Balch's extended absence would be good for both her and the college, and Pendleton was confident that Balch would return to the economics department for the fall semester. Pendleton had forgotten, however, that Balch's term of appointment expired that academic year. Upon realizing that detail, Pendleton wrote worryingly to Balch in the spring of 1918, informing her that "the situation has now somewhat changed." Pendleton feared that the appointment expiration would become problematic when Balch sought to return. "Had I remembered that," Pendleton wrote, "I should have realized that the attitude of the Trustees in regard to a reappointment might be different from that toward a continuance of an appointment made some years ago." The necessity of requesting a reappointment meant that the trustees of the college were free to renew or deny her contract without explicitly having to confront charges of academic freedom or Balch's pacifist activities.[1]

When Balch learned of the situation with her contract, she knew immediately that the Board of Trustees would examine her antiwar position and pacifist activities in their discussion of reappointment. So, in April, she attempted to explain her actions clearly and to relate her position to the trustees. Balch noted that her involvement with antiwar organizations did not violate any actual Wellesley College policies. She did not make direct accusations of a violation of academic freedom. Instead, she asserted that she had not strayed too far into the realm of radicalism. She defended her antiwar position as rooted in her Christian beliefs and confronted what she thought were the major objections to her political stand. In her letter to the board, Balch exhibited her ability to relate the truth but skillfully couch her position in a more acceptable framework. She affirmed that she was "entirely in sympathy with the purposes of our country in the war as expressed for us by the President." She was a patriot. However, she could not "reconcile war with the truth of Jesus' teachings."[2]

Balch opposed war generally, but, she asserted, her efforts had in no way worked "to obstruct the war, to work against enlistment or anything of the sort." Such actions, she believed, were "not only inexpedient and silly," but also "morally wrong." Knowing that some board members would no doubt worry about how her pacifism would influence her classroom teaching, she assured the trustees that she would never employ propaganda to "dampen patriotism" among her students. She even infused her case with a tinge of regret. She lamented that she could not join others who felt they were doing right in war, declaring, "One of the hardest things about holding that position that I do is that it is so hard to keep it clear of Pharisaism."[3]

Balch's statement to the board of trustees clearly showed her diplomatic skill. She toned down her own convictions without diluting them. However, she knew she had avoided a particularly contentious issue and so sent a supplementary letter outlining her position in the People's Council, certainly the most radical of her wartime affiliations. She confirmed that at that time she did not hold any office in the organization, and that it was a greatly misunderstood group. She explained that this resulted mainly from the group's formation meetings being in the center of a controversy between radical and conservative politicians in the Midwest when they were organizing their first meeting. The other reason Balch's association with the PCA provoked such a response resulted from the misunderstood belief that the group actively opposed the draft, which it did not. The group had, however, opposed conscription when it first formed, prior to the conscription law in the United States.

Most important, Balch claimed that that she had a right as an academic and as an American to belong to any organization without persecution. She concluded her letter to the board by asserting this right. She implored the trustees to consider how their decision would "far transcend" her particular case. "It appears to me to be very dangerous in a democracy for citizens," she wrote, "to feel that they are controlled in their decision as to joining or not joining a (legal) political organization by considerations as to retaining their opportunity to work." Was this not then a case of academic freedom? Pendleton passed Balch's letters on to the executive committee of the board of trustees that same week, but the committee took no action. Pendleton wrote to Balch that, despite her statement, "it does not look as if they would be favorably disposed."[4]

The board of trustees acted slowly. Pendleton encouraged the trustees to postpone the question of reappointment until the following academic year. After several meetings, the board agreed to do so. Balch, and her many supporters on the faculty, were hopeful that a year's delay would allow the board to cool off a bit. The war would most likely be over in another year and Balch's wartime activities would not seem so offensive. Some professors, like Mary Whiton Calkins in the psychology department, believed that postponement was the only acceptable decision in 1918, that the only other outcome would have been the failure to reappoint.[5] Balch agreed, and she hoped that in another year she would be invited to return.

Balch had many friends at Wellesley, and they all stood behind her, writing letters to the board and encouraging her to remain confident for another year, when "the madness will have subsided." Every member of the economics department signed a letter declaring Balch a vital member of their department. Even while on leave, they said, Balch had remained critical to the running of the department. Her colleagues described Balch as a treasured teacher who had "always been able to present her subject dispassionately, unmarred by any spirit of propagandism," and as "a scholar whose impartiality of judgment [had] not been shaken by strength of her personal convictions." Failing to renew her contract, they argued, would be an "irreparable loss."[6]

In January 1919, a Senate committee charged with investigating pro-German propaganda received a report from Archibald Stevenson, an official in Military Intelligence Division of the Army. "Stevenson's List" became known as a "who's who of pacifism," as it purported to name "the principal supporters of various radical and pacifist organizations."[7] Balch's appearance on that list placed her in the center of the radical group in the United States that needed to be carefully monitored. Balch's supporters among the faculty, however, remained undeterred by the Stevenson List and continued to campaign on her behalf.

Despite her support among Wellesley colleagues, Balch was plagued with anxiety and uncertainty. She doubted her own value, wondering to a friend, "How could I come back to [Wellesley] feeling that a large body of Trustees did not want me at the college and perhaps a large part of the students also?" Balch spent the year riddled with self-doubt in the face of the board's indecision. She worried that, should she be invited back, she would be "self conscious and ineffective" in her teaching.[8] Eased by many assurances from her friends, Balch tried to be optimistic and view the situation as a mixed blessing. After all, it would allow her another year to campaign for peace.

While the year's delay in Balch's return to Wellesley might have been welcome in some ways, it still left her without an income. All of her work with peace organizations had been voluntary, and she did not have a substantial inheritance to live on. Thankfully, Oswald Garrison Villard, a friend and fellow peace campaigner who happened to own *The Nation,* came to her aid. He offered Balch a position on his editorial staff and she eagerly accepted. She returned to New York and undertook her new position with as much zeal as she had for every new endeavor.

Balch was working in New York as the First World War came to a close. She was in *The Nation*'s offices the evening she learned that the Austro-Hungarian Empire had collapsed. Villard informed her of the news and implored her, given her expertise in Slavic cultures, to "write a leading article on the subject before the paper went to press in two hours' time." She complied, being "especially interested in the effect of the change on the nationalities."[9] Of course, she failed to fully grasp the lasting and devastating economic result that the disintegration of the empire brought about. At the time, she mainly focused on the end of the war, turning her mind toward the peace negotiations that would follow.

"An International Spirit"

The war officially ended on November 11, 1918, when the Central and Entente powers signed an armistice. Two months later, in January 1919, statesmen from twenty-six nations began holding peace talks in Paris. The "big three" leaders—Great Britain, France, and the United States—dominated the conference. David Lloyd George, the British prime minister; Georges Clemenceau, the French premier; and American president Woodrow Wilson ran the show. Official delegations gathered. Unofficial lobbyists labored to be heard. It quickly became apparent, however, that the British and French delegates were mainly interested in a punitive peace, and all other ideas, including most of Wilson's Fourteen Points, were brushed aside.[10]

The international women's peace network was determined to contribute to the peace proceedings. The International Committee of Women for Permanent Peace (ICWPP) had resolved in 1915 that they would next meet after the war, wherever the peace negotiations were held, "for the purpose of presenting practical proposals."[11] This resolution became problematic, however, because the victorious leaders chose to meet in France, where it proved extremely difficult for citizens from formerly belligerent nations to gather. ICWPP leaders ultimately settled on Zurich as the alternative location for their international congress. Still close to Paris, the women would send telegrams to the international leaders then discussing the terms of the Treaty of Versailles.

The women at The Hague in 1915 had also set out the plan for postwar organizing of delegations from each of its member nations. The international leadership selected two individuals from each member country who then chose an additional three activists from their own countries. These five women constituted a committee whose job it was to organize thirty women to attend the peace conference. The Woman's Peace Party in the United States, one of the largest member branches of the international organization, ended up sending twenty-seven women in total. The committee of five—Lucia Ames Mead, Florence Kelley, Alice Thatcher Post, Jeannette Rankin, and Lillian D. Wald—organized twenty-two other American women as delegates, among whom were Emily Greene Balch and Jane Addams.[12]

Prior to the meeting in Zurich, Balch went to Paris with a smaller group of the American ICWPP representatives in early April 1919. The women spent three weeks discussing aspects of treaty negotiations with the French delegates. They also attempted to meet with officials from the peace conference and food administration. While in Paris, the Americans also learned that their English colleagues were having problems obtaining their passports to Switzerland and that the French government had refused passports altogether to potential representatives. Despite such delays, Balch and her American peers went on to Zurich, where they faced the great task of arranging the agenda and organizing the conference.

Balch assumed a leadership position immediately upon arriving in Zurich. Arranging such a conference was no small task, and Balch proved her immense talent for such organization. She worked with the other leaders to select the preliminary committee members, construct a program of discussions and events, and define the rules of order. Additionally, these delegates faced the awesome chore of arranging the numerous resolutions each national group had prepared for submission for the congress's consideration. The women established three committees as the backbone of the congress: one dealt with "political questions" and another discussed "matters affecting the status of women"; a third committee was created to handle "questions of education" and other remaining matters. When the congress began its discussions, the first committee, dealing with political matters, created two subcommittees to discuss how to proceed, whether the congress accepted or refused the League of Nations Covenant in the Treaty of Versailles.[13]

Finally, on May 12, Jane Addams, the ICWPP president, opened the congress. She praised the difficult work the women pacifists had been doing in their own nations during the four years of war. She marveled at the fact that when the international board was organizing the resolutions to be discussed, the same themes emerged from voices in every country. This showed that many of the women shared similar war encounters, and where their experiences differed, they still expressed allied concerns over the future of international cooperation. Addams emphasized that this meeting of women need not pretend to obtain harmonious agreement. It was important to recognize that women's experiences during the war might result in a "sense of estrangement" among the delegates. Without any illusions that the congress would be entirely "free from animosity," differences of opinion must be expressed in an open forum. Still, in the face of disagreement, Addams encouraged the women to cultivate their "sense of goodwill and mutual understanding" in their discussions of "the uncertain future." The Swiss leader Clara Ragaz also keenly articulated the differences of opinion among the women and expressed the need for cooperation. "There are women who entertain different opinions as to the responsibility of different nations in this war, as to the connection of our economic conditions with the war, even concerning women's fault in the war," she stated. "But this difference of outlook does not prevent us from recognising a common share of the responsibility in its deepest sense and in its deepest causes."[14]

Addams and Ragaz were wise to call attention to the differences in experience and opinion among the Zurich delegates. Despite the spectrum of opinion, however, common concerns and themes emerged as the women deliberated in meetings throughout the days and evenings. In this environment of openness and honesty, the congress set out to debate resolutions, some of which were directed to the peace negotiations in Paris and others set as guiding principles for the organization.

The most immediate (and most divisive) topic for discussion related to the formation of a League of Nations. Two distinct camps emerged during the discussions: Lucia Ames Mead, the Woman's Peace Party leader from Massachusetts, headed the pro-League camp, which urged the congress of women to fully support the League of Nations Covenant as the best aspect of the treaty. Mead asserted that while most of the treaty was "unjust, imperialistic, and a severe handicap upon the Covenant," the League still offered the greatest hope. Although the covenant was far from perfect, Mead and her camp argued that it had "within it great possibilities of growth, and, in this acute crisis, is the best available alternative to the old system of alliances, balance of power and war." In opposition to that view, British delegate Ethel Snowden asserted that the covenant must be rejected outright, as its present form "so seriously violate[d] the principles upon which alone a just and lasting peace can be secured." The League of Nations, as the covenant proposed, merely perpetuated the rest of the flaws in the treaty.[15]

Florence Kelley of the United States presented a third perspective, offering a sort of compromise. She suggested that the congress of women explicitly support the idea of a League of Nations but publicly denounce those elements of the covenant that were "not democratic." Specifically, the League originally represented only the victors, allowed the colonial system to continue, and embraced a one-sided disarmament agenda. After significant debate, the congress adopted Kelley's compromise that supported the League of Nations *in principle* but objected to it in numerous ways. The congress condemned the covenant's omissions and made suggestions for improving the League in the future.[16]

Another issue at the heart of the Zurich congress discussions related to the blockade that the Entente nations had continued against Germany and which was perpetuating a famine in central Europe. Unlike most of the officials in Paris, the international peace women remained deeply concerned over the welfare of the people in the defeated nations. The women maintained that the "widespread unemployment, famine and pestilence" extending throughout Europe and Asia at the time was "a profound disgrace to civilisation, and a challenge to all men and women who believe in the brotherhood of mankind and in the duties of world citizenship." They unanimously passed a resolution charging the politicians in Paris to lift the blockade immediately "in order that food and raw materials may be brought to the unemployed and starving peoples" and that the world resources be organized to relieve and prevent famine.[17]

On Tuesday morning, May 13, the congress telegraphed this resolution, in an amended form, to officials at the peace conference in Paris and agreed to present the final resolution at their meetings in Versailles. Of the several telegrams they sent to Paris that week, only the resolution condemning the blockade received a response. President Wilson's reply, read aloud to the entire assembly in Zurich, related little other than acknowledgement of receipt and sympathy with their aims. "Your message appeals both to my head and to my heart," he said, "and I hope most sincerely that ways may be found, though the present outlook is extremely unpromising, because of infinite practical difficulties." Despite the lack of any action on the matter, Wilson's telegram produced an excitement in the crowd. Addams later recalled the reading of Wilson's words as "one of the most striking moments of the Congress," showing utterly "the reverence with which all Europe regarded the President of the United States."[18]

The women also discussed and accepted seven resolutions under the broad heading of "status of women." The most substantial was the creation of the Women's Charter. The women resolved to urge the inclusion of this charter in the peace treaty, recognizing that "the status of women, social, political and economic, is of supreme international importance." This document included principles such as suffrage, equal protection by law against slavery, women's "full personal and civil rights" in marriage (especially regarding property), equal parental rights, national rights of married women, equal opportunities for education, equality in the professions, equal pay, suppression of the trafficking of women, the responsibility of fathers for illegitimate children, and mothers' economic recognition.[19]

These resolutions highlighted the ongoing campaigns for suffrage in every nation. In a resolution entitled "On Women's Vote in Plebiscite," the congress insisted that the peacemakers insert into the treaty the clause: "That in any Plebiscite taken under the Treaty or Peace or a League of Nations women should have the same right to vote as men." In addition to women's political and economic equality, the congress passed resolutions concerned with such social and political issues as married women's nationality and even women's access to information about birth control.[20]

Another paramount issue for discussion in 1919 related to the revolutions spreading throughout Europe. These movements, many of which were based in socialism, sparked great excitement among many of the Zurich delegates. Support for violent revolutions, however, remained a volatile issue. In fact, the women only narrowly passed their resolution (60 to 55 votes) on the relation of pacifists to revolutionary movements. It read, in part: "We declare our sympathy with the purpose of the workers who are rising up everywhere to make an end of exploitation and to claim their world." After great debates over the language, the final resolution contained a weaker statement than originally proposed, toning down solidarity with the working class. Some women, however, wished to go further than a mere expression of support and reaffirmed their pacifist role in the revolutionary movements. They wrote, "Nevertheless we re-assert our belief in the methods of peace, and we feel that it is our special part in this revolutionary age, to counsel against violence, and above all to prepare the wealthy and privileged classes to give up their wealth and yield their special privileges without struggle, so that the change from a competitive system of production for private profit, to some cooperative system of production for human happiness, may be made with as little bloodshed as possible." These delegates saw their role not only as condemning violence, but also as assisting in the creation of a new socialist world order. Balch, however, thought this version of the resolution too weak and preferred the original wording that asserted a stronger revolutionary spirit.[21]

The women at Zurich wanted it understood that international congresses could work together, even across the divide of nations recently at war, and establish true cooperation for peace. One much-accounted story from this week involved the reception of French delegate, Jeanne Mélin, who finally arrived in Zurich on the last day of the conference. The German delegate Lida Gustava Heymann rose, crossed the stage, and embraced the French delegate. The congress erupted in applause. Heymann proclaimed, "A German woman gives her hand to a French woman, and says in the name of the German Delegation, that we hope that we women can build a bridge from Germany to France and from France to Germany, and that in the future we may be able to make good the wrongdoing of the men. We women of the world who all feel alike, who want to protect and not to destroy, we shall always understand one another."[22]

In the spirit of international cooperation for a better future, the gathering of women agreed that their organization needed to better represent its aims. Most important, the congress voted to change the name of their organization. Many delegates argued to keep the name of the organization formed at The Hague in 1915, the International Committee of Women for a Permanent Peace, by morphing it into the Women's International League for Permanent Peace. Others, however, felt it necessary to include the concept of freedom in their new organization. They eventually accepted the American delegate Catherine Marshall's urging of "the Women's International League for Peace and Freedom" (women referred to this mainly as the WILPF or the WIL). Marshall asserted that the "adoption of the new name" was "more inclusive" and focused "more toward the future" than the other names proposed.[23]

In determining its immediate post-congress activities, the assembly voted to send Addams, along with French delegate Gabrielle Duchêne and a small group, to the International Peace Conference in Paris to present their resolutions to the official diplomats. Addams later recalled, "It was creditable to the patience of the peace makers in Paris that they later received our delegation and allowed us to place the various resolutions in their hands." Of course, the women and their ideas were ridiculed in the press. As Addams described, "Only slowly did public opinion reach a point of view similar to ours."[24]

Indeed, within a few years, public opinion supported the line of thinking embraced by the small assembly of international women at Zurich in 1919.

WILPF Delegates, Zurich, 1919 (Balch on far right, sitting; to her right, also sitting, are Lucia Ames Mead, Jane Addams, Alice Thatcher Post, and Jeanette Rankin). Women's International League for Peace and Freedom Papers, Swarthmore College Peace Collection.

Ultimately, the congress condemned outright the terms of peace established at Versailles. The women regretted that the treaty "should so seriously violate the principles upon which alone a just and lasting peace can be secured, and which the democracies of the world had come to accept." It violated the principles of self-determination in favor of the ancient tradition of granting spoils of war to the victors, thus creating "all over Europe discords and animosities, which can only lead to future wars." Indeed, the women at the Congress were proved correct. The treaty unquestionably fueled the fire for another war. Balch and her peers at Zurich in 1919 warned the statesmen in Paris: "By the financial and economic proposals a hundred million people of this generation in the heart of Europe are condemned to poverty, disease, and despair, which must result in the spread of hatred and anarchy within each nation."[25]

The Treaty of Versailles was ultimately signed on June 15, 1919. When the women who had attended the Zurich conference learned the details, they were greatly disappointed in the peace negotiations. Still, they firmly believed that their gathering and the resolutions agreed upon there were of great significance to their future. Although their ideas failed to move political leaders, they were, of themselves, important. The Congress of Women at Zurich was the first group to publicly rebuke the terms of peace and condemn the League of

Nations Covenant. They had verbalized the true principles of peace, principles the organization would continue to promote. In her closing address, Addams had urged the women not to be discouraged, proclaiming, "If some of us who are looking at the terms of the Peace Treaty and the prospects for the future are not very happy, we must remember that the people who made the Peace Treaty are also far from happy."[26]

After the week in Zurich, there was a good deal for Emily Greene Balch to be unhappy about personally. Over the course of the week, although very busy with the conference, Balch undoubtedly had at the back of her mind the uncertainty of her future. Thankfully, she was surrounded by her friends and supporters when she finally received word from the Wellesley College board of trustees. In a very close vote, the board decided against reappointing Balch to her position. When she finally received the news, it was "not a surprise," though still "something of a shock." Balch "celebrated the occasion" by joining Emmeline Pethick-Lawrence, the head of the British delegation, and Madeline Doty, from New York, for a cigarette. She had never smoked before. "At Wellesley, at that time, smoking was strictly taboo," she stated. Now, she was taboo as well, and so it felt apropos. She did not take up the habit, however.[27]

Balch's later portrayal of these events, and the subsequent descriptions by historians, illustrated Balch as sad yet accepting, even a bit self-admonishing. In 1933, she authored an article in which she "grieved that the well-known liberality of Wellesley College should have been over-strained by me."[28] This later vision of her response to the decision was no doubt influenced by her ongoing positive relations with the college. In the months immediately following the trustees' decision, however, Balch insisted the situation demanded attention. She angrily informed President Pendleton that newspapers misstated that she had resigned. She wanted this untruth shown clearly for what it was.[29]

When Balch expressed her outrage to Pendleton, she also relayed her anxiety that the board's decision meant that, after twenty-one years of service, she would not receive her pension. She had not saved money for her retirement, and so the pension constituted a genuine cause for concern. Balch's childhood friend, Helen Cheever, then took action in such a way that enabled Balch a greater freedom in determining what her future employment would be. Cheever bestowed upon her an annual sum approximate to the amount of her pension. Characteristic of Cheever, though, she revoked Balch's pension when she found out that her friend was giving a significant portion of it away.[30]

In Zurich, after receiving the initial news of the board's decision, Balch did not have to wonder what her next professional step would be. The congress had agreed to set up an international headquarters for the Women's International League for Peace and Freedom. The delegation elected Balch to serve as its first international secretary-treasurer. Balch's new position charged her to shape the international framework for the new organization. Having proven herself at Zurich as an expert in the organizing of bureaucratic conferences, Balch, thankful for the opportunity, prepared herself for her move to Geneva.

Geneva, 1919–22

Balch's efforts to launch the international WILPF office in Geneva marked her professional transition, at age fifty-two, from academic to paid worker for the women's international peace movement. The delegates at the Zurich congress charged her with the daunting task of setting up an international office and organizing the daily functions of the international body. The new WILPF constitution stated that the organization's headquarters would be based in the same city as the League of Nations. The League decided to make Geneva its home base, moving there from its temporary offices in London in November 1920. Balch spent the autumn of 1919 working to build the physical and ideological framework for the new international organization and to arrange the establishment of an international center that came to be known as "Maison Internationale."[31]

As much as Balch thrived in this new environment, she put herself under a great deal of stress and remained overly critical of her own performance. Her friends and colleagues frequently reassured her as to her usefulness to the organization and also chastised her for working too hard. Two individuals in the postwar years stood out as central influences and steadying forces: Jane Addams and Helen Cheever remained in close, often daily, communication with Balch during her early days with the WILPF and came to understand her daily activities. Both women often expressed concern over her work schedule and potential health problems. Balch worked herself to exhaustion during this period. Jane Addams was undoubtedly familiar with handling multiple projects simultaneously and balancing her professional responsibility with the almost constant demands on her time. She counseled her friend, "You have a house beside the road in a very literal sense and you should not allow travelling pacifists to eat you up." Addams, suffering from poor health herself, focused more of her efforts on the international office rather than the American branch after 1919. Her friendship with Balch thus deepened through their shared commitment to the new international order.[32] Cheever, Balch's friend since childhood, strengthened her own commitment to support

Balch's work during these years. While Addams remained Balch's stalwart professional champion, Cheever's personal assistance to Balch became increasingly relevant to the success of the WILPF.

Between 1919 and 1922, Balch accomplished an astounding series of tasks. She efficiently accomplished her main charge, to set up the international headquarters. In so doing, she spent a good deal of time thinking about how the new international organization would actually function. She also established a relationship with the League of Nations, initiated new international publications, and designed the institutional framework necessary to enact the international resolutions from Zurich, such as food campaigns for war-torn countries and women's struggles for equality. In addition, she dedicated herself to expanding membership in the WILPF and studied how to establish more branches. In the midst of all of this, she also prepared for the next congress of women, scheduled for 1921.

Although Balch consistently downplayed her own importance in the international network, she was in fact essential to the WILPF during these years. Her understated sense of worth to the international movement during this period resulted from her self-doubt as much as her modesty. She worried, for example, that she took a paycheck from a mostly voluntary organization. Addams, then acting as the international president, discouraged Balch from feeling guilty about being paid to do the valuable work she was taking on. She assured Balch, "Please do not feel for one moment uncomfortable about your salary. It is all right and I say to every one who has any business to know that your salary was the same as that you had at Wellesley and I am sure that can but seem reasonable."[33]

Despite Balch's discomfort with her paid position, she needed the money. Having lost her salary and the hope of her pension from Wellesley College, she depended on the funds to maintain her modest lifestyle. The WILPF paid her a salary of $200 ($2,468.76 in 2008) per month. Balch stated that the amount was "a good rate at that place and time though not excessive by American standards." Further, she claimed, "Though living in Geneva was not dear, I spent a considerable part of my salary for the [Women's International] League in direct and indirect ways."[34]

A central part of Balch's and the WILPF's new vision focused on the workings of the League of Nations. The WILPF set up in Geneva with the specific intention of closely monitoring and, when possible, influencing the League's actions. Like most of her peers, Balch expressly disapproved of and was disappointed in the Treaty of Versailles. With the United States on the verge of rejecting the peace terms, including the League of Nations, American internationalists grappled with how best to serve their vision of powerful and effective international organizations. In the fall of 1919, Balch still struggled with how to confront her reservations about the peace terms and the League of Nations and still support any work toward an international organization of nations. She turned to Addams for guidance, asking, "Did you finally decide to favor ratifying the peace treaty unreservedly? And entering the L of N?" Balch confided her true stance to Addams, saying that she "personally would be thankful to see the Paris Covenant fall through if a more democratic Society of Nations could then be organized and as I *believe* one could and would be, I should be relieved to see the Paris L of N fall to the ground." Addams responded, "I have never favored ratifying the peace treaty unreservedly and have always said that I hoped the Covenant would go through as it seemed the best possible and that the Senate would insist upon changes in the treaty."[35]

The international women's movement, with Balch and Addams at the helm, had to work to shape what little the League offered. Balch encouraged WILPF members to have faith that their efforts would bring about a new world order. She declared, "It is . . . only by initiative, self-sacrifice and intelligence that we shall contribute to the coming of the decent world order that we hope to see follow—like spring after winter and green shoots from bare black boughs— the ugly, greedy, cruel civilization in which our life time has been cast."[36]

Balch had always believed in the power of democratically managed, large institutions to solve problems by systematically studying them and reaching a consensus about solutions. Her participation on various municipal government committees—in Boston and, especially, in her involvement with the Conference of Neutrals during the war—reinforced her confidence in such bodies. In that vein, Balch sustained a deep interest in how the League organized itself. She sought to learn from how it divided up its departments or organized its committees. Balch and the international WILPF office continued to work with and monitor the League throughout its short lifetime.

Balch dedicated the majority of her time to ensuring the smooth running of the international office and to initiating the organization's new publications. Balch worked continuously to organize the international WILPF office in Geneva. In September, she wrote, "It is hard to keep up with the work at the office. We have sent out over 350 foreign letters alone and besides correspondence, news sheets and trying to get on with the Zurich report, there is seeing people." She received a constant stream of visitors while trying to complete her daily chores with minimal staff support. Balch worked ceaselessly throughout the fall of 1919 to sort out the details of running an international office. One of the numerous tasks that added to her daily work involved discerning how to bank WILPF's funds in Switzerland in the postwar economy. After studying the issue, Balch informed Addams in December that the organization's funds would be better off in a New York bank, as Swiss banks were still tied to the unstable economies of the Central powers. As much as she hated not keeping their funds in Europe, Balch felt it best "to do the conservative thing" and keep the WILPF's funds in a more stable economy.[37] Balch's role as treasurer of the international organization increased an already substantial list of responsibilities.

Balch's position as an international leader often distanced her from the actions of the American branch of the Women's International League. The international office had no official position that required the branches to function a certain way, and this great autonomy sometimes caused friction, as evidenced by Balch's efforts to mitigate increasing factionalism. Although her energies focused on the international office, Balch remained concerned with the workings of her American counterparts at home. She frequently wrote to Addams and other WILPF leaders seeking more information from the troubled American branch. In October 1919, Balch complained to Addams that she felt "entirely out of touch" with the American section. She became upset with the lack of news from the Americans not simply because she felt lonely, but because she believed that the American branch was "the key to the pacifist situation." She meant that the United States was then struggling with multiple matters central to the international peace movement, including "military training, conscription, amnesty, Mexico, Hawaii, ratification or no ratification [of the Treaty of Versailles], Oriental mandate yes or no, Siberian prisoners, Russian and renewed German blockade, famine and the rest." With all of these issues for the American branch to confront, Balch expressed her frustration that little news reached her in Geneva other than the fact that Eleanor Karsten in Chicago "did not think there was anything to be done in America."[38]

In November 1919, when the national board of the Woman's Peace Party formally agreed to become the national council of the Women's International League for Peace and Freedom, the leaders gave their members the option to belong to either the national or the international organization, or both. The board knew, as did Balch, that the international organization needed to issue a broad appeal for membership if it hoped to draw from the array of peace interests in the country. Addams wrote to Balch that the national board planned to "urge as many people as possible to join the national and international" associations. Membership in both levels of the WILPF entitled individuals to receive the international news sheets Balch produced as well as information from their local and national sections.[39] Balch called on WILPF members from all nations to join the organization even if they disagreed on some questions. The organization only excluded those who advocated violence.

Of the early WILPF campaigns, the one of greatest interest to Balch and Addams centered on providing relief to the starving in war-devastated countries. Those nations particularly affected by the blockade—Germany, Austria, and Hungary—received much of the organization's attention. Addams conducted a speaking tour on behalf of the European Children's Fund, which was raising money for famine relief. In October 1919, Addams wrote Balch about the problem, emphasizing that the issue of famine relief must be an *international* one. She declared, "In time the nationalistic lines will no longer hold where starving children are concerned." This became a main priority of the international group; in fact, it became difficult to raise money to put toward any other part of the organization.[40]

By the end of 1919, the international office in Geneva was starting to run more smoothly, assisted by the establishment of a small paid staff. By December, the number of volunteers in the international office had expanded. Volunteers temporarily relieved Balch from much of the more mundane office work, such as letter writing, paper organizing, publication preparation, and general office management. The WILPF offices on the Rue du Vieux Collège, known as the *Maison Internationale,* opened early the following year and constituted not only an office but an international meeting house. Balch's efforts paid off in the creation of an international center, complete with office space, a library, facilities for lectures and meetings, a grand garden, and rooms to rent to members and friends who came to work with the WILPF.[41]

Balch also diligently worked to prepare a great number of publications, reports, letters, and memoranda, both to League of Nations delegates and WILPF members. She later claimed that letter writing and the editing of the report of the congress at Zurich alone consumed her entire first year. Balch, along with her two secretaries, produced a detailed report of more than four hundred pages. Knowing that this account, as well as being vital documentation of that important conference, provided a model for future reports, Balch made certain that it was thorough. She and her assistants compiled all elements of the conference into a coherent whole, written in English, French, and German.[42] During her first year in Geneva, Balch also oversaw the establishment of a new WILPF monthly publication, *Pax et Libertas* (this became *Pax International* in 1950). Again, Balch knew that this newspaper would be the standard for future editions.

In the first issue of *Pax et Libertas,* in February 1920, Balch addressed factionalism in the WILPF. She encouraged WILPF members to join as many organizations as they wished. Some WILPF members wanted only to support the League of Nations, while others wanted to focus on suffrage or on absolute pacifism. Rather than have these issues divide the WILPF membership, Balch dedicated her first column in *Pax* to encouraging members to participate in various organizations. She wrote to the president of the American section, Anna Garland Spencer, regarding the upcoming editorial. Balch confirmed her belief that the solution to factionalism within nations resided in her "practical policy," which allowed social justice organizations "to multiply freely and have as many organized groups in the same place as may happen to develop, each working in its own way but keeping in touch and cooperating."[43]

After attending the first sessions of the League of Nations in November 1920, Balch paused to write President Wilson of her impressions. Qualifying that her letter only related her own thoughts on the League, not those of a representative of the WILPF, she expressed her disappointment that the United States failed to participate in the vital work of the international organization. Balch wrote that after witnessing the Assembly in action, she grew more confident in the growing sense of internationalism. Even if other nations, including her own, were slow to fully participate, she claimed, "The world has in the Secretariat of the League a constant, quiet force at work creating a new type of public servant."[44] This force, Balch firmly believed, would triumph.

The WILPF's many campaigns in the postwar years kept Balch extremely busy. She managed to find time, however, to examine the changes in her life and seriously consider her perspective on the world. During those years of professional transition, Balch evaluated her personal, political, and spiritual views and made marked changes in her identity.

One substantial transformation for Balch related to her political outlook. She no longer identified as a socialist after World War I. She was careful to emphasize, however, that this was not because her political outlook "had moved more to the 'Right.'" Rather, she felt that socialism had changed into something else. Recalling her decision to distance herself from socialism, she wrote, "The word seemed to me to have come more definitely to connote the Marxian creed if not actual Party membership: the war had made me more sceptical [*sic*] of Governments as such and much more afraid of trusting them with new powers." The other lesson she learned from the war experience was that "tags which while often useful and necessary terribly obliterate vital shades of difference and in general suit only very simple situations."[45] Although Balch ceased to identify as a socialist, she remained committed to the economic concept throughout her life.

The Society of Friends

Balch reassessed her spirituality during this period as well. The news that the Wellesley trustees had ended her twenty-one-year teaching career had been unexpected. The blow to her professional plans and the change in her financial situation was eased by the WILPF's decision to pay her to act as its international secretary-treasurer in Geneva. Yet this transition, as much as she came to embrace it, necessarily altered how Balch viewed herself in the world. No longer a respected college professor who engaged in social reform activities, Balch had now been labeled an American radical. Her employer, through its trustees, had affirmed that claim. Further, the experience of the war had deeply affected American liberals and their sense of progress. It is not surprising, then, that during this period in her life Emily Greene Balch seriously reexamined her own spiritual outlook.[46]

While living in Geneva, Balch began attending Quaker meetings. The Society of Friends had a long tradition of social reform and pacifism, both of which resonated strongly with Balch, especially in the years during and following the First World War. After attending meetings for a year in Geneva and considering what she identified as a longer-term "drawing" to the denomination, she finally embraced "a definite desire to become one of them."[47] It happened that the majority of her colleagues at the time belonged to the Society of Friends. With help from her friends Edith Pye and Joan Fry, the London annual meeting admitted Balch as a member in February 1921. She specifically chose to join the English section rather than the American Society of Friends because the branch in the United States was then embroiled in theological disputes. Balch did not wish to involve herself in political quarrels in her religious life. Presumably, she struggled with enough of them in her professional life.

Undoubtedly, the Quakers' dedication to peace was a compelling issue for Balch, but her draw to the society represented more than an affirmation of her pacifism. Balch's religious conversion related directly to the Quakers' social reform outlook. Her experiences with peace activism during the war had reinforced her belief that all aspects of life must be directed toward improving one's world. Her religious conversion, however, occurred not during the war years, but during her early years with the WILPF, suggesting that her Quaker identity would be another aspect of her essential professional work. In 1933, she wrote of the Quakers, "It was not alone their testimony against war, their creedless faith, nor their openness to suggestions for far-reaching social reform that attracted me, but the dynamic force of the active love through which their religion was expressing itself in multifarious ways, both during and after the war."[48]

In early 1921, fully committed to the Quaker faith, Balch considered how to expand the network of WILPF women. As part of the WILPF's efforts to recruit more members and establish branches in other countries, she spent April and May touring areas of the former Austro-Hungarian Empire and the Balkans, witnessing the aftermath of the war in those lands. In addition to gaining a greater understanding of the situations in those regions, Balch successfully recruited many women to their international alliance. She described to the WILPF congress in 1921 the ways in which she had been fruitful, stating, "The visits I made in April and May to Prague, Agram [Zagreb, Croatia], Belgrade, Sofia, Bucarest [*sic.*], and Budapest" had "served to make many new connections and to strengthen old ones, and I hope that in the end it will prove its usefulness in the growth of our work in South Eastern Europe."[49] Following this tour for WILPF, Balch went to Vienna, where she stayed with her friend Yella Hertzka, the Austrian WILPF president. There the two women planned the organization's third international congress.

The Third International WILPF Congress, 1921

Balch and the international committee of the WILPF chose Vienna as the location for its international conference in 1921 because the city stood in the middle of where the war still affected people. The Austrian people suffered from a great shortage of food, high unemployment, and a turbulent economy. For Balch, the troubles in Austria weighed on her heavily; she described it as being "like lead on my heart." In her opening address, Jane Addams highlighted the importance of the conference's environment to their discussions, exclaiming, "We realize, as we come, that this country has suffered bitterly both from the war and from the terms of the Peace. But even here we hope that we may do something in the name of reconciliation."[50]

Yella Hertzka, the president of the Austrian section, welcomed the women to her war-devastated nation. She emphasized how terrible life had been in Austria since the armistice, which had sparked hope for many women that conditions would improve rather than further deteriorate. Hertzka urged the delegates to learn the true state of affairs in the former Central Powers, pointing out, "If you get to know only the parts of Vienna where the foreigners' hotels stand, you may easily get a wrong impression of the town. . . . You can only get a true idea of what war has meant if you go out to the workers' districts or if you see the dwellings of the workers or of the middle classes." She closed her speech by reminding the women of the city's place in the war's origins and looking toward a better future. She declared, "May this town from which the spark sprang that set the world ablaze, also be the place where the work for lasting peace shall be begun with best success."[51]

A photo taken at the congress shows Balch smiling, but looking older and more exhausted than in 1919. Yet she stood surrounded by the international leaders of the organization, all with a sense of purpose on their faces. The Vienna congress was important to the international movement of women and to Balch in particular because it articulated the issues that would remain of central importance to the organization for the decade. One prominent event during this conference was the debate over the organization's formal relationship to absolute pacifism. Other principal issues included the WILPF's activities regarding the League of Nations, international education, disarmament, and the colonies and mandate system.

Balch gave a report to the Vienna congress on the WILPF international office. She described the broad scope of the *Maison Internationale*, which served as more than just a headquarters. The building had "rooms to let to friends passing through Geneva and where we should like to welcome every one of you." Balch was careful to qualify, though, that the building could not accommodate them all at once. The Geneva office efficiently organized all of the materials from each of the national sections. She informed the delegates,

WILPF members, 1921 (Balch third from left, to the right of Jane Addams). Women's International League for Peace and Freedom Papers, Swarthmore College Peace Collection.

"We are so organized that we can act quickly yet in co-operation; suggestions received at Geneva can be acted on promptly and suggestions radiating from Geneva make it possible to secure simultaneous action from all quarters."[52]

Catherine Marshall of Great Britain reported on the international office's activities in relation to the League of Nations, which had opened its first assembly the previous November. Marshall began by recognizing the WILPF's criticism of the League from their Zurich congress. She concluded, "Time has shown us how right we were." Marshall focused on "how far the League, as it is, can be used to further pacifist and true internationalist aims" and "how far we, the Women's International League, are in a position to exercise any influence on the League of Nations in that direction." In the fall of 1920, Marshall had been part of a WILPF investigation that examined the workings of the League of Nations. She told the women in Vienna how that involvement changed her attitude toward the possibilities of that organization, stating, "I am personally convinced by our experience there, contrary to my expectations, that a very great deal can be done and was done."[53]

Marshall worked with Balch and the Swiss leader Marguerite Gobat to learn about the strengths and weaknesses of the League. Marshall concluded that the League could be modified on its three levels—the council, the assembly, and the secretariat. She believed the greatest potential for amending the League's work, however, was with the assembly. She declared, "Our idea was to encourage the Assembly, by seeing it get the support it needs from the public opinion in different countries to assert itself against the Council, and to be independent and courageous." In 1920–21, the WILPF presented eight proposals to delegates of the League of Nations and, according to Balch, experienced "two bits of visible success." These included "the appointment by the League of Nations of a Commission on behalf of Greek, Armenian and other women and children still captive in harems, and the placing of Mrs. Wicksell of Stockholm on the very importent [*sic*] Commission on Mandates." In addition to lobbying delegates, the WILPF leaders felt that the women's most important role in relation to the League of Nations was to arouse public awareness and opinion in its dealings. At the Vienna congress, specific actions and resolutions regarding the League of Nations were "referred to the International Bureau at Geneva and to the National Sections for study and action."[54] Although the women devoted much of the conference to the topic of the League of Nations, it did not usurp as much time as it had two years previously.

The mandate system and the colonies themselves were a subject of significant discussion at Vienna. Balch spoke convincingly against the "military use of native populations of colonies," arguing that utilizing native civilians as troops for imperial armies "is a menace to civilisation that is not fully realized." She asserted that this practice constituted a continuation of slavery and that using colonies in such a way did not strengthen imperialists but rather provoked "a most potent cause of wars."[55] It provided another reason for nations to go to war to gain their own colonies and colonized armies. The Congress swiftly passed a resolution condemning the use of colonized populations in this way.

Another notable topic at the Vienna congress related to "pacifism in practice." The delegates allocated several sessions to discussing the use of violence in support of self-determination, especially regarding national movements then being waged in Ireland and India. The women wrestled with how to officially embrace absolute pacifism. In the end, the congress passed a resolution condemning violence and adopting "the principle and practice of Non-Resistance under all circumstances."[56] However, the resolution noted, "The vote was an expression of individual opinion and purpose, and was not to be taken as binding in Sections." Although the organization embraced the principle of nonresistance, individual members were not required to commit to absolute pacifism, the condemnation of violence under all circumstances. Fanny Garrison Villard had traveled from the United States to propose that the WILPF incorporate absolute pacifism into the constitution. When the women refused—after much discussion—Villard returned to the United States and helped to found the Women's Peace Society, based on absolute pacifism. Balch supported this decision, believing that there was room in the movement for multiple organizations.

After the Congress, Balch returned to the offices in Geneva for a few months before traveling home to Jamaica Plain for a brief visit in November and December of 1921. During this period she learned that, at age fifty-four, her health was in serious decline. She wrote to Addams that winter that she had seen a doctor in Boston, who had told her what she already knew: she suffered from exhaustion. Despite this information, Balch apologized to Addams for not keeping up with WILPF work while in the United States, although she had given numerous speeches on behalf of the organization. Telling of the fact that Balch had been overworking herself, she declared that she had "not been accomplishing much." She continued, "I have spoken, however, at Wellesley College (on WILPF), Women's City Club, League of Democratic Control, Liberal Club Radcliff [sic] (with Mrs. Mead), and WIL Boston." She added that she "also presided and spoke at Monday's meeting of the WIL here" and that she had scheduled "2 other engagements."[57] To Balch, this constituted little work in comparison to her productivity in Geneva.

Balch returned to Geneva in 1922 for what would become her last year of full-time work for the WILPF. Expressing her frustration with the focus on the office and fears of her own utility, she wrote to Addams, "I have moments of great distress of mind feeling we might be doing more, yet not sure *what,* to push forward on big lines. I never seem to have time for any but the little things and that is so stupid."[58] Balch's work in the Geneva office may have been overshadowed with minute tasks, but without question the many advances made during the first three years of the WILPF were due almost entirely to her.

Helen Cheever, 1920–24

Balch's professional life in Geneva demanded most of her time. She was thrilled to participate in the formation of an international structure at a time when she and others hoped institutions such as the League of Nations marked a new order in relations between nations. Yet she depended on the emotional support of her friends and family back in the United States. She corresponded frequently with her siblings and worried over her sister Annie's deteriorating mental health. In addition to her family, Balch continued to turn to her dear childhood friends, especially Helen Cheever and Frances Hayward. Cheever, Balch's close friend since her days at Miss Ireland's School for Girls, stood out as her great advocate and ally during her years in Geneva. Cheever believed herself indispensable to Balch's personal and professional life; in fact, it is unlikely that Balch could have maintained her international office and perpetuated the peace agenda of the WILPF during the early 1920s without Cheever's support.

During the autumn of 1919, as Balch's work burdens increased, her physical and emotional health suffered. Addams, the main recipient of Balch's letters during this time, worried over Balch's health and admonished her colleague, "Do try to go slowly. Fraulein [Lida Gustava] Heymann wrote that you looked thin and overworked and I am sure you know that none of us want that." Addams was particularly concerned about Balch's emotional state. She came to believe that her colleague would greatly benefit from Cheever's joining her in Europe and wrote of this to Aletta Jacobs, saying, "Miss Balch seems to be in fairly good spirits although I think she has been pretty lonely at times. It is hard to change . . . residence from one country to another." She expressed her relief that Cheever planned to join Balch that winter, thinking, "It will be a much pleasanter arrangement."[59]

Cheever also believed it would a better situation for Balch. Planning her journey to see Balch, Cheever wrote to Addams, "I hope my companionship and her desire to make me comfortable may have their influence upon her own comfort and health." Of course, Cheever supported Balch's professional responsibilities as well. She reassured Addams that she would not interfere with the work for the WILPF, that she was "going nominally to assist Emily." Cheever remained quite clear about her value and purpose in this voyage, asserting her belief that just "being with Emily will be of itself an assistance to her."[60]

Although Cheever had planned to spend the winter of 1919 in Geneva with Balch, a series of miscommunications and Balch's own apprehensions about Cheever's presence in Europe delayed the journey. During a confusing interim, Addams learned that Cheever might not travel to Geneva, and Addams wrote to Balch, "I can't tell you how sorry I am. . . . I had counted great things from her companionship and the establishment of a household of your own. Of course you know the situation better than anyone else but I do hope that you will soon feel that it is perfectly safe for her to come."[61]

During that winter, Cheever spent more time learning of Balch's social reform interests. In early 1920, she still had little involvement in the Women's International League, or with international affairs generally. Her community work, though extensive, tended toward local efforts. She was dedicated to Denison House (an involvement initiated by Balch) and remained very active in work for children in the Boston area. During the winter of 1919–20, Cheever visited Addams at Hull House, during which time she came to a greater understanding of the WILPF and its work. She wrote to Addams of her appreciation for that visit, particularly because it imparted a better sense of the meaning of Balch's efforts.[62]

Cheever finally sailed for Europe late in February 1920 and met up with Balch in Geneva in March. She stayed for the better part of a year. That winter the two women sent a joint letter home to their school alumni group, describing their life together in Geneva. Balch wrote of her work for the WILPF in Geneva and of Cheever's care and company, "I cannot tell you how devoted she has been, what a constant comfort and pleasure, only I have let her quite spoil me."[63]

With Cheever caring for her, Balch seemed to fare better. Cheever wrote to Addams, assuring her that Balch was resting and exercising on weekends. Though she refused to take a long vacation as Cheever wished, Balch conceded to weekend getaways to the country. "Emily's love of nature, and her ability to absorb herself in the happiness of the country life, enable her to make it really restful." Cheever was not without worry, however. She continued, "I am aware that her head is tired, because I have to choose the time very carefully when I can talk to her at length about American or my own affairs."[64]

Cheever also wrote about the office in Geneva and about the people there. The diversity of national backgrounds of individuals in the office, she felt, contributed to the international interests of the organization. Because of so many connections to individuals from war-torn nations, she wrote, the peace workers seemed "terribly close to the suffering of the starving people." Though she supported the WILPF, Cheever never became as ardent a supporter of its mission as Balch. She wrote to Addams that she planned to stay in Geneva, at least through the summer because "E's work seems to me so worth while." Revealing her own hesitations, however, Cheever continued, "Any difference of opinion I have evaporates when I am with her. She is so reasonable and so loving and her standards are such a comfort to be living near to, physically at any rate. Even if one cannot reach them spiritually." Even though she never entirely committed to the WILPF, as her letter indicated, Cheever still shared Balch's joy over the potential of the work being done in Geneva. To their girlhood friends in Boston, Balch wrote to describe the excitement of postwar Europe, as political activity transformed from newspaper stories into "actual men struggling to realizing new aims, partly common to their aims, partly divergent."[65]

Cheever returned to Boston in February 1921 and began her own work with the Massachusetts branch of the Women's International League for Peace and Freedom, though a motivating factor for doing so might have been an ongoing professional tie to Balch. She became the state chairman in November and continued her involvement in both Balch's life and work through the organization. Given Cheever's suggested reservations regarding the mission of the WILPF, her choice to become a state chair seems curious. Either Balch successfully convinced her of the value of the work or Cheever became involved as a way to become closer to Balch. Either way, throughout 1921, Cheever's concern for Balch's health increased and she became more vocal to Addams about what she felt was best for her friend.

Cheever frequently chastised Balch to rest more or to take frequent and longer vacations. When Balch failed to heed these pleas, Cheever turned to Addams. In letters to Addams, Cheever tried to convince her to force (or at least to strongly encourage) Balch to take more breaks. In December 1921, when Balch was home in Boston for the holidays, Cheever wrote to Addams detailing her concern for Balch: "If you think Emily Balch could properly take two or three weeks more vacation than that allotted her, I wish you would write her promptly to that effect."[66] Failing to heed Cheever's plea to extend her vacation, Balch returned to Europe in early 1922.

In the fall of 1922, Cheever successfully arranged another temporary living situation with Balch. Although she had returned from Geneva less than a year previously, Cheever believed Balch functioned best under her care. In September 1922, Cheever wrote to Addams of her intentions to resign her chairmanship of the Massachusetts WILPF immediately in order to prepare for her move to Geneva. Citing Balch's health as her central concern, she wrote, "I have cabled her that I will go to her if [my] health permits. And I feel that in order to be able to do so, I must give up the work of the WIL as quickly as possible, and spend the time in regaining my strength." Her own health also being an issue, Cheever emphasized that that her doctor advised her not to strain herself, and so she determined that her "usefulness to the WIL" would be "confined to being with Miss Balch."[67]

Cheever set sail on October 19, 1922, heading for Geneva via Italy. She arranged for the two of them to spend four months in Egypt. Just how successful she had been at convincing Balch of her need for vacation was evident in Balch's letter to Addams that she would not be available to meet with her. On hearing that Addams would be attending a meeting in The Hague, she replied, "And here am I going off to Egypt with Helen Cheever. It seems too absurd." However, she opted not to rearrange her own schedule, saying, "It seems to me that I ought to continue with the plan for the two reasons that, having undertaken it and got everything arranged for the sake of trying to rejuvenate my energies, to change now and go to the Hague to meet you would undo the business of resting."[68]

Cheever never hid her pure adoration and admiration of her friend. She praised Balch as a "sweet flower to me, never arrogant or showy, always modest and lovely in every aspect." She felt that Balch inspired her to be a better person. In return, Cheever believed herself best suited to take care of Balch, in such a way as allowed her to do the work she loved. Cheever wrote of her desire to provide for Balch: "I can at any rate so behave with you that you shall find peace and rest and freedom when with me, freedom to be and do all that is in you, and I can use my companionship in a sincere effort to be no hindrance to you, and to become better myself."[69]

During their months in Egypt, Cheever revealed her desire for the two women to continue living together. Balch wrote to her sister Anne, "Helen would like to hitch up together permanently." Balch debated how such an arrangement might affect her and concluded, "I don't think it is a good plan." Unable to discern what exactly about the proposal so discomfited her, Balch realized that she did not entirely like the way she felt with Cheever. She described this to her sister, saying that Helen "utterly spoils me and at the same time while I love her deeply and enjoy a great deal with her she is the only person I know with whom I am really irritable and you know that a state of controlled irritation is not a gracious one."[70]

Why was Cheever able to unleash Balch's less reasonable side? Perhaps Cheever knew and understood her friend so thoroughly that Balch felt comfortable enough to let her guard down. Perhaps Cheever's pushiness needled the even-keeled Balch beyond her usually high tolerance. Perhaps Balch could, as she suggested, never handle being loved so thoroughly. Balch confided in her sister, "Perhaps a psychoanalyst would say that it is an obscure reaction against the sense of how much I owe her, or of her giving me more love than I can quite digest, or her constant and unconscious tendency to dominate in small matters."[71] Whatever the reason, Balch could not agree to spend the rest of her life as Cheever's companion.

Everyone in Balch's life seemed to agree that Cheever could be overbearing, especially where Balch was concerned. That Balch never exactly gave her friend the sort of arrangement she desired never deterred Cheever from bestowing unyielding affection and support on her. Balch's school friend and college roommate Alice Gould wrote to Balch praising her efforts in Geneva, but also indicating how imperious Cheever could be. Gould noted, "I think you are [one] of those who work best under the warmth of approval and admiration, so I am glad you should get it; I only hope that Helen Cheever has not glutted you with it. This inelegant word is the only one I can think of."[72]

Cheever's proposition that she and Balch set up a household together was not an uncommon occurrence for women of their generation. Balch and Cheever had grown up during a time when romantic friendships between women of their class was not unheard of. In the last quarter of the nineteenth century, financially independent or career women entered what was termed "Boston marriages," as such arrangements seemed more particularly prevalent in New England. The sexual nature of these relationships mostly remains unknown; undoubtedly some were and others were not.

What is clear is that many women established caring primary partnerships with other women. Several of Balch's friends lived within such relationships—Jane Addams and Mary Rozet Smith, Vida Scudder and Florence Converse, Katherine Coman and Katharine Lee Bates—and so Cheever's proposal would have come in no way as shocking. It wasn't the institution as such that Balch struggled with, but the individual.[73]

Balch, later in her life, made subtle efforts to deny the idea of her own lesbianism. She authored a brief, unpublished essay on her life as an unmarried woman in which she expressed great regret at never having achieved the "the fullness of life" through marriage and motherhood. While the extent of her feelings toward Cheever or other women remains unknown, she did surround herself with women who were in committed relationships with other women. Further, it was clear that Cheever loved her deeply and wanted a more constant and committed relationship, and Balch ultimately rejected that. Despite that fact, Cheever continued to try to interject herself into Balch's life whenever possible, maintaining an intensity and passion for her friend that was never quite reciprocated.[74] Whatever Balch's rationale for declining Cheever's offer, the two women continued to spend time together. They would spend another extended holiday in California for four months during the winter of 1923–24, while Balch was recuperating from illness and working on a book.[75]

By the autumn of 1922, it was clear that Balch could no longer continue in Geneva. Even with the long respite at Cheever's insistence, Balch's health continued to suffer. She issued her resignation. Addams had appealed to Balch to stay on, dramatically stating, "I can't bear to go on without you" and offering her the position of "traveling secretary," even if part time.[76] Notwithstanding Addams's pleas, Balch submitted her resignation in order to devote more time to improving her declining health. (Although she never clarified the precise nature of her health problems, she frequently referred to exhaustion and nervous disorders.) She continued to work on behalf of WILPF but never again in a full-time capacity. Undoubtedly, though, the endless hours she put into establishing the international office and framework in Geneva became her greatest legacy to the WILPF.

In the middle of the decade, Balch dedicated as much time as possible to WILPF activities. She lived in Washington, D.C., for most of 1924, working part time for the WILPF. While living in the capital, she worked with the national secretaries, Amy Woods and then Dorothy Detzer, on several campaigns. That city hosted the international women's congress in 1924, and Balch, backed by her experiences organizing the earlier meetings, proved a great help to the national leadership. She then spent most of 1925 traveling. Though her travel was partly for health reasons, she devoted a portion of her time to engaging interest in WILPF. She visited North Africa, the Middle East, and the Balkans. She then went to Greece, Turkey, Belgium, and Budapest.

When Balch returned to the United States in late 1925, she set up her permanent home in Wellesley, Massachusetts. Friends from her teaching days at the college, Agnes Perkins and Etta Herr, built a house at 19 Roanoke Road and offered her the in-law suite. When she moved in December 1925, Balch christened the home her "Domicheck," a Czech term meaning "the little house." She kept this as her primary residence until her death, though she continued to travel a good deal on behalf of the WILPF.

Although in the mid-1920s Balch allotted a smaller portion of her time to WILPF activities than she had after the war, her work from that period represents some of her greatest accomplishments. She continued to promote the WILPF abroad and to encourage other nations to establish branches. Increasingly, though, she directed her keen mind on questions closer to home, namely the situation in Haiti.

Haiti, 1926–27

The principle of self-determination resonated strongly with Balch and the WILPF women. At the Zurich congress, the women had discussed the necessity of self-government for colonized lands. At Vienna, the delegates spent much of their time examining self-determination as it applied to Ireland and India, as well as other nations then struggling against colonial rule. In 1925, Haitian WILPF members approached the international executive committee and requested that the WILPF explore the state of affairs in their country, where a U.S. military occupation had been in force since 1915.

The committee then turned to the U.S. section of the WILPF and asked them to organize an investigatory committee. Not surprisingly, WILPF leadership chose Balch to head up the mission. She quickly organized an interracial committee of "six disinterested Americans."[77] This group included Charlotte Atwood, Zonia Baber, Paul Douglas, Addie Hunton, and Grace Watson. The group set out for Haiti in February 1926.

The committee approached its mission in much the same way that Balch had managed her study of the Slavic peoples from 1906–08. During three weeks in Haiti, they worked to interview as many and as broad a representation of people as possible. They then returned to the United States, where they met with Americans as well as Haitians of various backgrounds. Interviewees included businessmen, French priests, missionaries, government workers, doctors and teachers. In the United States, they also met with individuals who exhibited a spectrum of beliefs about what the American role in Haiti should be. In chapters written by different members, the committee's report detailed how American policies affected various areas of Haitian life and governance, including the land, health, education, public works, race relations, public order, judiciary, the press, prisons, and the validity of charges of abuse against the American occupiers. In 1915, the United States had justified its occupation by pointing to the threat of the war in Europe. Balch's commission proved this justification completely false, pointing out that Germany had no real chance of or interest in occupying the island in 1915, and other nations—namely France—also seemed unlikely to invade, given their involvement in the European war at that time.[78]

Balch and her colleagues reported on the social and political history of the situation in Haiti as of 1926, as well as the economic and military context of the American occupation. To begin with, they wrote that the United States' occupation of Haiti clearly violated the tenet of self-determination. An outbreak of revolutionary violence in Port-au-Prince in July 1915 had given the

U.S. Marines a "pretext," as Balch worded it, for beginning an occupation. The Haitian people were then subjugated to the rule of American-friendly dictators Dartiguenave and Borno, and the "order" imposed by American military forces.[79]

The committee revealed that American intervention in Haiti had only enhanced any political corruption already present. The American government, in order to occupy the country, signed a treaty with Haiti, which allowed for expanded American involvement if the Haitians violated the agreement in any way. However, Balch's group observed that the treaty, hardly an honest pact, was instead "forced through under duress."[80]

The United States forced a constitution on the country, which the Haitian Assembly refused to ratify in 1917, and in response American military forces prevented the Haitian congress from convening. The WILPF delegation clearly detailed this history and its relationship to the current situation. The "real power" in Haiti lay solely with the American occupiers.[81]

Balch chronicled the extent of American political corruption in Haiti. She exposed numerous examples of tampering with elections, withholding official salaries, and intimidating journalists. American actions, she declared, "spell despotism."[82] Americans exercised total legislative and budgetary control over the country. American officials acted as political despots in Haiti—that was clear. But Balch and her committee were curious to know if American involvement in any way improved the country.

Their inquiries revealed that in most areas of life, the American occupation had not improved the quality of life in Haiti. In presenting a demographic study, Balch reported that "the average value consumed in a Haitian peasant family amounts to $20.00 a year per capita. . . . Translated into life-terms this means not only living at the very bottom of the scale as regards range of wants and satisfactions, but too often, undernourishment."[83]

The committee also investigated charges of American abuses against Haitians as well as alleged improvements to health and sanitation, education, and race relations since the occupation began. They carefully noted that abuse was more widespread during the beginning of the occupation but by 1926 occurred less frequently or had vanished altogether. One of the greatest outrages of the occupation was the use of forced labor. The committee confirmed that, after the occupation, Americans utilized forced labor to build roads, but noted that these workers were now paid. Although the claim of forced labor was no longer valid, Haitians correctly argued that other injustices continued. These claims included martial law, restriction of the press, and the free reign of American marines to commit atrocities. Balch argued that the American government did not take such charges seriously, asserting that the government-sponsored investigations into them were "primarily a defense of Americans in Haiti."[84]

The WILPF committee also carefully studied health and sanitation. They found that the prevalent diseases in Haiti included "fevers, chiefly malaria; those caused by intestinal worms; syphilis and yaws; tuberculosis." These were also the primary causes of death. Interestingly, the study reported, "There is more good feeling, and less hard feeling among Haitians toward the Service d'Hygiene, than toward any other branch of the American Occupation." Despite American success in improving hygiene and sanitation conditions, the American attitude toward this service did not assist their efforts. The committee asserted, "When Americans learn to work *with* and not merely *for* Haitians, and not until then will their efforts be truly fruitful."[85]

The report also disclosed, not surprisingly, that "the American Occupation has done little or nothing for education in Haiti." This, according to Balch, resulted from a mutual distrust between Haitians and American officials. Americans refused to properly fund Haitian schools, fearing that Haitians would only mismanage the funds. As a result, teachers remained ill paid and poorly trained, while illiteracy soared at an "overwhelming" rate. The investigatory committee recommended that the government sponsor Haitian men and women with potential to go abroad for study. They also recommended that the government be provided with the funds to pay teachers a decent salary.[86]

The subject of race relations in Haiti was of special interest to the interracial American group. Balch and Addie Hunton, a prominent African-American woman, reported that "Haitians are like the colored people of the United States in having an African inheritance with an intermixture, of greater or less volume, of white blood and Western civilization." Despite this, they noted that Haitians differed substantially from African-Americans, having obviously different historical experiences. The report noted, "There was almost nothing before the Occupation to make Haitians racially self-conscious or to create an 'inferiority complex' with its inconsistent but equally natural resultants—a morbid lack of self-confidence and self-assertiveness." The committee found that white Americans' racial prejudice made the problems with the occupation even more severe. The committee observed, "The traditional attitude of the white American to black men is merely intensified in Haiti by the fact that the country is the black man's." The committee strongly recommended that only Americans without racial prejudice be involved in the interactions with Haitians.[87] Of course, this perspective is far more revealing about American attitudes toward race in their own nation than in Haiti. First, they believed that Americans without racial prejudice existed. Moreover, Americans, both black and white, saw their own country reflected in Haiti, rather than seeing Haiti itself.

The committee concluded that Haiti presented "a clear challenge to all who believe in the fundamental principle upon which the United States is founded, that government should rest upon the consent of the governed." American involvement with that small nation revealed that the United States' own democratic principles were in peril. The committee testified, "There has been for some time a drift toward imperialism, a movement veiled and therefore the more dangerous, dangerous to the liberty of our neighbors, dangerous to our own democracy." It was possible, the committee argued, to assist Haiti without occupying the island. The committee made a set of interim recommendations about American policies in Haiti but mainly advised that the United States immediately end the occupation. Balch and her colleagues asserted that terminating the occupation was the only option.[88]

Balch's study of Haiti was prophetic in its findings as well as its conclusions. It persuasively argued that Haiti exemplified a growing trend of American imperialism. Drawing comparisons with American involvement in the Philippines, Balch and her commission discovered that Americans were not in any great way improving the lives of Haitians. What, then, was their claim to occupy? The United States, despite its culture of noninterventionism, had entered the imperialist race. Balch and her peers documented the dangers of this trend. Not only did the committee expose American wrongdoing in Haiti, it warned that American self-interests threatened to devastate a country.

Balch presented her commission's findings to President Calvin Coolidge when the group returned in the spring of 1926. Though the American government took no immediate action, eventually President Hoover sent an official inquiry, the Forbes Commission, in 1930. This commission confirmed the accuracy of Balch's study, reporting similar findings and recommendations. The United States did not officially end its occupation of Haiti until 1934, and the legacy of American intervention in Haiti during a period of supposed isolationism remains momentous.

Balch's experience in Haiti strengthened her conviction that the United States and other powerful nations could, if they so wished, assist small countries without monopolizing political and economic control. It also enhanced her belief that any assistance to nations struggling from economic troubles or revolutionary violence must be aided by the international community and not by just one particular nation. She saw the American presence in Haiti during the 1920s as an opportunity for the United States to form a new type of relationship, a nonimperialist one, between strong and weak countries. She commented, "There are more ways of helping a neighbor who is in trouble than knocking him down and taking possession of his property and family."[89]

After returning home from her mission in Haiti, meeting with President Coolidge, and publishing the report, Balch went to Europe in 1928 on another recruitment drive for the WILPF. She also campaigned throughout England, Wales, and Ireland to promote the Kellogg-Briand Pact. Balch spoke passionately on behalf of the international treaty aimed to replace armed conflict among nations with international law. The U.S. Secretary of State Frank Kellogg and French Foreign Minister Aristide Briand designed the multilateral treaty to this end. Though it was widely considered an unrealistic effort, Balch and numerous other pacifists responded with enthusiasm.

The Kellogg-Briand Pact represented the culmination of pacifist efforts during the 1920s. Although its authors more than likely had ulterior motives and the treaty ultimately proved useless in preventing war, the pact set an important precedent for turning to international law and viewing war as a crime.

WILPF Executive Committee at the *Maison Internationale,* 1928 (Balch standing, second from right). Women's International League for Peace and Freedom Papers, Swarthmore College Peace Collection.

Balch embraced what hope the treaty offered and vigorously campaigned in Europe in 1928. After a brief tour, she returned to Geneva, where she spoke before the League of Nations. There she presented WILPF's position on munitions in China in addition to promoting the Kellogg-Briand Pact.

Balch's many experiences between 1918 and 1929, both in her personal life and with the WILPF, deeply entrenched her in the international peace movement. In the 1930s, Balch further assessed her approach to social reform, both locally and internationally. On the home front, she faced the tragedy of the Great Depression. In Europe, she confronted the spread of right wing ideologies and armies. In 1933, writing her recollections of her experiences during the First World War, Balch commented on the dangers she saw emerging and threatening yet more war in the 1930s: "More and more it becomes evident that the political nationalistic tension is all intermingled with the social-economic unrest. If France and Germany fear one another, and territorial problems like those of 'the Corridor' and Hungary are danger points, not less certainly is there a threat of conflict between left-wing Revolution and right-wing Fascism, and between these and evolutionary social-economic democracy."[90]

6. "The World Chose Disaster," 1930–41

The 1930s were a frightening decade for many involved with the international peace movement. Emily Greene Balch and her fellow WILPF members became increasingly alarmed as each year brought more episodes of violent struggle and the growth of right-wing dictatorships. They endeavored to direct international attention toward the greatest threats to peace; Balch named those threats specifically as Italy, Germany, and Japan, all of which maintained "a nationalist-militarist point of view." Spain joined the list of nations to be carefully watched when a civil war there broke out in 1936. In addition to these "obvious danger spots," Balch considered any nation with imperialistic designs to be a potential threat to international stability. She did not excuse her own country in her scrutiny, and she publicly condemned the United States for its control of the Philippines. In Balch's view, it did "not take a prophet to foresee" what the rapid war preparations would lead to. Despite the escalation toward war, Balch emphatically reminded people, "War is not inevitable in the sense in which an earthquake is."[1] She and the WILPF closely monitored developments in Europe and Asia and worked aggressively to support alternatives to war and encouraged that threatening regimes be met with international arbitration rather than violent opposition.

The first event signaling an imminent change in international relations occurred in Asia. Japan attacked the Chinese province of Manchuria in September 1931 in its first effort to extend its empire throughout Asia. By occupying this land and installing a puppet emperor in the newly declared independent state, Japan obtained the profits from the area's vast stores of raw materials. Thus commenced Japan's imperialistic conquest, as the nation continued to push across the Chinese mainland.

When Balch learned of the incursion into Manchuria, she issued appeals to both the League of Nations and the United States government, imploring both to respond quickly and condemn Japan's actions. She traveled to Europe that year to lobby the League of Nations directly to lead an international punitive campaign against Japan. The most the League consented to do was to issue a public condemnation of Japanese hostilities, in part fearing Japanese withdrawal from the League. Balch was understandably disappointed in this result. She then went to a peace meeting at the Trocadero Palace, where she was shocked to witness the speakers being driven off the platform by a Parisian right-wing "mob." Observing the demise of internationalism in Europe, Balch sailed home in December 1931, as she recalled, "full of anxiety, as was every thinking person."[2]

Back in the United States, Balch dedicated much of her attention in 1932 to seeking a government condemnation of the situation in Manchuria. She lobbied the American government to issue an official acknowledgement that Japan had violated multiple international treaties, thereby violating the integrity of the Kellogg-Briand Pact and the Nine Power Pact. She implored the president to recognize that "preserving faith in the usefulness of treaties is of more far-reaching and fundamental significance."[3]

Balch authored a "Memorandum on Manchuria" in January 1932, in which she outlined her proposals for the occupied province. In it, Balch suggested that Manchuria be secured and governed by an international administration. She understood that because of the rich resources of Manchuria, an international administration must be careful not to cater to the national interests of one particular country. The administration, she believed, "should be a body of paid experts." Her plan, as she well recognized, depended upon the "good will and perhaps yielding of cherished positions on all sides."[4] She hoped that the international community would embrace this plan and, most important, that the United States and Russia, neither of which belonged to the League of Nations, would work with the member states of the League to effectively govern the province. In retrospect, though we may view her ideas as naïve, the courage and steadfastness with which Balch relentlessly endeavored to preempt catastrophe through international arbitration nevertheless deserves recognition.

Balch and the American branch of the WILPF also highlighted the American government's partial responsibility for the conflict. They centered their lobbying on the issue of armament sales to the region. Balch wrote to President Hoover in January 1932, demanding that the president issue a request for congressional legislation "to forbid the shipment of arms to Japan" and "to declare loans to Japan as contrary to public policy." Hoover refused. That same month, the WILPF leaders in Geneva learned that Britain, France, and the United States had agreed not to forbid shipments of arms to Japan and China, then at war. The WILPF leaders decided to continue the campaigns in their home countries but became bitterly disappointed by ongoing sales to the belligerent nations.[5]

In Balch's view, the "most grievous fault" was that the United States, knowing of the great dangers abroad, could "think of nothing better to do than to wash her hands and draw aside."[6] Japan, with no serious international recrimination and still able to buy arms from the United States and its allies, continued an aggressive march across China. The Japanese did not feign interest in remaining within the society of nations, and in March 1933, Japan withdrew from the League of Nations. Although Japan was the first nation in the 1930s to succeed in its violent conquest, other nations quickly joined her camp. While still campaigning for international intervention in the matter of Japanese aggression, Balch turned her attention to Italy.

In its quest for an extensive colonial empire, Italy invaded Ethiopia in October 1935, after almost a year of building up a military presence in the area. The incursion created another problem for the League of Nations. Many European nations were vying for Italian allegiance, fearing an imminent war with Germany. This fact undoubtedly contributed to the League's ambivalent response. Although the League took more extensive action than it had in the case of Japan, it still failed to meet the expectations of the international peace community. It issued sanctions against Italy, which it named as the aggressor, but neglected to include items in the sanctions that would actually cripple the nation, such as an oil embargo. It also forbade its member states from providing arms to Italy, but these actions proved ineffective. The League's inadequate efforts failed to stop the Italian offensive. Italy incorporated Ethiopia into its empire in June 1936. The League officially condemned Italy's position in the war, which ultimately led, in part, to Italy's withdrawal from the League of Nations in December 1937.

Much as they had with Manchuria, the Women's International League issued appeals for the U.S. government to work with the League of Nations in objection to Italy's aggression. Many WILPF women, though not all, promoted a private boycott of Italian goods, but this endeavor produced limited results. Women's peace advocates utilized their extensive network of international women to issue a powerful, transnational condemnation of Italy's belligerence. Balch even sent a telegram to the queen of Italy imploring her to intercede and halt the Ethiopian war. This action brought press coverage but, in the end, proved to be a futile effort. Though undoubtedly dismayed by their campaign's lack of effectiveness against Japanese and Italian aggression, WILPF women refused to let up their battle against escalating militarism.

The imperialistic aims of Japan and Italy warned of a shifting trend—one of increasing loyalty to dictatorial regimes and the rise of governments seeking to build colonial empires. The growing Nazi movement in Germany was the most prominent example of this trend. As early as 1931, Balch, returning to her alma mater, the University of Berlin, noticed the changes in Germany. She voiced her early concerns over the rising popularity of Adolf Hitler. After delivering a lecture at the university, Balch met with Helmut von Gerlach, a leading German pacifist and opponent of Hitler. Also present at that meeting was her old friend from the American pacifist movement, Louis Lochner. These men explained the popularity of Hitler's National Socialist German Workers Party and the militaristic outlook among many Germans. Two years later, in 1933, when Hitler assumed the post of chancellor, Balch recorded her "great anxiety." Particularly, she worried for her German friends and wondered how Hitler would contribute to the "critical condition of international relations."[7]

After the meeting in Berlin, Balch began to criticize the changing culture in Germany publicly. She held the German people responsible for Hitler's rise and the actions set in motion by his government. In a letter to the editor of the *New York Times* in early 1933, she voiced her sadness concerning the German people. Pointing to the suffering of Jews and leftists under the Nazi government and her own concern that Hitlerism would give way to a Communist dictatorship, Balch said that she found it "even more disturbing" that "such great masses of the German people are choosing the way of illegality, class and racial prejudice and personal cruelty."[8] While Balch held the German people partially to blame for Hitler's rise to power, she also pointed to the international community and the legacy of the First World War as responsible for establishing the conditions in which Germans turned to Hitler.

Balch's ideas to reduce the appeal of fascism in Germany were controversial yet insightful. They revealed the depth of her objectivity and conviction that equality and internationalism would produce a stable situation. Foremost among Balch's early ideas concerning Germany was her call to bring the nation into the international community by increasing its rights within the League of Nations. Germany had belonged to the League since 1926, but the League still enforced the terms of the Versailles Treaty, which prevented Germany from rearming. Balch argued that the international community needed to officially support German rearmament in order to monitor its arms development effectively. Giving Germany equal status among the nations of Europe, Balch asserted, would produce less popular support for Hitler's agenda by decreasing the power of his nationalistic rhetoric, as he "could no longer represent Germany as encircled, victimised, in danger of attack."[9]

Balch's argument to allow German rearmament may seem strange in light of the fact that one of the WILPF's central campaigns was global disarmament. Balch reconciled these seemingly contradictory positions by using the example of German armament to criticize the global attitude toward disarmament. She contended that the legacy of World War I for Germany illustrated the problematic effect of only disarming defeated nations. Balch reviewed the decision of "the military experts" at the close of the World War I to prevent Germans from rebuilding its military capabilities. In short, she firmly believed the armament issue would fuel another war. The problem with the decision, Balch showed, was that only one side was made to give up arms. This meant that any nation in such a weakened military position would eventually fight to rebuild its depleted stores. She concluded, "If indeed what was sauce for the goose had been sauce for the gander, the criteria could have been accepted for all."[10] Balch's proposal to allow Germany to rearm was not taken seriously, but its validity was reflected in Germany's decision to withdraw from the League of Nations in 1933, mainly in order to rearm.

Balch continued to monitor events in Germany throughout the decade, but by the mid-1930s yet another conflict arose to claim her attention. The Spanish Civil War began with a coup in July 1936 under the leadership of General Francisco Franco against the Republican government of Spain (the Republicans). The ultimate victory of Franco's army (the rebels) in April 1939 established his dictatorial regime. The war sharply divided the international community. One side (the democratic nations) distanced itself from the conflict, whereas the other side (Germany and Italy) supported Franco's army. Franco's rebel forces, supported by both the Roman Catholic Church and Nazi Germany, also contained internal divisions, but not to the same extent as the Republicans. Balch argued that the international community must help establish a coalition government, that a victory for either side would lead to chaos. Regardless of who won the civil war in Spain, Balch maintained, the country would suffer, as "the victors would be likely to fall to fighting among themselves."[11]

Balch remained keenly aware that Spain represented the looming division in sentiment throughout Europe. The most prominent ideologies reflected democracy, socialism, communism, or totalitarianism. In her writings on the subject, Balch highlighted the ways in which Nazi Germany and Fascist Italy backed Franco (mainly by supplying arms), the Soviet Union similarly supported the Republicans (though with caveats), and the democratic governments mostly ignored the leftist (though legally elected) government. She emphasized that Franco's army drew its strength from its European backing, while the Republicans suffered from internal divisions and a lack of support from other nations. This fact meant that the policies in Great Britain and the United States, for example, actually contributed to Franco's triumph and ultimately to another war in Europe.[12]

"The only hope" for a swift end to the Spanish Civil War, according to Balch, centered on the international community. She contended that a peace could be brokered "only through friendly offices from the outside, since while fighting is in progress, neither side can afford to propose to initiate talk of a settlement for fear of weakening its position by seeming to want peace." Taking her usual approach, Balch urged a negotiated peace. During the first year of the Spanish engagement, Balch proposed that the international community, either through the League of Nations or an independent coalition, negotiate a peace and set up a non-party, or else a coalition government, in Spain. As with her proposal regarding Manchuria, Balch acknowledged the need for "painful concessions from both sides," but she stressed that there would be great benefits, "the chief of which would be the cessation of the progressive suicide of Spain, and of the use of the country as the terrain for the struggle between fascism and communism."[13] Despite the exhausting lobbying activities initiated by Balch, the Women's International League for Peace and Freedom and many other international peace groups, no negotiated peace was reached. Spain, like China, Ethiopia, and Germany, became another battleground for totalitarian dominance and imperialist conquest.

The WILPF in the 1930s

The events of the 1930s presented unfathomable obstacles to peace, and Balch, leading the international WILPF through the turbulent decade, worked tirelessly on its behalf to present plausible alternatives to war. Balch recognized the peril created by the view that violence was the only means for solving conflict and described the world as being "in danger of immediate catastrophe." She found it "scandalous" that the world appeared dominated by peoples who were "normally hostile, instead of normally friendly and cooperative."[14] In the years leading up to the Second World War, the WILPF women continued to stress the importance of international institutions, such as the League of Nations and the World Court, as keys to preventing global calamity. Almost collapsing under the strains of the international situation and internal divisions, the WILPF remained intact largely through the intelligent leadership of Balch.

In 1931, Balch became the president of the United States section of the WILPF, but her central loyalty remained with the international office. Throughout the decade, Balch continued to emphasize the importance of the international aspects of the WILPF's work to her American peers. Urging American members to focus their attention on international matters, as she herself did, she declared, "Our League is international not only in name, but in nature." The main purpose of the WILPF, Balch insisted, centered on promoting "the cooperative and friendly relation between peoples." Although such a goal seemed utopian, as even Balch acknowledged, it nonetheless remained "so necessary." She understood that human beings were inextricably linked to each other, and only by working for each other's mutual benefit could the world progress. Balch's internationalist perspective linked individual lives to national government decisions. She declared, "There is no village so remote, no savage tribe so inaccessible that it is not affected by the decisions of those in the seats of power in foreign capitols."[15]

Balch's fervent internationalism stood in stark contradiction to a popular view in the United States that equated neutrality with nonintervention. Many pacifist women actively supported many policies forwarded by noninterventionists, such as the Neutrality Acts, which forbade arms sales to belligerent nations. But they objected to the principle of isolationism, which they saw behind these measures. Balch agreed that the American government "should have no military alliances nor war commitments." Rather than simply limit American involvement in the European war, however, the WILPF wished to see the United States become an active mediator to end and prevent war. The WILPF International Committee promoted "collective, non-military measures against an aggressor." Specifically, the organization promoted peaceful alternatives such as withdrawing ambassadors from, refusing loans to, or prohibiting imports from nations that threatened war. Whatever the international situation, Balch and the WILPF believed that the first response from the global community must be to strengthen and utilize instruments of internationalism.[16]

Throughout the tumultuous 1930s, Balch and many of the WILPF leaders continued to look to the League of Nations, despite "its failures, weakness and mistakes," as the appropriate body "for the pacific settlement of disputes." It had not effectively combated Japanese and Italian aggression. The withdrawal of Japan and Germany in 1933, and Italy in 1937, would affirm that the League's prospects for mediating a peace in the future were diminishing. International peace activists feared that the collapse of the League of Nations would undermine all future efforts for internationalism. The WILPF therefore refused to give up on the admittedly weakened League and urged its members to "cooperate closely in every phase of the work at Geneva."[17] Only by protecting the fundamental principles of the League of Nations did the WILPF envision being able to confront militarism with international plans free from the interests of any one nation.

Early in the decade the WILPF focused mainly a proposed League of Nations conference on arms reduction. In 1932, Balch was among the WILPF leaders who believed total disarmament was a possibility. WILPF members in various countries gathered millions of signatures to present to the representatives at this conference. In so doing, they raised public awareness of the disarmament campaign. The initial popular interest in the subject was perhaps the greatest achievement of the campaign. Most support for disarmament subsequently fell away when a European war became imminent.

The League of Nations convened its Conference for the Reduction and Limitation of Armaments in Geneva in 1932, the early sessions of which Balch attended. She witnessed a group of international women as they presented the representatives with more than eight million signatures in support of armaments reduction, six million of which had been gathered by WILPF members. The multitude of signatures confirmed to some representatives the importance of their discussions, which lasted until 1937 (though they convened only sporadically after 1933). Despite the conference's long duration, delegates fell into petty arguments and ultimately accomplished nothing. Balch recalled sitting in sessions with the growing realization that the discussions would all come to naught. She blamed the conference's failure on the call for *reduction* in arms rather than *total* disarmament. Although universal disarmament might seem utopian, as Balch conceded, it was the only way disarmament could actually happen. The conference, she argued, only "demonstrated the insurmountable difficulties of a partial and piecemeal solution."[18] She foresaw the problems that would emerge once representatives agreed on a certain amount of reduction. The question then became how much of a reduction and under what terms. The disagreements that then transpired were endless. For Balch, total disarmament was not only necessary for the future of the human race, but it was also the only outcome that could be reached without resorting to menial bickering.

In 1932, the Women's International League for Peace and Freedom also held its international congress in Grenoble, France. This congress held discussions on the usual retinue of subjects, including international education and the establishment of new WILPF sections. The women also heard reports from members in Poland concerning the recent incursion against Ukrainians. The topic that overshadowed all others, however, was that of arms reduction. The WILPF's seventh congress chose what Balch called the "too prophetic title" of "World Disarmament or World Disaster." Balch later remarked, "As everyone knows, the world chose disaster."[19] Even though the WILPF women grieved over the dismal outlook of international disarmament and arms reduction talks, they remained optimistic that the mere existence of those proceedings would set a precedent and that future discussions of disarmament would prove successful. They clung to the six million signatures as a sign of hope that the people wanted disarmament. In reality, the WILPF continually pointed to this feat because it was one of the few examples of acts that unified its membership during the decade.

The WILPF in Turmoil

The WILPF's prolonged internal struggles resulted, in part, from its dire financial situation during the 1930s. In the previous decade, the international office and the national sections of the WILPF strained to remain financially solvent. The Great Depression of the 1930s transformed the organization's financial turmoil into crisis.

One way in which the organization tried to stay afloat was by restructuring membership dues. Women could join the Women's International League on two levels; they could pay their annual dues to the international office in Geneva and/or to their national section, should their nation have one. While the international leadership continued to defend the importance of both membership levels, Balch increasingly worried about the sustainability of the vital international work. She wrote to a fellow American WILPF member regarding the urgent need to maintain and increase the international membership, because those members paid a $5 annual fee directly to the office in Geneva. Balch was confident that an increase in these membership dues would sustain the office through the difficult financial period.[20] She was correct. The additional dues helped: the international office remained open, in part, as a result of Balch's difficult campaign drive to recruit international members during the Depression.

The membership dues contributed to the ongoing work of the international office, but the WILPF's greatest financial windfall during this period occurred when Jane Addams donated the entire sum of her Nobel Peace Prize in 1931 to the international office of the WILPF. The reported sum of twenty thousand dollars ($280,242.18 in 2008), along with a careful reduction in office costs, helped sustain the international office for most of the decade. The contribution also eased the burdens of the American Section, which sent substantial sums to the international office. The sentiments of Cor Ramondt-Hirschmann, the Dutch WILPF leader and a member of the international executive committee, revealed the extent to which the international office had been dependent on funds from the United States. She wrote to Balch, "We will have to express to Miss Addams our great gratitude that she, in this way, is making it somewhat easier for our American Section."[21]

Addams's decision to allocate her donation to the Geneva office rather than the American branch also illustrated that she shared with Balch the conviction that the work of the international office was paramount.

The WILPF troubles extended far beyond financial troubles, however. Disputes over pacifism and war relief work had plagued the organization for the previous two decades. The arguments had reached a peak in 1926, when the international congress held in Dublin debated whether or not to disband the organization entirely. The WILPF survived that crisis, but in 1932 it experienced its deepest schism yet. The British section of the WILPF, one of the largest national branches, threatened to secede from the international body because the majority of the British members believed the Geneva office exhibited an increasingly revolutionary outlook. These British women expressed dissatisfaction with the ideological differences within the WILPF and demanded significant changes or else threatened to form an independent organization.

This difference of opinion only became a serious problem when, in the late 1920s, the WILPF leadership had removed most of the decision-making power from the national sections and placed it in the hands of the small international executive committee. This centralization of authority did not easily allow the two schools of thought to maintain their "very loose" connection. Eventually, one group would come to dominate the international committee. By the early 1930s, the international office seemed solely to promote revolutionary change.[22] This faction of British women elected as their spokeswoman Kathleen Courtney, with whom Balch had a longstanding, amicable professional relationship, as well as a friendship.

Courtney delineated the ways in which the differences between the revolutionary and evolutionary perspectives affected the work of the organization. The two viewpoints, for example, viewed the WILPF's campaigns for disarmament in different ways. Those like Balch, who advocated what Courtney termed revolutionary change, advocated that the organization support only total disarmament. Courtney and her colleagues, however, embraced the idea of incremental disarmament through arms reduction. Both of these perspectives had been able to work together when power lay with the national sections, but when the international office determined that total disarmament would be the center of its campaign, it weakened the work of those seeking arms reduction. Courtney reminded the international committee of the British Section's powerful petition campaign in Britain, in which activists gathered the majority of the six million signatures presented to the League of Nations conference in 1932. She claimed that her group's achievement resulted from its ability to act independently—and specifically by being able to

promote incremental arms reduction. Courtney asserted that had the British
section been beholden to the international office during its campaign, the
women "should have gained a very small number of signatures." Courtney
concluded that the WILPF's stubborn adherence to total disarmament meant
that the women's group was not taken seriously at the conference. She proclaimed, "It is to me rather tragic that after 18 years of existence, when at
last a Disarmament Conference is called in Geneva, the WIL should as an
international body count for nothing in the discussions."[23]

Severing the British women's tie to the international structure, Courtney
recognized, would be a great loss to both the "evolutionary" and "revolutionary" factions. Nonetheless, she and her peers grew increasingly distraught
with the outlook of the international office and its increasing centralization
of decision making. Moreover, Courtney felt that the British section did its
"most valuable work" independently and not "on the lines adopted internationally." A "friendly" separation of the two groups, Courtney believed,
would help both camps maximize their potential in every country where the
WILPF was active. Although Courtney suggested a complete break between
the two factions, she acknowledged that such a severance was unlikely to
happen. As an alternative to "the present drifting" apart of the two sections,
she urged the executive committee to reconsider its present organization and
establish a "very loose connection between the various national sections" as
had originally been the case.[24]

Balch responded to Courtney's complaints, arguing that the WILPF must
maintain the strengthened international committee, even if doing so caused
discontent. She dismissed Courtney's British contingent as a small faction
without much widespread support. However, Balch conceded that those
members sincerely believed that their complaints were shared by the majority.
Given that, it was best to address their claims and "clear up the points they
raise . . . to make the way smooth for our future collaboration."[25]

Balch defined "the crux" of the problem not as ideological difference but
as a struggle for power between the international office (the executive committee and the officers) and the national sections and their leadership. She
likened the clash to that in the United States concerning the issue of vesting
more power in the federal government or enhancing individual states' rights.
She viewed this power struggle as natural and did not think it should lead to
the splitting up of the organization. She offered a simple solution: the organization would focus on those activities on which they could all agree. This still
skirted the issue of power. Where questions of policy became controversial,
however, Balch maintained that decision-making power must still lie with
the international leadership. Although she preferred "*not to have a fixed*

rule," Balch welcomed any solutions the international committee thought would be best for the health of the organization. Though she consented to support whatever agreement the committee reached, Balch stated her belief that the British suggestions "might sometimes work badly."[26]

Jane Addams, still the international president of the WILPF in 1932, supported Balch's position regarding the British section. She wrote to Kathleen Courtney, expressing her sincere hope that the British section not succeed from the international body. Addams cautioned Courtney that the peace movement's reputation could be damaged should the British section split off. She reminded her British colleague that all of the other international women's organizations chose not to meet during or immediately after the previous war because of the likelihood of great disagreements among their membership, while the WILPF continued its important work during such turbulent years. Addams warned that British action would result in a public perception that women's organizations could not withstand difficult times. Despite her convictions on this point, Addams asserted that the organization would do better to disband than to try to function with so much discord. Demonstrating her brilliant political tact, Addams insinuated that the British contingent would be blamed should the international network fall apart. She then cautioned, "There is a great difference between the disbanding of an organization in its own Congress by the mutual consent of a majority of its members and the disintegration of an organization by the withdrawal of the largest and perhaps the most valuable of the national sections." Addams, like Balch, suggested that any decision concerning the future of the WILPF should result from collective, international agreement, the very notion that the British contingent did not support.[27]

Despite her claim to the contrary, Courtney did not represent all of the British section. Balch, Addams, and the other international leaders carefully cultivated their relationships with those British members who remained within their ranks during this schism. Addams praised Edith Pye, a British member who agreed (despite the British section's threatened secession) to become an international co-chair of the WILPF's International executive committee. Addams wrote to Pye that her loyalty to the international office was brave "in face of the embarrassment which may be caused [her] by the protesting action of the British Section." Addams also related Balch's hope that, should Courtney and her contingent withdraw from the League, "there [would] still be enough people to carry on the British Section and to maintain the international connections."[28]

Ultimately, Courtney and her peers in the British Section backed down and did not secede from the WILPF. As the war intruded on the WILPF schism, the British contingent and the international office worked through their differences in order to assist its members in threatened nations. The WILPF members continued to struggle with a disparity in their ideologies, but the war, and the multiple challenges it issued to the peace movement, drew together the various factions at least for its duration.

Another challenge for the WILPF during this era related to the acceptance of communist members. Balch outlined her perspective on communists in the international peace movement to Frederick Libby, head of the National Council for Prevention of War. She reiterated the position she had held since 1919 concerning differing ideologies among members in the international peace movement. Balch proclaimed, "At Geneva and here [the United States] I have long stood for cooperation with peace organizations that include members with whom I disagree on other issues than the peace policies in which we are working together." She stressed that working across ideological differences for shared goals enhanced the overall efforts of the peace movement. However, Balch refused to involve herself in party politics. She averred, "I do not believe in working with the 'Communists' or any other political party," although she did not object to working with individual Communists. She explained, "To me there is a crucial difference between working with the Communists and with a peace organization which is known to have Communist members [*sic*]." The central distinction for Balch lay in the main purpose of an organization. She believed that a peace organization that welcomed individual Communist members still advanced its objectives. However, Balch argued that attempts to insert the pacifist agenda into the Communist movement only injured the peace movement by providing "priceless ammunition to all those who try to spread the impression that pacifism is all mixed up with communism."[29] Many WILPF women strongly opposed Communist involvement in their organization, fearing that it would weaken their already limited effectiveness by drawing further criticism. Balch, in contrast, promoted the WILPF as a nonpartisan and inclusive organization.

The WILPF's internal struggles continued throughout the decade, but the organization, thanks greatly to Balch's diplomatic skills, remained intact. Edith Pye credited Balch as central in keeping together the WILPF's diversely opinionated membership during the 1930s. Pye recalled, "I saw how her helpful and concilliatory [*sic*] spirit kept the members of the League together, in spite of differences of language, nationality and in our aims, though not always as to methods." She emphasized Balch's diplomatic abilities as central to gaining the admiration of her struggling membership. She wrote, "She always tried to reconcile one side with another. Sometimes she failed because there was no point upon which minds could agree but always her love and her sincerity were sincerely felt and of immense help in the finding of a way out of some of the difficult situations."[30]

Jane Addams also believed in Balch's skillful diplomacy, and even more fervently in the dedication of the WILPF's members to the organization. She wrote to Balch in 1934 of her conviction that the organization would persevere despite the differences among its members. Prevented by illness from attending the congress at Zurich in 1934, Addams wrote on its eve to Balch regarding the troubles among the members, and her certainty that WILPF women put their cause above their petty squabbles. Addams declared, "I have such confidence in the underlying character of our members that I do not believe the congress will be as difficult as we feel. But that perhaps is whistling to keep my courage up."[31]

Balch's involvement with the international office intensified in the spring of 1934. Under great economic stress and therefore forced to reduce its spending, the international office could no longer afford to pay its international secretary in Geneva, Camille Drevet. Balch had served in that capacity from 1919 to 1921 and agreed to fill the position voluntarily for six months.[32] Balch sailed for Geneva in March 1934, but remained in that station for nearly a year and a half.

In the eighteen months that Balch spent in Geneva, she served in many of the same capacities that she had from 1919 to 1922, but she exhibited that her role had extended solidly into a leadership position. She did not hesitate to solidify her philosophy and the mission of the WILPF. One example of Balch's policy and program implementation was her proposal that the WILPF adopt an official position on continuous mediation as its standard response to war should another war break out. It remained controversial within the peace movement to discuss war policy in the absence of major conflict, but Balch did not balk at the prospect. She recognized that the heightened tension in Europe might result in war and believed the WILPF must develop a policy should that occur. From Geneva she petitioned the American government to adopt a plan for continuous mediation, reminding the White House of its failure to do so in 1915.[33]

Balch's poor health had necessitated her early resignation from her first stint as international secretary, and she carefully monitored her health during her second term in Geneva, even though her responsibilities were not as daunting as they had been after the First World War. Helen Cheever had played a crucial role in Balch's previous service as secretary, and though less involved in Balch's daily activities, Cheever continued to care for her. Referring to Balch's vacation in the spring of 1935, her younger sister, Alice, wrote to her, "I was thankful you went South for your recuperative trip and know that we have Helen to thank for it as she told me she was planning to make it possible. We are all grateful to her."[34] Balch's more careful attention to her well-being during her 1935 work in Geneva reflected her own maturity concerning her health as well as how the organization had grown to a level that it demanded less of the principal figures' energies.

Knowing Jane Addams

Balch was still in Geneva in May of 1935 when she learned that her dear friend Jane Addams had died. She took the news with characteristic reserve, but without a doubt she deeply mourned the loss. The two women had known each other since 1892, when Balch first heard Addams speak in Plymouth, Massachusetts. From their settlement work, to the labor movement, and then developing the international women's peace network, Addams and Balch had been good friends and devoted colleagues. Eleanor Moore, the secretary of the Australian branch of the WILPF, upon hearing of Addams's death, directed her condolences to Balch. She wrote, "Among the thousands who will feel that they have lost a precious personal friend, you and I are counted. Your connection was closer than mine, but my own love for her makes me understand yours."[35]

In her public remembrances of her friend, Balch expressed the great veneration Addams had earned through her peace and social reform work, and she recalled her friend's great devotion to the community. She said of Addams, "Her relation to her friends and colleagues, drawn together from so many countries to this work in common, was one of deep affection and confidence." Like Balch, Addams culled the wisdom she had gained from her experiences in the settlement movement and applied it to her work in international relations, as Balch herself noted: "Her Hull House experience had enriched her understanding of and liking for people of the most differing temperaments and origins and her power of making herself understood by them." Balch's fondness for her friend, matched by a great appreciation for Addams's ideas and life's work, allowed Balch to easily promote Addams's legacy as one of the America's greatest peace leaders. She never failed to mention Addams's influence on her own work and her contribution to the international peace movement. Addams, in many ways, was Balch's role model and mentor, as well as dear friend. "To have known her," Balch expressed, "is an inestimable privilege."[36]

Addams preferred the public spotlight more than her friend did, but Balch became just as influential in their peace circle. Addams claimed many of the peace movement's landmark achievements first, such as becoming the first international president and then the first American woman to win the Nobel Peace Prize in 1931. Though Balch modestly downplayed her own critical role in the women's international peace movement, her achievements often mirrored Addams's. Balch's brief biography of Addams could serve as a description of Balch herself. She wrote that Addams's "concern for peace was not something that began when the War forced the issue. . . . It was a deep part of herself, at once her philosophy and her life."[37]

Peacemaker Returns

Balch returned to Massachusetts in October 1935 and continued to agitate for American involvement in peaceful mediation. Balch's international reputation, as well as her refined diplomatic character, led to reconciliation with Wellesley College in 1935. Although she had voiced her feelings to the president and board of Wellesley, Balch had never publicly professed her outrage and disappointment at her dismissal in 1919, desiring to maintain a connection with the institution she loved so dearly. Despite these efforts, Balch remained distanced from the college for more than a decade following World War I. To her tremendous delight, the college invited her in 1935 to deliver the Armistice Day address to the student body. Wellesley not only welcomed her back, but it did so in recognition of her leadership in the international peace community.

Balch used her speech to focus the students' attention on the precarious situation in Europe. She described three perspectives on war—that of governments, of the peoples of the world, and of the international peace network. She emphasized the importance of understanding all three of these outlooks in order to comprehend how the world was again headed for war so soon after the last global catastrophe. Believing that governments did not want war but instead perpetuated the conditions that led to it, Balch pointed to the increase in arms production, as opposed to efforts to reduce arms, as proof of governments' propensity for engaging in war. She spoke of arms buildup as the result of secrecy between nations and the concern that another government might be creating even "more terrible weapons." Lastly, Balch emphasized that while governments might not necessarily want to engage in war, they had imperialistic hopes and tended to seek those outcomes that could only be achieved "by war or indirectly as a result of the changes consequent to a war."[38] Thus, governments fostered the need for war.

Balch maintained that the people of every nation, on the other hand, both "educated and simple," primarily opposed war and did so "actively" to an unprecedented degree. Interestingly, Balch claimed that people's general aversion to war had little to do with the efforts of the organized peace movement. Rather, she believed it resulted from "a natural ground of revulsion from war" which was "more profound." Balch argued that since governments truly did not wish to see an outbreak of war and the "unexampled mass of popular opinion [was] opposed either to all war or at least to governmental war," the world had a fair chance of successfully avoiding "the dangers of a catastrophic war."[39] At least she still held that hope in late 1935.

Balch then described the third group, or the "collective peace system," which included independent international peace groups, such as the Women's International League for Peace and Freedom and the League of Nations. The collective referred to all of those networks that were "designed not merely to hold back an evil but to build up a new type of world society." Balch also included "agreements[,] pacts and alliances" in this collective network. She cited both the Kellogg-Briand Pact and the Nine Power Pact as vital contributions to the peace effort, especially since they were supported by the United States. The collective peace system, Balch insisted, had the potential to put in place permanent alternatives to war. In theory, both the people and their governments supported this possibility.[40]

Balch closed this landmark talk with an appeal for action. She proclaimed, "The forces making for peace are profound, not superficial, in part new in type, hard to estimate." She remained hopeful that, despite the recent victories of dictatorships in Italy and Japan, people would not allow another global war to be waged and would seek a peaceful solution. She emphasized that it was "entirely unhistorical to claim that all the great historical changes" were products of war. Rather, great consequences could also result from processes and international institutions focused on peace. Pointing to the need for involvement in the peace process, she implored the Wellesley students to seek out their role in the current world crisis: "In all of this we are not mere spectators: we are actors, all responsible, in one degree for the future. Let us try to be worthy to live in the period of human history which because it is most self-conscious and purposive is perhaps of all ages the most vital."[41]

Balch's Armistice Day speech at Wellesley College cogently summarized her conception of the international peace movement during the 1930s, as well as her firm conviction that the people's will would defeat governmental interests. While she expressed immense gratitude at being formally reconnected with the college, she did not balk to recruit the young women to the peace movement. Balch's words in 1935 portrayed her as more firmly dedicated to the peace agenda than ever before. Although the coming years presented another widespread and catastrophic conflict, against Balch's expressed hopes in 1935, she continued to agitate for international diplomacy.

The Second World War, however, brought new challenges to Balch and the women's network.

WILPF and the Efforts to Assist Refugees

Balch traveled to Prague in 1936 to attend the WILPF international executive committee meeting. She did not return to Europe again until after the war. Although she remained in the United States, Balch closely monitored developments in Europe, just as she had implored the Wellesley students to do. She dedicated most of her time from that period onward to the WILPF refugee committee to establish safe havens for WILPF refugees and asylum seekers. The Nazi government persecuted leftists and peace advocates, and so the WILPF in the United States and Great Britain initiated campaigns to rescue their members. Although Balch and her peers sympathized with the countless others suffering within the Nazi regime, the WILPF believed it would achieve greatest success by concentrating only on its own membership. Balch argued, "As regards refugees our immediate duty and responsibility is toward our own members and those involved with them." The WILPF experienced limited success liberating its members from occupied countries, but Balch lamented that the effort "was too generally futile owing to the policy of the American State Department."[42] Angered by American immigration restrictions, Balch nonetheless persistently lobbied her government to accept more refugees.

The WILPF refugee campaigners stressed the urgency of their task, pointing to the increasing number of examples of unlawfully victimized groups. As early as 1934, WILPF leaders petitioned German officials on behalf of their members. Dorothy Detzer, the national secretary of U.S. WILPF at the time, wrote to the German ambassador in Washington, describing the WILPF's "horror" over the "accounts of the barbarous mistreatment of certain German women." Detzer had inquired about the welfare of seven women (WILPF members who were included in a group that was being tried for treason) and objected to their harassment. She protested on behalf of Charlette Adel, Lillie Adel, Edith Baumann, Erika Destzer, Kaethe Kirchnick, Ilse Schnichler, and Kaethe Schuften. Detzer and the WILPF asserted that these women were not treasonous, but were being persecuted "simply on the ground of their opinions."[43] To date, the outcome of these women's trials cannot be confirmed. The WILPF recognized early the risks of holding progressive opinions in Nazi Germany, and its members worried about how to get their German peers out of danger.

The low immigration quotas in the United States posed an immediate problem for the American WILPF refugee committee members. Balch ve-hemently argued that the government must reform its "rigid restrictionist laws" in order to assist refugees. She further contended that refugees must be viewed as "assets" to the United States, consistently pointing to the advances immigrants had made in the nation.[44] Her outlook was frequently met, how-ever, with the nativist, antiforeigner attitude prevalent among Americans in the 1930s. This anti-immigrant perspective was only intensified by the economic burdens of the Great Depression. Balch confronted the popular fears that immigrants constituted little more than competitors for American jobs by arguing that, in fact, their role as consumers made them valuable to the American economy. Balch's condemnation of American immigration policies and popular anti-immigration sentiment met with little response. Despite such immense social and political obstacles, Balch and the WILPF refugee committee carried on their efforts throughout the 1930s and early 1940s to extract their peers from deteriorating conditions in Europe.

A crucial component of the WILPF refugee committee's work centered on securing affidavits from influential and affluent individuals to assure the government that the women would not pose an economic burden to the na-tion. As part of this process, Balch and her peers issued endless requests to wealthy friends and acquaintances asking them to sponsor certain refugees until they could find work. Balch later recalled, with regard to the work for the refugees, the exhaustive hours securing the "coveted affidavits." Her papers from this period are stuffed with thousands of letters attesting to the fact that she worked endlessly to procure the affidavits for the WILPF women to come to the United States or to allied nations in Europe. The WILPF also set up a refugee fund in order to assist women once they reached their destination. Thus, between those who agreed to sponsor refugees by signing affidavits and the small but useful refugee fund, the women that the WILPF were able to extract from occupied Europe had a financial safety net when they reached their destination.[45]

Despite its meager capacity, the WILPF refugee fund assisted some women. One was Dr. Helene Stöcker, who, with WILPF help, managed to escape Berlin. The WILPF continued to assist her as she moved between England, Switzerland, and Sweden. The refugee fund was able to provide limited as-sistance to Stöcker, in the form of "50 Swiss francs, equivalent to about 17 $ a month" ($264.03 in 2008). Balch later sponsored Stöcker's move to the United States. The WILPF refugee committee backed her as best they were able, though their limits were clearly evident in the fact that the group had to scrounge money from at least four different funds just to facilitate Stöcker's transatlantic journey. Another woman the WILPF assisted was Yella Hertzka, the Austrian WILPF leader and close friend of Balch's since the early years of the organization. The WILPF successfully moved her to England by 1940, where she refused assistance from the WILFP fund: she did so knowing that those funds were scarce and that she would more likely need them once she made it to the United States.[46]

During the war years, the WILPF continued its modified efforts to liberate their members from Axis nations. It achieved mixed results. One prominent success story was Gertrud Baer. Baer was the leader of the German branch and, with the aid of the international body, escaped from Hitler's Germany to England. After an orchestrated effort involving numerous WILPF members, Baer arrived safely in the United States by the summer of 1940 and spent the war years in New York City, where she ran an outpost of the international office. She and Balch published the international newsletter, which the Geneva office was no longer able to produce. Balch later credited Baer's work during this era as vital in "awaking and maintaining an international spirit not only among WILPF members but also among outside subscribers."[47] Liberating Baer from Germany had most likely saved her life and also allowed the WILPF to continue to benefit from Baer's leadership.

The Nazis executed the majority of the WILPF's Czech leaders, but the WILPF refugee committee saved at least one, Marie Schmolkova. The organized efforts for her liberation began in May 1939, when Kathleen Courtney cabled Balch that "urgent requests" were needed "from abroad stating personal knowledge of character and impartial humanitarian work." Balch responded to this call and immediately issued a letter to all of the WILPF's members to follow her lead. She then cabled the British consulate in Prague: "Passionately urge release my old friend Marie Schmolkova to come to America. Affidavits already supplied. Plea based on her widely known service to humanity."[48] Although the details of her release are unclear, the WILPF successfully lobbied for Schmolkova's exit from Czechoslovakia. She made it to England, where she died during the war.

The WILPF also had its share of disappointments in its efforts to assist refugees. One heartbreaking instance was the attempt to extract Rosa Kulka, along with her sister Julia and their nieces Ella and Suse, from Czechoslovakia. Kulka, a local WILPF leader, began a friendship with the American WILPF leader Ellen Starr Brinton at the 1937 international congress. That year, Kulka began seeking assistance from her friends in the United States for her family to get out of Czechoslovakia. Balch aided Brinton's efforts to find refuge for the Kulkas in the United States. Throughout 1939 and 1940, Balch corresponded with Rosa Kulka and recruited many of her friends to petition the U.S. State

Department to consider the case. Balch confided to Brinton that her efforts were not looking hopeful. Eventually, Balch secured affidavits for the women but met with the obstacle of immigration quotas. The State Department refused to make an exception. Brinton wrote to Balch in April 1939: "Apparently the trouble is *quota numbers* and not finances or relationship." Brinton and Balch did not relent in their efforts, however, and the Kulkas recognized their dedication. Rosa Kulka related to Balch her family's gratitude for "our American friends, but most of all to you," and the Kulkas referred to Balch as their "friend and kind protectress."[49] The Kulkas remained hopeful that Balch would find a solution despite the increasingly dismal news they received.

Balch did put forth tremendous effort on their behalf. She even recruited the support of Massachusetts Senators Henry Cabot Lodge Jr. and David Walsh. Both issued letters of support to the State Department but neither prevailed to win the Kulkas entry into the United States.[50] By early 1941, the Kulkas no longer replied to their friends in the American WILPF; Balch and her friends correctly feared the worst. After the war, Brinton confirmed that at least three of the women perished in concentration camps and the last never surfaced. Balch's efforts, and those of her WILPF colleagues, remain powerful examples of the WILPF's extensive networking on behalf of refugees and the profound consequences of their failures to obtain refugee status.

* * *

The WILPF members demonstrated their admiration and respect for Balch's leadership in 1937, when they elected her as their new honorary international president. Balch did not attend the international congress that year because she was caring for her sister Anne, who was ill. Replying from Massachusetts, Balch expressed her gratitude to the entire WILPF membership: "As you all know I was very much touched and gratified by the vote by which I was made Honorary International President. I thank you all." Although it was an honorary position and thus no absolute set of responsibilities was attached to it, Balch, like Addams, did not serve merely as a figurehead. She worked tirelessly to lead her organization and maintained her dedication during the war.[51]

By the late 1930s, Balch and her colleagues held little hope that governments would avoid an all-out war. She outlined the succession of disappointing events that culminated in a formal declaration of war, stating, "No one could fail to see the disaster ahead, or rather already occurring." Balch was utterly disillusioned by the failure of the international community to respond early to Japanese and German aggression or to find a suitable solution in the Spanish Civil War. She felt "deeply grieved" at the failure of what she termed "the anti-Fascist powers," which had refused to place moral and economic pressure on those aggressor nations.[52]

Between 1936 and 1939, Balch had issued very few public comments concerning the developing conditions in Europe and Asia. There was a striking discrepancy between how much Balch wrote about events in the early 1930s compared with the dearth of material she produced concerning events later in the decade. This resulted, in part, from the fact that Balch tended to see those events as the consequences she had warned of since 1919. She was not surprised, for example, at the Austrian *Anschluss* in March 1938, when Germany absorbed Austria. She had believed it was a likely outcome, given the Treaty of Versailles restrictions of such unification, in addition to Germany's exclusion from the international community. WILPF members then worried for the future of Czechoslovakia, correctly arguing that it would soon fall to Nazi Germany as well. When Balch did comment publicly, she characteristically continued to vocalize the need for international cooperation.[53]

Another possibility for Balch's seemingly increased public silence might be that it became more difficult to distinguish between Balch's personal views and the organizational outlook of the WILPF by the early years of the Second World War. Both Balch and the WILPF's leaders continued to reiterate those solutions that had always been paramount to Balch: international agencies and mediated peace. As Nazi Germany extended throughout Europe, for example, Balch and the WILPF repeated the need to examine the root causes of war. In terms of specific and immediate solutions, Balch's consistent response to increased hostilities centered on calling peace conferences and instituting economic boycotts. However, it seems likely that by 1938, she had accepted the inevitability of a war, because she focused her efforts almost exclusively on extracting refugees from occupied areas. Balch saw her work as central to preventing all future wars, and she became increasingly upset as world leaders ignored the pleas of the international peace movement. When the war formally broke out in Europe in September of 1939, Balch confided to a friend, "I feel stunned and callous. We foresaw it, we foretold it, but that makes it no easier."[54]

7. "The Things I Leave Undone," 1942–61

The United States entered the Second World War in December 1941, following the Japanese bombing of Pearl Harbor. Balch later pointed to this as the moment that began her "long and painful mental struggle" over which she "never felt that she had reached a clear and consistent conclusion." Unable to reconcile her pacifist outlook with the horrors unfolding before her, she asked how to achieve a balance "when in your own mind an irresistible force has collided with an immovable obstacle?" For Balch, the war years allowed her to refine her opinions on absolute pacifism, that is, the total opposition to war under any circumstances. Early in the war she wrote to a European peer about her personal struggle with pacifism in light of the war, confiding, "As to my own position on the pacifist issue I have been and am very unhappy."[1] Balch gradually moved further from the absolute pacifism that most of the American WILPF leaders embraced and toward a more relativist approach that was popular with the European leaders. She came to see the danger of the Axis forces and the spread of totalitarianism as a far greater threat to civilization than the use of violence to confront that threat.

Balch's opinions about the Second World War differed considerably from her ideas about the First World War. This resulted, in part, from her view of the causes of those wars. In 1914, from Balch's viewpoint, the world witnessed a power struggle within an acutely divided race for greater empires. Nationalistic ambitions of the 1930s also reflected imperialistic desires, but Balch came to believe that Hitler and his ideology presented a great and immediate threat to civilization as a whole. In her own recollections of her position during World War I, she continued to struggle with what would have happened had the Entente powers lost. She did not ever question, however, that the spread of Hitler's racist and militarist ideology posed one of the greatest threats the world had yet witnessed. In her view, because the Allied nations had failed to prevent the war, they needed to defeat Hitler.

Nonetheless, Balch continued to advocate for a negotiated peace until 1941 and then vehemently objected to the "unconditional surrender" mandate issued by the Allies. She developed her own mixed position that partially supported the war while also protesting it. She refused to buy war bonds, but she did contribute money to "community war-funds" because they apportioned most of their proceeds "to wholly peaceful social aid."[2] Essentially, Balch maintained that her pacifist outlook, which had never been entirely absolutist, changed between the wars because of the causes and the stark differences between those wars, not because of any marked change in her personal philosophy. She never wavered in her conviction that the best approach to international conflict was through collaborative diplomatic approaches.

Balch's position on the war was a complicated and often misunderstood one. This resulted from her frequently confusing positions, such as her staunch opposition to military conscription compared with her support of military training. Since the First World War, Balch had adamantly objected to the draft, and she continued to do so. By 1940, the American public was swept up in a debate over the issue of compulsory military training. Balch reasoned that if the military provisioned arms, it was "inconsistent . . . not to prepare the men to use [them]." Training young men in military skills, Balch argued, was not the same as compelling them to fight. Balch's promotion of military training is surprising given her general objection to the culture of war. This resulted from both her complex feelings toward the Second World War and her leadership position in the international peace movement. "To oppose training is to expose the pacifist movement to condemnation in public opinion," she reasoned.[3] Balch's concern for public opinion about the peace movement is notable, given her previous involvement with various unpopular groups. She refused to embrace any particular viewpoint in order to gain popularity, however, as is evident in her continued opposition to conscription.

Balch had always been a relativist, and so her qualified stance on pacifism is not as out of character as it might seem. Although her wartime perspectives sometimes confused her WILPF colleagues, she defended her position as in accord with the spirit of the WILPF. Balch's limited support for the war sometimes ostracized her, especially among her American peers. She wrote to Clara Ragaz in Switzerland in 1941 that many American members firmly, and incorrectly, believed that "the WILPF *always* stood for absolute pacifism."[4]

The philosophical differences that emerged within the WILPF during World War II certainly challenged Balch, but she refused to resign in order to make the situation more comfortable for others. She persisted in her belief that the WILPF must include "peace-minded women of very different shades of opinion." She insisted on a more tolerant atmosphere, stating that the "growing trend toward absolutist pacifism should not cause those who do not accept [it] to withdraw." She even authored a WILPF resolution at the national United States meeting in 1941 that reemphasized the political diversity within WILPF membership. As long as members objected to war as a method of international relations, they were free to "come to different conclusions on important points of current policy."[5]

Thinking Beyond the War

In 1942, in the midst of the Second World War and the WILPF's internal struggles with absolute pacifism, Emily Greene Balch turned seventy-five. Her peers in the international peace movement honored the occasion with a celebratory dinner, held in Philadelphia. The WILPF commemorated Balch's life of service to peace and social reform and acknowledged her contribution to reconceptualizing work for peace. The speech that Balch delivered that evening, entitled "Towards a Planetary Civilization," outlined her "social philosophy" and articulated her vision of peace, showing how her philosophy had evolved. Her speech also embodied those topics to which she would dedicate the remaining nineteen years of her life: embracing global citizenship, promoting international agencies, and confronting the Cold War.

Balch refused to allow her vision of peace to be defeated by the experience of World War II. She asserted that even the painful experience of war was one step in a greater historical trend toward "planetary civilization." She optimistically viewed the "planetary barbarism" of the war as merely a "forerunner" to a world in which individuals would view themselves as global citizens. Her presentation implored her fellow peace activists to view their mission holistically; she described the process of her own realization that war was "intertwined with our whole economic and social system" and with our "scale of values." As such, Balch asserted that the work for progress and peace must be multifaceted. The movement must be broadened to seek the replacement of all forms of injustice with "organized cooperation" for a "common interest."[6]

Balch also strived to persuade her audience that the peace movement must re-envision itself and, in doing so, continue to expand the definition of peace. Balch's concept of peace had changed since her early days of social reform. As she increasingly came to understand the need for the presence of social and economic justice, she argued that peace must not be understood merely as a negative concept. "Peace is too small a word," she declared. As commonly understood, peace was "too negative in its considerations."[7] By only seeking to eradicate war, Balch argued, the peace movement would fail to examine and eliminate the causes of war. Social and economic justice must exist in order to envision a world free from violent international conflict. Balch's vision for the future demanded a broader interpretation of human relations. She would devote her remaining two decades to that vision for peace. Balch's conceptualization of peace and ideas for international organization constituted both the heart and the backbone of the Women's International League for Peace and Freedom, which she had worked so diligently to create and advance.

As the war drew to a close, Balch turned her focus to international relations in the postwar world. The use of the atomic bomb ignited in Balch a horror of military technological developments. However, she utilized the horror to further illustrate the necessity for total disarmament and the establishment of international agencies for peace. She did not remark on the Marshall Plan to provide aid to war-devastated Europe, though she had previously, and characteristically, discussed the need to create an international body that would distribute postwar aid. After careful consideration, Balch fully supported the new plans for the emerging United Nations (UN). Although she was one of the last to let go of the dream of the League of Nations, she hoped that the UN would prove itself more effective and that it would eventually establish new international agencies. She persisted in her belief that only through international organization and management could the world avoid the conflicts that resulted from imperialistic ambitions or competitions over resources. Balch, however, was not an unconditional advocate of the UN. She worried that it might come to represent a "resurgence of nationalism and power politics."[8] She keenly observed the increasing distance between the Soviet Union and the West and wondered whether the UN would come to merely serve the interests of the West in a polarized world.

Emily Greene Balch and the Nobel Peace Prize

Many in the world of peace advocacy, whether or not they agreed with Balch's wartime position, deeply respected and admired their aging leader. In 1945, the Women's International League for Peace and Freedom established the Committee to Sponsor Emily Greene Balch for the Nobel Peace Prize, with Mercedes Randall acting as chairwoman. This committee solic-

ited recommendations from colleagues from every side of Balch's professional life. They obtained letters praising Balch from prominent individuals,
including Oswald Garrison Villard of *The Nation* and Clarence Pickett of the
American Friends Service Committee. The eminent American philosopher
John Dewey campaigned vigorously for Balch's nomination, authoring a
request to the English pacifist Sir Norman Angell that he formally present
her name to the Oslo Committee. In his appeal to Angell, Dewey shared
his impression that Balch "has played a historic part in the peace efforts of
our time." Angell agreed.[9]

On November 14, 1946, while recuperating from bronchial asthma at a
Massachusetts hospital, Balch learned that the Norwegian Nobel Institute
awarded her the Nobel Peace Prize, an honor she shared that year with Dr.
John R. Mott of the Young Men's Christian Association. She commented, "I
am surprised and very much delighted." With characteristic modesty, she
transferred the spotlight from herself to the WILPF, stating, "I am happy in
thinking that not I myself but the Women's International League for Peace
and Freedom, with which I am identified, is the true recipient."[10] Balch's
response relayed both humility and insecurity about her relationship to the
movement. She had never described Addams's 1931 award as a representative
victory for the WILPF.

Balch, seventy-nine years old and quite ill in the hospital, was unable to
attend the award ceremony in Oslo that year. She reflected on the great legacy
within which she now stood. She sent a telegram to the German-American
Socialist Newspaper, *New Yorker Volkszeitung,* discussing her peace heritage.
She voiced her admiration for Carl von Ossietzky, the German pacifist who
spoke out against Hitler and who received the Nobel award in 1935, though
the German authorities refused to allow him to accept it. He died the following year in a concentration camp. She related that receiving the prize
meant remembering the work of others like von Ossietzky. She explained,
"In remembering Carl von Ossietzky today . . . we are remembering a man of
heroic courage and devotion. He defied the Nazi power at its height and paid
a bitter penalty." Remaining modest in the response to her lifetime of work
toward peace, Balch never elevated herself above others whom she admired,
commenting, "It is a sobering thing to follow him and Jane Addams and
so many other noble and rich personalities in the list of those who, due to
Nobel's generous thought, have received the honor of this Peace Award."[11]

The WILPF honored Balch upon her receipt of the Peace Prize. As well as
holding a celebratory dinner in New York in 1947, the leaders of the WILPF
published their thoughts on Balch's accomplishments in the American branch's
publication *Four Lights.* Gertrud Baer praised Balch's years of dedication. She

Emily Greene Balch,
c. 1946–47. Emily Greene
Balch Papers, Swarthmore
College Peace Collection.

extolled her friend, claiming, "Your close workers . . . have benefited from the
strength of your spiritual 'rich and noble' personality, from your exceptional
ability to see the many facets of a politically intricate question and to find a uni-
fying formula—international statesmanship at its best." Baer recalled Balch's
work during the formative years of the organization, stating, "In those early
days, work at International Headquarters in Geneva was a real venture. It was
genuine community work—anonymous, pioneering, daring."[12] Admiration
for Balch as one of the organization's pioneers abounded in the publication.
The recent resentments over Balch's lack of absolute pacifism seemed to be
in the distant past.

Two years later, Balch, recovered from her illness, journeyed to Oslo to
deliver her Nobel laureate lecture, which she titled "Toward Human Unity,
or Beyond Nationalism." After surveying the trends that characterized her
nearly eighty years of life, she considered peacemaking on both the individual
and the collective level and declared, "Peace workers or pacifists have dealt
mainly with two types of issue[s], the moral or individual, and the political
or institutional." On an individual level, she discussed the obvious "personal
refusal of war service." She expressed her great admiration for those who

communicated their personal peace activism, stating, "I believe that it has been an invaluable witness to the supremacy of conscience over all other considerations and a very great service to a public too much affected by the conception that might makes right."[13]

In Balch's discussion of international institutions, she also clarified her position on world government. She emphasized that the path to peace lay with international institutions, but not governments. "World government," she claimed, posed "very real dangers." Her protest rested in her distrust of governments generally, not from a lack of internationalism. She continued, "I see governments as a peculiar historical kind of organization which is not necessarily the last word in human wisdom." Most important for Balch, "Governments seem to have a bad inheritance behind them," she said, " . . . with lust for power and with much too great concern for prestige." Balch hoped that the international peace movement would continue to support the United Nations and other international bodies designed to reduce and resolve world conflict.[14]

Crucial to the success of any international institution, Balch believed, was the work of international peace organizations like the Women's International League for Peace and Freedom. Balch highlighted the importance of continued work toward disarmament and the need for effective trusteeships and mandates. She closed her Nobel lecture by promoting her vision of internationalizing aviation, waterways, and the polar regions. Balch dreamt of the establishment of multiple international agencies to regulate all aspects of international life that tended toward conflict. In her final decades, she focused her attention almost exclusively on developing such projects.

The Cold War and Beyond

Throughout her eighties, Balch's responses to the cold war were mostly rhetorical. She did not posit specific solutions to end the Korean War, for example, but rather continued to address the root problems of war. She focused on the need to understand alternative viewpoints and establish international modes of cooperation, rather than competition, in order to progress in a way that would not result in total global destruction.

Balch believed that the greatest danger of the Cold War to Americans stemmed from the culture of fear that it sparked in the United States. In a 1954 address to the WILPF, she declared that McCarthyism threatened to destroy free thinking. She expressed her "surprise" that so many Americans had embraced "the cult of fear and suspicion." Yet Balch inspired her colleagues by reminding them to focus on their triumphs and look toward the future. The WILPF had withstood multiple challenges to its global perspective and mission, and Balch remained confident that it would withstand the repressive cold war culture as well.[15]

Balch refused to think that a third world war was inevitable, but she did remain concerned over the deteriorating relations between nations. In 1955, she became increasingly anxious over the growing animosity between the American and Chinese governments. She drafted a Christmas message to the Chinese people that year, which she subsequently delivered to many of her American friends and also broadly published in popular magazines. This "letter of love" expressed Balch's desire for peace and friendship between the two nations, despite their differences. She wrote, "I am an American and what you perhaps call a capitalist. Need that be a barrier to love? It does not hold back mine." She wished that people not "be divided by ideologies." Most interesting, she noted American culpability in poor perceptions of them by the Chinese people. "You may know bad Americans. There are such. But there are also here friendly, right-meaning people who want to make the world better for everyone. There are bad people and good people, I suppose, in every country."[16] Such sentiments demonstrated how Balch continued her efforts to act as a diplomat among citizens of various nations.

In 1955, at age 88, Balch once again expressed her conviction that human interaction, across national and ideological identities, remained the key to establishing a secure and lasting peace. She criticized popular newspapers during the cold war for being "full of the word 'co-existence.'" She argued that such an interpretation of peace, as separate existence without any interaction, was impossible. International relationships, she maintained, were always changing. After all, only ten years previously the United States had provided financial assistance to Russia to fight against their common enemy, Nazi Germany. The cold war would gradually give way to another phase of international human interaction. Balch observed, "Inanimate objects can exist side by side without affecting one another. Not so human beings."[17] This rather unconcerned philosophical perspective on the Cold War was rooted in her firm belief that the global human community would find a way to avoid total destruction.

Balch had always advocated that the path to peace required a broader acceptance of international agencies. Distrusting governments as tools to secure international cooperation, Balch believed that only those organizations that were truly international in nature and in mission could ensure peace. In her final years, she directed her lobbying efforts specifically toward the internationalization of those arenas that she felt held the greatest potential for future conflict, namely, the air and seas. By the 1950s, however, Balch conceded that commercial interests were too strong to continue to advocate for the international management of the air. She continued to hope for the possibility of naval internationalization and even drafted multiple proposals to the United Nations asking for studies of the possibility. While advancements toward internationalizing the air and seas failed to materialize, Balch lived to witness what she considered a great step toward internationalization: she had also been an advocate for internationalizing the planet's polar regions, and in December 1959, twelve nations, including the United States, signed the Antarctic Treaty, which specifically outlawed weapons testing and ensured an international effort that Antarctica would be utilized only for peaceful purposes.

Balch was encouraged by such international agreements, but as she grew older, she continued to worry about the future of international relations. She maintained great hope in the potential of humankind but worried, on a personal level, that she had not done enough with her life to see her dreams realized. She revealed this inner perspective in a small book of poems that she had published amidst the chaotic demands of her life during the war. In this book, *The Miracle of Living,* Balch reflected on her life. Her poems exhibited her wit and insight, yet the publication differed from her more concrete intellectual endeavors. In this little book, she provided a window into her innermost thoughts. She had, for example, finally reconciled herself to her old age and reflected on her most personal joys in life.

One short poem, "Harried," displayed her attitude toward the rigorous schedule she maintained despite her age, and revealed her deep fear that all of her efforts would not be enough. This poem, set in the context of other reflections on aging, told her friends that, though the troubles of the world and her duties in the peace movement exhausted her, she constantly worried of the tasks still ahead:

> When I feel hunted all day long
> And fagged at set of sun
> I am tired not by the things I do
> But the things I leave undone.[18]

Balch's earnest desire to fill each of her days with important work never wavered, even as her body aged. Close to the end of her life, her family placed her in a nursing home in South Natick, Massachusetts. Even this did not slow her down. Frances Hayward, the first friend Balch made as a child in Jamaica Plain, encouraged Balch's seemingly endless drive to continue. When both women were in their nineties, they exchanged letters frequently. The women came to believe that they would fare better under each other's care. Balch somehow managed to sweet talk a doctor at the nursing home into driving her to Maine so that she might stay with Hayward. Not surprisingly, the journey proved too much for Balch and she soon returned to Boston. This vignette of two women in their nineties, convinced of their own fortitude, revealed their determination not to let age stop them from living each day as thoroughly as they wished.[19]

All of the energy and the dedication in the world could not deny the inevitable. Emily Greene Balch died on a Monday evening, January 9, 1961, one day after her ninety-fourth birthday. Rallying until the end, Balch left this world as quietly as she entered it, but having been a profound force during the time in between. She had been fundamental to the life and work of Jane Addams and other settlement and peace workers; she had been an influential teacher and revered friend, a respected scholar and visionary thinker. She left a powerful legacy. Although many of her dreams remain unrealized, future generations may be inspired by her fortitude and dedication to establishing a better, more peaceful world.

Conclusion

"If We Have a Long Road Ahead of Us,
We Have Also Come a Long Way"

After Balch's death, her community in Boston and the peace network throughout the world recognized the loss of a leader, the woman Jane Addams had once referred to as the "'goodest person' she had ever known." Balch's family and fellow WILPF members endeavored to continue her legacy as a good, kind, and simple woman. Her friend and WILPF colleague Hannah Hull related a favorite Balch story about one cold Boston day just before Thanksgiving, when Balch stepped outdoors after having stopped to warm herself with a cup of hot chocolate at a local drugstore. As she left the store, she met a young woman who worked for the Salvation Army and was asking people to donate pennies to help feed the hungry on Thanksgiving. Balch insisted that the woman accept a cup of hot chocolate for herself and a few minutes inside to get warm. Balch then stood in the woman's place and asked passers by for pennies while the woman warmed herself inside. Recalling this story, Hull exclaimed, "A far cry this, from being envoy to kings and potentates, to begging pennies on a city's street!"[1]

Many of Balch's friends and co-workers shared the admiration conveyed in this popular portrayal of Balch, and they crafted her legacy in that image. They told the story of a woman whose moral convictions and dedication to service drove her choices and ideas. These factors are undeniably important to understanding Balch's character. But her true personality, of course, was much more complex. From an early age, Balch wished to live a useful life in the service of something greater, but she also struggled against her own high standards and ambitions. By understanding the more complete and complex version of Emily Greene Balch as described in these pages, we can more easily relate to her and be inspired by her visionary ideas. Balch was driven by a strong moral impulse. But she also struggled, as most do. She worked diligently to balance her intellectual longings—her desire to immerse herself in a world of books—with the need to serve her community. Her scholarship reflects this struggle. She produced methodical, analytical studies, but always on subjects of great, and sometimes immediate, relevance to her world.

Balch grew into a woman with brilliant ideas and a remarkable talent for mediating intense or problematic discussions. Her personality and this particular talent were unquestionably shaped by her times. She was an intelligent and ambitious woman who was fortunate to have a family that encouraged her to feed her intellectual curiosity. She was one of the few women of her generation to receive a college education. Yet she was born too early to have a great many choices on how to apply her mind. Because of the limited options for educated women of this era, Balch came to live and work in a world dominated by women. She grew up with five sisters and then attended educational institutions for women. She taught for twenty years at a women's college and then became a leading figure in the international women's peace movement. She worked among women who depended on each other and built strong networks of support.[2]

Although Balch thrived among networks of insightful and influential women, she did not balk at the public sphere, which for much of her life was reserved for men. She twice chose to pursue her education abroad in places where it was not popular or common for women to do so. In fact, neither Paris nor Berlin offered degree programs to women. But Balch was determined to make the most of her experience, to challenge her mind and learn from the best. She went where the men went. Even after her miserable experience as a woman trying to get a legitimate education in Paris, she again subjected herself to a struggle when she chose to study in Berlin. Although Balch is primarily remembered for her work within the women's international network, she was not unknown to peace and diplomacy circles more broadly. She was a frequent presence at the League of Nations and a known figure in Washington. She met with several presidents, tasked with informing each of the progress of one of her projects.

Balch's public life raises a crucial question: was she truly a radical, or was she a moderate who associated with radicals? Despite the fact that Balch dedicated most of her time to organizations and works for social reform, she did not have a radical's nature or approach to social change. While many during her life and since have labeled her as such, I argue that Balch was actually a moderate, especially in her temperament and her approach to her work. Only the conservative times in which she lived forced her reformist views toward the radical end of the political spectrum. Her main reform activities focused on settlement, organized labor, and the peace movement. She firmly believed in women's right to vote but never became an outspoken suffragist. Some might point to the brief period she identified herself as a socialist as proof of radicalism. Her socialism, limited as it was (she herself professed never to have accepted Marx's theories), was an intellectual manifestation of her understanding of the world during her time. Most of her associations with radical organizations, namely the People's Council of America, occurred during the First World War. Both her contemporaries and many historians since have defined Balch as a radical, at least during the First World War. During that period, in the context of the antiwar movement, she was. However, a deeper insight is that Balch thoroughly understood radicals, conservatives, and moderates. She consistently attempted to see all sides of a situation and remain neutral, in search of a solution to the concrete problem at hand.

Balch's studied moderation was present in her scholarship as well as her activities. Her early work studied municipal regulations and government administrations. She analyzed how governments worked to assist the community or the nation. As a young scholar, Balch was primarily interested in the role of government and how specific programs affected actual people. This was evident in her study of French public assistance programs, in various reports commissioned for the city of Boston, and in her thesis paper in Berlin. By age thirty, Balch focused her scholarly ambitions on the field of economics. She wrote her own textbook for the courses she taught at Wellesley College. Not long into her professorial years, however, Balch's intellectual curiosity led her to the newly emerging field of immigration studies. She researched and authored a tome on Slavic immigration to the United States. During the First World War her ability to synthesize information and produce insightful compromises truly matured. She compiled *Approaches to the Great Settlement,* which presented various perspectives on how to mediate and end that war. Through her work with the Neutral Conference for Continuous Mediation, she authored a compelling work on colonialism. After World War I, her work with WILPF allowed her to continue to think and write about international affairs. In *Occupied Haiti,* Balch focused on one example of the greater problem of American imperialism.

Balch's ideas did not transform as much as evolve between 1919 and 1945. She grew to better define and articulate her pacifism. She wrote countless and insightful responses to the international events that ultimately led to World War II. Those in power refused to embrace such ideas, and Balch came to believe that war was the only response to the threat of fascism. This, however, did not negate her conviction that social justice and economic justice were as necessary components of a lasting peace as the simple absence of violent conflict. Above all, Balch continued to argue for strong and effective international administration.

The evolution of Balch's ideas is best exhibited in her discussions of a new international order. Like most American progressives, Balch was forever changed by the First World War. While the Progressive movement mainly died out in the United States, Balch took its ideals to a global stage. She envisioned a new world order in the postwar era and tried for the rest of her life to realize that vision. She consistently promoted international institutions and internationalization programs. Many of her dreams would ultimately manifest themselves in forms she had not directly advocated, such as the European Union.

She was an early critic of what scholars and advocates have come to see as the costs of globalization. In 1926, Balch pointed to the various aspects of economic interdependence among nations and saw in that reality a potential for a new form of internationalism, though she was careful to note that such interdependence held "both menace and promise." She recognized that it would "be a slow and difficult process" to transform economic interdependence into social awareness and understanding among the people of all nations. "We drink our tea from China and our coffee from Arabia or Brazil," she wrote, " . . . without any sense of community . . . or any sense of personal relation to the coolie who picked the tea leaves."[3] The key, as Balch saw it, was increasing this sort of awareness and removing national profit. So, she argued, we must reform systems of currency and advance internationalizing projects, creating transnational administrations to oversee the waterways and the skies. Understanding that this was a long, slow process, Balch continued to promote this new international order until her death in 1961.

Balch's advocacy on behalf of internationalism was an outlet for her personal identity as well. Balch's greatest contribution to the international peace movement, and perhaps her most powerful legacy, was her complete commitment to global citizenship. Toward the end of her life, she eloquently voiced her personal acceptance of this identity: "I am a good American but far more deeply and happily I feel myself a citizen of the world. I am at home wherever there are people. Wherever I go I know I shall find cruel sly dishonest unpleasant people and everywhere I shall find magnanimous generous people, men with keen minds, friendly honest open serviceable people who want to help, who want to make friends."[4]

Balch's commitment to global citizenship reinforced her efforts. Her sense of community extended beyond national borders, and so did her concern for individuals. Time and again, in the face of what many believed to be imminent global destruction, Balch maintained an air of calm. This, in part, resulted from her understanding that most international tensions eased with time. She never forgot that when she was eighteen years old, she was stuck on a ship in the midst of preparations for a war that never came to be.[5] She believed, despite surviving two world wars, that the world could rid itself of war and that an international community could work together for the global good. Whenever Balch began to despair about the state of the world and the lack of influence of the peace movement, she consistently returned to the metaphor of springtime. She found comfort in the knowledge that there was always another level of new growth that was only invisible because of the circumstances of the present.

Emily Greene Balch, both personally and professionally, helped to elevate the world in which she lived. She strove to create community everywhere she traveled. No doubt many will view Balch's ideas as utopian and so without any practical application. But her experiences remind us that such ideas do sometimes come to fruition. In 1952, she remarked, "If we have a long road ahead of us, we have also come a long way." Yes, the road to progress might be slow, but it is not impassable. Balch brilliantly pointed to the example of technological progress, which had transformed her world in ways impossible to imagine fifty years before. "Technical progress has made practicable what until now was utopian." Balch saw hope in this example, continuing, "This does not mean that the revolutionary changes involved can be brought about either easily or quickly, but it means that they can be brought about."[6] This example, still relevant today, serves as a constant reminder that the long road to internationalism will eventually reach its destination.

Notes

Abbreviations for Individuals

AB	Anne Balch (oldest sister)
ABG	Alice Bache Gould
ABS	Alice Balch Stone (sister)
EGB	Emily Greene Balch
FNB	Francis Noyes Balch (brother)
FVB	Francis Vergnies Balch (father)
HC	Helen Cheever
JA	Jane Addams
MB	Marion Balch (sister)
MKS	Mary Kingsbury Simkhovitch
MMR	Mercedes M. Randall
NNB	Nelly Noyes Balch (mother)

Abbreviations for Manuscript Collections

ABGP	Alice Bache Gould Papers, Massachusetts Historical Society, Boston, Massachusetts
AUAMP	American Union Against Militarism Papers, Swarthmore College Peace Collection, Swarthmore, Pennsylvania
DDP	Dorothy Detzer Papers, Swarthmore College Peace Collection, Swarthmore, Pennsylvania
DHR	Denison House Records, Schlesinger Library, Radcliffe Institute, Harvard University, Cambridge, Massachusetts
EGBR	Erin-Go-Bragh Records, Schlesinger Library, Radcliffe Institute, Harvard University, Cambridge, Massachusetts
EGBP	Emily Greene Balch Papers, Swarthmore College Peace Collection, Swarthmore, Pennsylvania

ESBP   Ellen Starr Brinton Papers, Swarthmore College Peace Collection, Swarth-
          more, Pennsylvania
HSP   Helene Stöcker Papers, Swarthmore College Peace Collection, Swarthmore,
          Pennsylvania
JAP   Jane Addams Papers, Swarthmore College Peace Collection, Swarthmore,
          Pennsylvania
KDCP   Kathleen D'Olier Courtney Papers, The Women's Library, London Metropoli-
          tan University, London, England
MCTP   M. Carey Thomas Papers, Bryn Mawr College Library, Bryn Mawr, Pennsyl-
          vania
MKOP   Mary Kenney O'Sullivan Papers, Schlesinger Library, Radcliffe Institute, Har-
          vard University, Cambridge, Massachusetts
MMRP   Mercedes M. Randall Papers, Swarthmore College Peace Collection, Swarth-
          more, Pennsylvania
SBC   Balch Family Records, kept by Si Balch
WCA   Wellesley College Archives
WILPFP   Women's International League for Peace and Freedom Papers, Swarthmore
          College Peace Collection, Swarthmore, Pennsylvania
WPPP   Woman's Peace Party Papers [segment of WILPF collection], Swarthmore
          College Peace Collection, Swarthmore, Pennsylvania

Introduction

1. Given Balch's relative obscurity in the historical literature, it is not surprising that this is the first in-depth, scholarly analysis of her life. All Balch scholarship benefits, however, from Mercedes Randall's 1964 tome on her friend Emily Greene Balch, entitled *Improper Bostonian*. While Randall's work embodies a colossal effort to present the life and ideas of Balch, it suffers from the author's closeness to her subject. Mercedes Randall was a colleague of Balch's in the peace movement and was her literary executor. *Improper Bostonian* has been, until now, the central reference for any discussion of Balch. It provides an exhaustive narrative of Balch's life, yet it lacks objective analysis.

2. The most significant works in peace history, as they relate to the period under consideration in this work, include: Alonso, *Peace as a Women's Issue*; Early, *World Without War*; Carrie A. Foster, *Women and the Warriors*; Catherine Foster, *Women for All Seasons*; Kuhlman, *Petticoats and White Feathers*; Patterson, *Search for Negotiated Peace*; Rupp, *Worlds of Women*; and Steinson, *American Women's Activism*.

3. Balch, "Our Call," 3.

Chapter 1: "The Service of Goodness," 1867–85

1. The Balch family can accurately be described as upper middle class, in terms of both their financial state and their social status. Throughout the last decades of the nineteenth century, Francis Vergnies Balch frequently (but not consistently), appeared in the yearly who's who of Boston society, the *Boston Social Register*. Unlike much wealthier families, such as their close friends the Cheevers, individual family members were not listed.

Emily Greene Balch did not appear in the *Social Register* until January 1905, but then she remained in the listings for several years. Inclusion in this publication indicates that, although not vastly wealthy, the Balches were generally considered part of the upper crust of Boston society. See, for example, *Social Register* (Boston) vol. 4, no. 4 (New York: Social Register Association, August 1890), 32; *Social Register* (Boston), vol. 8, no. 5 (New York: Social Register Association, November 1893), 10, 21; *Social Register* (Boston), vol. 12, no. 8 (New York: Social Register Association, August 1898), 58; *Social Register* (Boston), vol. 8, no. 5 (New York: Social Register Association, November 1898), 9, 21; and *Social Register* (Boston), vol. 17, no. 5 (New York: Social Register Association, November 1902), 11, 29.

2. Emily was the second living daughter of Francis and Nelly Balch. They had another daughter, Ellen, who died in 1874, at age three. See Family Tree, EGBP; Catherine Porter Noyes, Diary, EGBP (not a part of the microfilmed collection).

3. He extrapolates this from data he collected from the Boston Directories for those years. Binford, *First Suburbs,* 130.

4. See Balch, "Draft Autobiography."

5. von Hoffman, *Local Attachments,* 25–26.

6. Ibid., 2, 33–34; Abbott, "Vital Statistics," 72; Kuczynski, "Fecundity," 143; Warner, *Streetcar Suburbs,* 6.

7. With regard to immigration and class in Jamaica Plain, see von Hoffman, *Local Attachments,* 24, 30; and Warner, *Streetcar Suburbs,* 48, 93; with regard to Emily's memories of immigrant domestic servants, see EGB, Recollections of childhood, EGBP; Randall, *Beyond Nationalism,* 50.

8. Randall, *Improper Bostonian,* 31; EGB, Journal entry, 15 July [unknown year], EGBP.

9. NNB, Diary entry, 30 November 1861, and 24 August 1862, EGBP.

10. NNB, Diary entry, June 1865, EGBP; quoted in Randall, *Improper Bostonian,* 31.

11. In Emily's recollections of her father she failed to identify the exact age at which her father moved to Jamaica Plain. She wrote only that the family resided "in what was then a desirable residential part of Boston. The purchase of the 'Rose Bank' place in Jamaica Plain meant removal to what must then have been the country." EGB, "Francis Vergnies Balch," n.d., EGBP.

12. Balch, "Oration," 15.

13. Bruce, *Twentieth Regiment,* 140.

14. John Gray, "Proceedings at Bar Meeting Held at Boston, March 26, 1898, Upon the Death of Francis Vergnies Balch," Supreme Judicial Court of Massachusetts [hereinafter, "Proceedings"], 4. In EGBP.

15. John Gray stated that Balch "was admitted to our (the State of Massachusetts's) Bar on April 9, 1861, but had little or no practice until seven or eight years later." Ibid., 4.

16. Felix Rackmann in Gray, "Proceedings," 18–19, 21; Balch, "Draft Autobiography;" Randall, *Emily Greene Balch,* 10.

17. The siblings spent some of their holidays over the years writing a family alphabet, in which each family member was described in a poem. In 1903, the entry for Emily read: "E is for Emily / wise from her toes; / To the tip of her grave professorial nose. / The traveller, the scholar [*sic*], the organizer, / And yet we all dare to be flippant with her." F. N. Balch and P. K. Balch, "A Balch Family Alphabet," 1903, EGBP. Francis never remarried and depended on Anne's assistance to raise the children. Only one letter survives, from Anne

to her brother Frank, that discusses the fact that their father considered taking his cousin, Agnes Balch, as a wife. Anne claims that Francis consulted her as to whether this would be a wise choice and that she discouraged the idea. AB to FNB, 31 July 1939, SBC.

18. In his history of Jamaica Plain, von Hoffman wrote, "Throughout the nineteenth and early twentieth centuries, members of Jamaica Plain's oldest and wealthiest families, such as the Balches . . . attended and supported the First Church." *Local Attachments,* 123.

19. Dole, *My Eighty Years,* 187, 195; EGB, Diary entry, 18 June 1876, EGBP.

20. Dole, *My Eighty Years,* 189–90, 207.

21. Ibid., 141. Dole remained an ardent pacifist, publicly opposing both the Spanish-American War and the First World War. His understanding of human relations resonated in young Balch. As an adult, she commented on her admiration of his pacifist principles, calling him an "honest pacifist," even more so because during times of war he chose to live with the unpopularity of his opinions and "remained honest" to his beliefs. EGB, Thoughts on C. F. Dole, EGBP.

22. Balch, "Draft Autobiography." As an adult, Balch continued to pray that she be strong enough to keep this vow of service. One of her privately recorded prayers read, "Use me I pray as a living instrument of service." EGB, Prayer, 7 May 1911, EGBP.

23. Balch, "Draft Autobiography."

24. No information about Balch's first schoolhouse survives. It appears that a woman ran the school out of her home and supported the institution by charging tuition. This type of private school was not atypical in mid-nineteenth-century New England. The older Balch children did attend school at Mrs. Walker's in Jamaica Plain. This fact is confirmed in brief references in a letter from Emily's younger sister, Alice Balch Stone, as well as in Emily's own draft autobiography manuscript. See Kaestle and Vinovskis, *Education and Social Change,* 17; ABS to MMR, 8 February 1962, MMRP; and Balch, "Draft Autobiography."

25. Louisville Square is located between 80 Pinckney and 89 Mt. Vernon Streets in Boston's Ninth Ward. ABS to MMR, 2 August 1962, MMRP; *Boston City Directory,* 1897; Balch, "Draft Autobiography."

26. EGB, ed., *Catharine Innes Ireland, 1838–1925: A Memorial,* 1929, EGBR. Note: Ireland's first name is misspelled in the title to this memorial, though spelled correctly as Catherine throughout the text.

27. EGB, *Ireland.*

28. One teacher who was particularly adored by the students was Miss Elizabeth Simmons, who taught mathematics and Latin. Other teachers integral in developing Emily's educational and intellectual interests included Fraulein von Seckendorf, who taught German literature, and M. Lévy, who taught French. Ibid.

29. The Cheevers were consistently listed individually in the *Social Register* for Boston (see ch. 1n1). At her death in 1960, Helen Cheever's personal estate was valued at approximately $425,000. The only nonfamily members to whom she devised a portion of her estate were Emily Greene Balch and another friend from her days at Miss Ireland's, Katherine Patten. HC, Will dated March 16, 1933, proved May 13, 1960, docket no. 407833, Suffolk Probate and Family Court, Boston, Mass.

30. Balch, "Draft Autobiography."

31. EGB, Diary entries, 6 and 7 April 1885, EGBP.

32. Balch admitted she had a "natural taste for language." During her life she added to this impressive list of languages the study of Dutch, Swedish, Polish, and Russian. EGB, Autobiographical notes.

33. William Allen, later a professor of history at the University of Wisconsin, was married to Mary Lambert Allen, the cousin of Balch's beloved "Auntie," Catherine Porter Noyes. Balch also identified the third girl in their party as Minnie Spaulding. EGB, Autobiographical notes; EGB to AB, [undated] 1885, and 12 May 1885, EGBP.

34. Dulles, "Historical View," 12.

35. EGB to FNB, [1885], EGBP; EGB, Autobiographical notes.

36. Balch's first biographer, Mercedes Randall, pointed to this experience as the key to what kept Balch "unruffled and unalarmed during the numerous 'war scares' she was destined to live through in later life." It could be further argued that the greater lesson of this threat of war centered on the value of diplomacy as well as the precarious nature of "threats." EGB, Autobiographical notes; EGB to FNB, [1885], EGBP; Randall, *Improper Bostonian*, 61.

37. EGB to AB, 12 May 1885, EGBP.

Chapter 2: "Characteristic of My Generation," 1885–96

1. Balch, "Confessions."

2. Ibid.

3. Jill Conway correctly argues this, showing that many women of Balch's age and class "could not accept conventional marriage because their minds had been trained along lines which required discipline and independent effort, and they expected to put this training to a practical use which was not to be found within the narrow confines of domestic life." "Perspectives," 7–8; regarding this generation of American women who entered college, see also Solomon, *Educated Women*.

4. Balch's papers do not contain the original diary entry indicating the possibility of Balch studying the law, but they do include her diary abstract confirming the information. EGB, Diary abstract, 17 February 1885, EGBP; EGB to AGB, 19 July 1885, ABGP.

5. The 0.24 percent figure refers specifically to women who enrolled in colleges during the 1870s. See Knight, *Citizen*, 434n53; EGB, "Change in Educational Opportunities for Women," n.d., EGBP.

6. Although this is how Balch recalled Benjamin Gould's reasoning, in truth Gould at first agreed to let his daughter attend the college in Cambridge in 1885. After some time and numerous letters between father and daughter, Gould retracted his decision, citing his concern for the toll her studying for the entrance exams had taken on his daughter's health. After Alice agreed to rest for a period, Gould eventually acquiesced and allowed her to enter Bryn Mawr the following year, 1886. Although no clear answer exists for Benjamin Gould's change in attitude toward the Harvard Annex, it did not seem to result from a fear of social recriminations for educating his daughter. More likely, the decision stemmed from what he called his disapproval of "the scheme" at the annex. That is, he objected to the fact that the college offered women the same courses as men. Benjamin Athorp Gould to ABG, 3 August 1884; see also correspondence between ABG and Benjamin Apthorp Gould, 1884–85, ABGP.

7. Mercedes Randall was highly critical of the relationship between Balch and Thomas, asserting that Balch "does not seem to have succumbed like so many of the Bryn Mawr students to the spell of Carey Thomas's sparkling and magnetic personality." She outlined the differences between them, claiming that the two "were at opposite poles. Carey Thomas admired physical beauty, Emily Balch loved also the beauty of the inner person; Carey Thomas had assurance and high spirits, Emily was inclined to be deprecatory and to lean to quietness; Carey Thomas moved at a quick, impatient pace, Emily . . . contrived an infinite leisure." Randall continued in this way, attempting to demonstrate that Balch was humble and quiet and Thomas the opposite. This shallow analysis fails to understand that the two had an important relationship. Although Thomas may not be considered a pivotal influence in Balch's young life, it was the dean's ideas on women and higher education that shaped the philosophy and culture at Bryn Mawr, ideas from which Balch greatly benefited. Further, Thomas's biographer, Helen Lefkowitz Horowitz, described how Thomas felt great affection and admiration for Balch. It was Thomas, after all, who campaigned to give Balch the first Bryn Mawr European Fellowship in 1889. Randall, *Improper Bostonian*, 64–5; Horowitz, *Power and Passion*, 241.

8. Horowitz, *Power and Passion*, 225.

9. ABS to MMR, 2 August 1962, MMRP.

10. HC to EGB, 28 February [1887 or 1888] and 5 May 1887, EGBP.

11. M. Carey Thomas to Mary Gwinn, 11 November 1887, MCTP.

12. Balch, Autobiographical notes.

13. Balch was quoting the English poet William Morris, from "Prologue of the Earthly Paradise." Balch, Autobiographical notes; Campbell, *Women Wage-Earners;* and Riis, *Other Half.*

14. Cornelia Meigs totaled the Bryn Mawr class of 1889 as twenty-four graduates. Meigs, *What Makes a College,* 52.

15. M. Carey Thomas to Mary Gwinn, n.d., MCTP.

16. Balch, Autobiographical notes; EGB to Bessie Balch, [1889], EGBP.

17. Balch, Autobiographical notes.

18. Ibid.

19. See Jean Brunhes, "Obituary: Émile Levasseur," *Geographical Journal* 38, no. 4 (October 1911), 437–39; Balch, Autobiographical notes; EGB to FVB, 25 January 1892, EGBP.

20. Balch, "Draft Autobiography."

21. Balch, Autobiographical notes.

22. Balch, *Public Assistance, 9.*

23. Ibid., 177.

24. Ibid., 9, 22–23, 41.

25. Ibid., 59, 65, 68.

26. Ibid., 75–77.

27. Ibid., 82.

28. Ibid., 90, 93–94.

29. Ibid., 118, 139–40.

30. Ibid., 158–60, 177; Balch, Autobiographical notes.

31. Balch, *Public Assistance,* 168, 174.

32. Green, "Review," 108; Foley, "Review," 677.

33. See Foley, "Review," 676–78.

34. Balch, "Draft Autobiography."

35. Balch, Autobiographical notes.

36. Ibid.

37. Balch, "Draft Autobiography."

38. See Holloran, *Boston's Wayward Children*, 56–62; and *Who Was Who in America*, s.v. "Birtwell, Charles Wesley."

39. Balch, Autobiographical notes.

40. Ibid.

41. Regarding settlement houses as Americanization efforts, see Hingham, *Strangers in the Land*, 238–39.

42. The College Settlements Association's first annual report did not name the four alumnae, but Mina Carson identified three of the four figures as Vida Scudder, Helen Rand, and Jean Fine. Carson, *Settlement Folk*, 40–41, 56; College Settlements Association, Excerpts from Annual Report, 1890, DHR.

43. Addams and others, *Philanthropy and Social Progress*. It is also interesting to note that the core subject of this summer session at the School of Applied Ethics related to the changing field of economics. Balch's academic and social interests were at the core of popular discussions about social progress in the 1890s. Balch wrote to her father from the conference that summer, stating, "Among my gains count foremost Miss Addams and perhaps Miss Coman." Both women became central figures in Balch's career. EGB to FVB, [1893], EGBP.

44. Balch, Autobiographical notes.

45. Denison House Chronology, DHR; "South End House" in Woods and Kennedy, *Handbook of Settlements*, 125; "Social Recovery," in Woods, *City Wilderness*, 258.

46. Records of the Executive Committee of Denison House, 2 October 1892; and Denison House Chronology, DHR.

47. Vida Scudder, "Early Days at Denison House," 1937, DHR.

48. "Report of the Headworker," Fall 1893, DHR.

49. The Executive Committee's "Report on Residents" for the years 1892 and 1893 confirm that Balch never resided in the house, even for a brief period (DHR; Balch, Autobiographical notes).

50. Denison House, Pamphlet, "Information to Candidates for Residence," n.d., DHR.

51. "Settlement Purposes submitted to the United Settlements of Greater Boston. An Outline from Denison House," 24 February 1940, DHR.

52. Denison House, Pamphlet, 10 August 1895, DHR.

53. Carson, *Settlement Folk*, 79.

54. Executive Committee Minutes, 23 July, 9 August, and 5 November 1895; also, 1 August and 2 September 1898, DHR.

55. EGB, Draft Manuscript for *A Heart that Held the World: An Appraisal of the Life of Helena Stuart Dudley and a Memorial to Her Work* (Boston, 1939), EGBP.

56. Executive committee minutes, 2 October 1894, DHR.

57. See Semmel, "Sir William Ashley," 343–53.

58. Little correspondence from Balch's time in Chicago exists. One letter, however, confirms that she intended to stay in Chicago for eight months (EGB to FVB, [1893], EGBP).

Small established the first Department of Sociology in the United States. In 1892, the year before Balch's arrival, the department opened at the University of Chicago. Notably, Small also studied at the University of Berlin, where Balch would next venture. Although it cannot be confirmed, it seems likely that he encouraged her to journey to Berlin for the next phase of her education.

59. See Rodgers, *Atlantic Crossings*, 86.

60. Ibid., 85; EGB to AB, [November 1895], EGBP.

61. Balch described a few of these men in a letter to her sister, carefully noting how interesting, cultivated, and attractive each was (EGB to AB, 12 October 1895, EGBP). See also Simkhovitch, *Neighborhood;* and Rodgers, *Atlantic Crossings*, 84, 85–86; Thwing, *American*, 40; and Ross, *Origins*, 55.

62. EGB to FVB, [1895], EGBP.

63. Balch, "Draft Autobiography;" EGB to family, 13 August [1895]; EGB to FVB, September [1895], EGBP.

64. EGB to FVB, 8 September 1895 and undated [1895], EGBP.

65. EGB to FNB, 15 and 29 September 1895, EGBP.

66. Balch, "An Artist of Life," 20.

67. Simkhovitch, *Neighborhood*, 39, 41–42, 46.

68. Ibid., 47, 50.

69. EGB to FNB, 29 September 1895; EGB to FVB, 22 September 1895, EGBP.

70. EGB to FVB, n.d. 1895, EGBP (emphasis in original).

71. EGB to AB, 12 October 1895, EGBP (emphasis in original).

72. Balabkins, *Not by Theory Alone*, 29.

73. Blaug, "Introduction," in Blaug, *Gustav Schmoller.*

74. Balch, "Draft Autobiography."

75. Ross, *Origins*, 173.

76. Gustav Schmoller's ideas and methods were incorporated into American scholarship by his many students. The American economist who continued Schmoller's ideas and methods in the United States was Thorstein Veblen. He described a particular aspect of Schmoller's methodology that Balch reflected throughout her scholarship, both as an economist and as a peace organizer. Veblen described the German habit of "treating a given problem from these various and shifting points of view, [which] at times gives a kaleidoscopic effect." Veblen, "Gustav Schmoller's Economics," *Quarterly Journal of Economics* 16 (November 1902): 90. Reprinted in Blaug, *Gustav Schmoller*, 1–25.

77. Balch, "Draft Autobiography.

78. EGB to FVB, February 1896, EGBP.

79. Simkhovitch, *Neighborhood*, 50; EGB to FVB, undated [1895], EGBP (emphasis in original).

80. EGB to FVB, 25 February 1896, EGBP.

81. Adolph Wagner disparaged the English style of economics, yet he also differed from Schmoller's Historical School. Wagner's views promoted policies of state socialism, and so he tended to be even more radical in his promotion of state involvement than the German Historical School. Daniel Rodgers claims that Balch's lectures as a professor at Wellesley College most reflected Wagner's ideas. While she incorporated elements of the state socialism model into her teaching, her ideas reflected a combination of her schools

of thought. EGB to FVB, 25 February 1896, EGBP (emphasis in original); Balch, "Draft Autobiography"; Rodgers, *Atlantic Crossings*, 90.

82. EGB to FVB, 26 April 1896, EGBP.

83. EGB to Unknown, unknown date [1896], EGBP.

84. Simkhovitch, *Neighborhood*, 53.

85. Balch approximated that eight hundred delegates met in London, though the *Times* (London) estimated an additional four hundred individuals in attendance. Balch, "International," 107; "The International Workers' Congress," *Times* (London), July 29, 1896; Edwards, "International Socialist Congress," 460–61 (emphasis in original).

86. Daniel Rodgers argues that the women's attendance at the congress exemplified the ideological influence of the German professors on their American students. Rodgers, *Atlantic Crossings*, 88.

87. Balch, "International," 109; *Times* (London), "The International Workers' Congress," July 29, 1896.

88. Balch, "International," 110; Edwards, "International Socialist Congress," 461.

89. Balch, "International," 112.

90. Ibid., 111, 114.

91. EGB to AB, 7 July 1896, EGBP.

Chapter 3: "Twenty Happy and Busy Years," 1896–1914

1. Balch, "Draft Autobiography," Balch, Autobiographical notes.

2. Kate Edelman to MMR, 28 May 1957, MMRP.

3. For information on American women who attended undergraduate institutions in these years, see Solomon, *Educated Women*, 62–77. In its early decades, despite financial insecurities, Wellesley College accepted only highly qualified students. See Horowitz, *Alma Mater*, 85.

4. Kate Edelman to MMR, 20 May 1957, MMRP; Horowitz, "Coming of Age," 227.

5. Si Balch (EGB's great-nephew), interview with author, January 2009; Pam Wheeler (EGB's great-niece) email to author, 28 February 2009.

6. Kate Edelman to MMR, 20 May 1957, MMRP.

7. Francis Balch's estate, divided among six siblings, presented a complicated mess for the children to sort out, and Balch felt incapable of being involved. Although Balch never mentioned the exact amount of her inheritance in her records, her father's will, dated February 27, 1896, directed his estate to pay each of his six children six hundred dollars ($15,329.39 in 2008 dollars) immediately upon his death. The bulk of the inheritance, however, existed in the form of a trust, which held most of Francis Balch's property and which paid each child a quarterly payment. The value of this payout is unknown, but we do know that the amount did not constitute enough to allow Emily to live independently without an income. EGB, Journals of Daily Activities, 29 April 1899, EGBP; FVB, will dated 27 February 1896, SBC; and Inflation Calculator, http://www.westegg.com/inflation/; EGB, Journals of Daily Activities, 20 June 1898, 1 January 1899, and 15 July 1899, EGBP.

8. Palmieri, *In Adamless Eden*, 130. One history of the college, written for its centennial anniversary, described Balch's cohort as the "radicals." See Ella Keats Whiting, "The Faculty," in *Wellesley College*, Jean Glasscock, ed., 100; Converse, *Story of Wellesley*, 121.

9. Wellesley College Board of Trustees Executive Committee Meeting Minutes, 24 January 1900, WCA.

10. Wellesley College Board of Trustees Executive Committee Meeting Minutes, 23 September 1896, 27 October 1897, 25 January 1899, 29 January 1902, 6 May 1903, 30 January 1907, and 6 May 1912, WCA; and Inflation Calculator, http://www.westegg .com/inflation/.

11. Balch, "Draft Autobiography." In her study of the faculty at Wellesley College, Patricia Palmieri also noted Balch's shift in her support of schools of economic theory and confirmed what I indicated in chapter two, that Balch's ideas and research were as equally rooted in the German historical school as the Austrian School. Palmieri wrote, "Influenced by her mentors and her work with Coman, Balch lost her initial fascination with Adam Smith and abandoned abstract economic theory for the inductive method of German historicism." Palmieri, *In Adamless Eden,* 170.

12. *Calendar of Wellesley College, 1898–99* (Boston: Frank Wood, 1898), 57; *Calendar of Wellesley College, 1896–97* (Boston: Frank Wood, 1896), 55; and *Wellesley College Calendar, 1906–07* (Boston: Frank Wood, 1906), 61.

13. Wells, *Future in America,* 175; Balch, "Hecuba," 146; and Balch, "Draft Autobiography."

14. Balch, "Draft Autobiography."

15. *Calendar of Wellesley College, 1897–98; 1903–04;* and *1906–07* (Boston: Frank Wood, 1897, 1903, 1906); See EGB, Lecture Notes, [1896–1911], EGBP.

16. Balch, "Draft Autobiography"; EGB interview by MMR (27 March 1953), MMRP; Mary A. Wyman to MMR, 1 May 1953, MMRP.

17. Wellesley College Board of Trustees Executive Committee, Minutes of Meeting, 30 January 1907, WCA; Balch, "Draft Autobiography"; *Wellesley College Calendar, 1901–02* (Boston: Frank Wood, 1901).

18. Balch, *Outline of Economics.* She revised the original 1899 edition in 1901. All citations in this work refer to the 1899 edition.

19. Balch, *Outline of Economics,* 5.

20. Ibid., 13.

21. Ibid., 12; Balch, "Economic Role," 622.

22. Balch, *Outline of Economics,* 29, 30.

23. Daniels, *Outline of Economics.*

24. Balch, *Study of Conditions.*

25. See Baldwin, Balch, and Rutan, *Strike;* Balch, "Draft Autobiography."

26. Balch, "Draft Autobiography."

27. Balch, *Our Slavic Fellow Citizens,* vii. References in this work cite the 1969 edition.

28. Ibid., 8.

29. Stolarik, "From Field to Factory," 97–98; Balch, "Draft Autobiography."

30. Balch, *Our Slavic Fellow Citizens,* 5.

31. Balch, "Draft Autobiography."

32. Balch, *Our Slavic Fellow Citizens,* vi.

33. Ibid., 10–16, 20.

34. Ibid., 28.

35. Ibid., 151, 120–22.

36. Balch, "Draft Autobiography"; Balch, *Our Slavic Fellow Citizens,* 76, 174.

37. Balch, *Our Slavic Fellow Citizens,* 87, 167.

38. Ibid., 94–95, 106.

39. Ibid., 58, 82.

40. Balch, "Draft Autobiography."

41. Balch, *Our Slavic Fellow Citizens,* 253, 280–81.

42. Ibid., 217–18.

43. Ibid., 235–39.

44. Ibid., 282, 288.

45. Ibid., 349–50, 362.

46. Ibid., 398.

47. McKenzie, "Reviewed Work," 125–26; Kelsey, "Reviewed Work," 233.

48. Balch, "Draft Autobiography."

49. College Settlements Association, Excerpts from Report, November 1891; Denison House, Report of Residents, 1897–1898, DHR.

50. Scudder, "Challenge of College Settlements," 1–2.

51. Balch, "College Settlements," 12–13.

52. Although Balch was a dedicated social reformer, she very rarely publicly espoused any political affiliation. Always an admirer of her father, a follower of Sumner's radical branch of the Republican Party, Balch likely supported the Republicans as well. She left few indications, however, and her politics were probably more issue based than party affiliated. In one instance, while she was still living abroad, she wrote to her father about the presidential election of 1896, when William McKinley defeated the populist Democrat, William Jennings Bryan, and subsequently reorganized the Republican Party. McKinley closely aligned the Republican Party with American business. The campaign, following an economic depression in the United States, focused on economic reform. Although Balch never revealed her thoughts on Bryan's free silver ideas, she showed no love for McKinley. She wrote to her father, "You say nothing of home politics. I imagine you will have to vote for McKinley. I trust there will be good scattering of gold and silver votes in the different sections and in different classes of the populations." Her letters indicate that she had seriously considered the many issues involved, though she never specifically endorsed a candidate. Her language here suggested that McKinley would be her father's choice simply due to his party affiliation. She remained vague about her own support for any particular political party. EGB to FVB, 26 July 1896, EGBP; Balch, Autobiographical notes, and "Draft Autobiography." Balch's friend, colleague, and fellow socialist Vida Scudder cited the same influences in her autobiography. See Scudder, *On Journey,* 162.

53. Balch, quoted in Randall, *Beyond Nationalism,* 50.

54. See Nutter, *Necessity of Organization,* 40; and Deutsch, *Women and the City,* 170–83.

55. EGB, "Mary Kenney O'Sullivan—In Memorial," MKOP.

56. EGB, "Mrs. Kehew" draft, n.d., EGBP. Mercedes Randall highlighted the importance of Kehew in Balch's life. She claimed, "Many of the traits which were to make Emily Balch influential in the peace movement and which she passed on to two generations of her colleagues there, she herself derived, by the contagion of respect and admiration, from Mary Morton Kehew." The two did share qualities that are immediately recognizable. They

both excelled as diplomats and organizers. Also, although Balch frequently held leadership positions, she did not necessarily aspire to them. As Kehew "preferred to be behind the scenes," Balch also quietly went about her reform work, rarely drawing undue attention to herself. Further, although Balch became an international leader and even received the Nobel Peace Prize, she never, it seems, went out of her way to be in the spotlight as did, for example, Jane Addams. Randall, *Improper Bostonian,* 115.

57. Balch, Autobiographical notes.

58. Balch, Autobiographical notes; see Henry, *Trade Union Woman,* 59–62.

59. Nutter, *Necessity of Organization,* 131, 133, 150–51.

60. Scudder, *On Journey,* 162; Balch, "Draft Autobiography"; "Well-meaning but Misguided," *Boston Daily Globe,* February 6, 1909; "Socialism and Christianity: Each Needs the Other, Prof Scudder Says," *Boston Daily Globe,* February 8, 1909. Hillquit and Berger were leaders in the right wing of the Socialist Party and Berger was the first Socialist elected to congress. Balch, "Draft Autobiography."

61. See "Organizations to which EGB Belonged," EGBP.

62. Balch, Autobiographical notes.

Chapter 4: "Tragic Interruption," 1914–19

1. Addams, *Peace and Bread,* 3.

2. *New York Evening Post,* September 30, 1914; for a discussion of how the peace movement changed after the events of 1914, see Patterson, *Search for Negotiated Peace,* 1–18.

3. Addams, *Peace and Bread,* 3; Balch, "Working for Peace," 12.

4. See Daniels, *Always a Sister,* 125–27.

5. Balch, "Working for Peace," 12.

6. EGB to MB, 8 August 1914, EGBP (emphasis in original).

7. Balch, "Working for Peace," 12; EGB to George Viereck, 9 November 1914, EGBP.

8. Lillian Wald to EGB, 22 September 1914, EGBP.

9. Ibid.

10. Paul Kellogg, "Minutes: Meeting at Nurses' Settlement," 29 September 1914, EGBP; Addams, *Peace and Bread,* 4.

11. Degen, *Women's Peace Party,* 38.

12. JA to EGB, 13 and 26 March 1915, EGBP.

13. It remains unclear how Balch financed her trip to The Hague, as she later was unable to recall how she did so, and none of her papers from the time mention these arrangements. It seems most likely that she did use a portion of her inheritance from her father (indicating how important she felt the trip was), as that was how she paid for her trip the following year to Stockholm. See "Ideas on Money and Incomes," MMR Interview with EGB, March 1954; EGB to Ellen Pendleton, 30 March 1915; Ellen Pendleton to EGB, 1 April 1915, EGBP.

14. FNB to EGB 7 April 1915, EGBP.

15. FNB to EGB, [1915], EGBP (emphasis in original).

16. International Congress of Women (ICW), *Report of First Congress, The Hague, 1915,* 3 [hereinafter, cited as *Report of First Congress*].

17. "Check Husbands at Door: Delegates to Woman's Peace Congress Hold Farewell Dinner," *New York Times,* 13 April 1915; Lochner, *Always the Unexpected,* 52.

18. EGB, 1915 Journal to The Hague, EGBP: Lochner, *Always the Unexpected,* 52.

19. Lochner, *Always the Unexpected*, 53–54.

20. EGB, 1915 Journal.

21. Ibid.

22. Emily Greene Balch, "Journey and Impressions of the Congress," in Alonso, ed., *Women at The Hague*, 6.

23. Ibid., 7.

24. Ibid., 8.

25. Emily Greene Balch, "At the Northern Capitals," in Alonso, *Women at The Hague*, 48–49; Balch, *Envoys' Interview*.

26. Quoted in Randall, *Improper Bostonian*, 167; Addams, *Peace and Bread*, 11; EGB to FNB, 16 May 1915, EGBP.

27. Balch, "At the Northern Capitals," 51.

28. Ibid., 52.

29. EGB to JA, 19 August 1915, JAC. EGB to Oswald Garrison Villiard, 28 September 1915, reprinted in Randall, *Improper Bostonian*, 199.

30. Report recorded by Rexford L. Holmes, reprinted in Lochner, *Always the Unexpected*, 55.

31. *Yearbook of the Woman's Peace Party: The Section for the United States of the International Committee of Women for Permanent Peace, 1916*, WPPP, 47, 31; see also "Mrs. H. Ford Gives $10,000 for Peace," *New York Times*, November 23, 1915; and "Pleas Flood White House," *New York Times*, November 25, 1915.

32. See Knight, *Jane Addams*, ch. 6.

33. Lochner, *Always the Unexpected*, 59.

34. Lochner, *Always the Unexpected*, 60; Addams, *Peace and Bread*, 24.

35. Lochner, *Always the Unexpected*, 60.

36. Balch, "Stockholm Conference," 141.

37. Ibid.

38. Ibid., 142.

39. Balch, "International Colonial Administration," 1916, reprinted in Randall, *Beyond Nationalism*, 87.

40. Balch, "A Plan for a Rehabilitation Fund Contributed By Neutral Countries as a Substitute for War Indemnities," 1916, reprinted in Randall, *Beyond Nationalism*, 92.

41. Lochner, *Always the Unexpected*, 64.

42. Ibid., 63.

43. Balch, "Working for Peace," 13. *Approaches to the Great Settlement* did not display any new aspects of Balch's scholarship. It was a compilation of the less publicly acknowledged perspectives on the peace settlement that emerged during the war years. It demonstrated Balch's keen abilities as an editor as well as her ongoing commitment to scholarship, even while she was a full-time activist.

44. Wilson originally asked Addams to meet with him, but he invited Balch to join them when he learned that she had returned the United States so that she could detail the proceedings for him. Woodrow Wilson to JA [telegram], 5 August 1916, EGBP.

45. The second point of the WPP platform, adopted in 1915, read that one "purpose of this organization" was the "limitation of armaments and the nationalization of their manufacture." Degen, *History*, 41.

46. *Yearbook of the Woman's Peace Party*, 31–34.

47. Crystal Eastman to EGB, 25 February 1916, AUAMP.

48. Balch, "Working for Peace," 13.

49. Ibid.

50. Frances Witherspoon to MMR, 12 October 1956, MMRP.

51. Emily Greene Balch in *Congressional Record* 55, reprinted in Randall, *Beyond Nationalism*, 98–100.

52. Balch, "Working for Peace," 13.

53. Schott, *Reconstructing Women's Thoughts*, 72. This was the lowest point in Addams's popularity. As she continued to head the Woman's Peace Party, her great reputation among Americans morphed into an image of anti-Americanism.

54. Like those in Massachusetts, many members of the WPP in other states also discontinued their public campaigns against the war and shifted their focus to supporting the troops and promoting the formation of an international organization. The New York state branch did not reelect Carrie Chapman Catt to the state board in 1917 after she declared that her suffrage organization, the National American Woman Suffrage Association, stood ready to assist the president in the war effort. Catt then immediately resigned. Degen, *History*, 211–12.

55. "War-Time Program of the American Union Against Militarism," May 1917, AUAMP.

56. Lillian Wald to Crystal Eastman, 27 August 1917; Crystal Eastman to Lillian Wald, 24 August 1917, AUAMP.

57. EGB to Crystal Eastman, 17 June 1917, AUAMP.

58. EGB to Crystal Eastman, 20 September 1917, AUAMP.

59. See Steinson, *American Women's Activism*, 267–68.

60. It must be noted that Balch later claimed that she originally joined the PCA at the urging of Oswald Garrison Villard. Having also resigned from the AUAM, Villard focused his attention on the young PCA but still worried about its potential radicalism. He informed Balch that he would continue to support the organization only if she agreed to join its ranks as a moderating force. Balch wrote, "He wanted a balance wheel of some one older and more sober than the young staff. He recognized their originality and devotion, but felt that they needed a steadying partner." It is also interesting to note that Balch explicitly pointed to her involvement with the PCA as her main offence against the Wellesley trustees. She continued, "I accepted although it was a delicate position and it entirely wrecked my position with Wellesley." EGB to Ellen Starr Brinton, 2 March 1938, EGBP.

61. Steinson, *American Women's Activism*, 275–76.

62. MB to MMR, 31 August 1959, MMRP.

63. Ethel Vaughan, Minutes from the twenty-eighth meeting of the Erin-go-Bragh, 27 December 1917. EGBR.

64. Balch, "Working for Peace," 14.

Chapter 5: "A Basis for a New Human Civilisation," 1918–29

1. There is no indication that Balch had remembered the end of her appointment before she made her decision to request her leave of absence. That information might allow us to know more certainly the extent of her dedication to the wartime peace movement. Her actions after the board's decision, however, indicated that Balch would

have remained in New York for most of the war, even though it meant a higher likelihood that the trustees would not renew her appointment. Ellen F. Pendleton to EGB, 20 March 1918, EGBP.

2. EGB to Ellen F. Pendleton, 3 April 1918, EGBP.

3. Ibid.

4. EGB to Ellen F. Pendleton, Supplementary letter, 3 April 1918; Ellen F. Pendleton to EGB, 10 April 1918, EGBP.

5. Ellen F. Pendleton to EGB, 24 April 1918; Mary Whiton Calkins to EGB, 23 April 1918, EGBP.

6. Anna Youngman to EGB, n.d. [1918]; Department of Economics to Wellesley College Board of Trustees, 29 April 1918, EGBP.

7. See "Will Advocate Law to End Propaganda: Senate Committee Investigating German Activities Soon to Submit a Report," *New York Times*, January 31, 1919.

8. EGB to Katharine Lee Bates, 8 May 1918, EGBP.

9. Balch, "Working for Peace," 14.

10. For an excellent account of the peace conference, see Macmillan, *Paris 1919*.

11. "Resolutions Adopted by the International Congress of Women at The Hague, May 1, 1915," in Alonso, *Women at The Hague*, 76.

12. The other delegates were Kate Waller Barrett, Marion Tolden Burritt, Mary Chamberlain, Marion B. Cothren, Madeleine Z. Doty, Grace Drake, Constance Drexel, Rose Morgan French, Catherine Eastman Fuller, Florence Holbrook, Alice Riggs Hunt, Lucy Biddle Lewis, Rose Standish Nichols, Lydia Lewis Rickman, Clara Savage, Mrs. Stock-Millar, Elizabeth Sweeney, Mary Church Terrell, Mrs. John Jay White, and Carolena Wood. See WILPF, *Report of the International Congress of Women: Zurich, May 12–17, 1919*, 461–562. Hereinafter, this report will be referred to as *Zurich Report*. Where no author is noted, it can be assumed that Balch acted as such, as she compiled the report.

13. For more organizing details of the congress, see Balch, Preface, in WILPF, *Zurich Report*.

14. WILPF, *Zurich Report*, 3, 16.

15. Ibid., 54–56, 60. At this point in the discussion, the covenant of the League of Nations still allowed Germany and Russia admission into the council of the League, giving them a voice in this international mechanism. In its final version, however, defeated nations were refused a seat in the League. Germany eventually joined in 1926.

16. Ibid., 69.

17. Ibid., 63.

18. Ibid., 162; Addams, *Peace and Bread*, 92.

19. WILPF, *Zurich Report*, 95–96.

20. Ibid., 97, 10.

21. Ibid., 126–27.

22. Ibid., 154. Other significant topics of conversation at the Zurich congress that are not discussed in this work included political asylum and international education. See WILPF, *Zurich Report*, 105–7, 131–35.

23. Ibid., 146.

24. The entire delegation that the congress elected to send to Paris included Jane Addams, Charlotte Despard, Gabrielle Duchêne, Rosa Genoni, Chrystal Macmillan, and Clara Ragaz. Balch was nominated, but lost; Addams, *Peace and Bread*, 93.

25. WILPF, *Zurich Report*, 242.

26. Ibid., 237.

27. The board of trustees met on April 21, 1919, and after "prolonged discussion" they failed to carry President Pendleton's motion to appoint Balch for a three-year term. Pendleton wrote to Balch on May 8 seeking confirmation of her telegrams relaying the sad news. Wellesley College Board of Trustees, Minutes of Meeting, 21 April 1919, WCA; EGB interview by MMR, March 1954, transcript, EGBP.

28. Balch, "Working for Peace," 13.

29. It appears most likely that Balch's September letter to Pendleton was originally intended for publication or wider distribution. The draft of the letter in her papers is only addressed to Pendleton, but subsequent letters refer to the September draft letter to the board of trustees, in which Balch sought advice from colleagues at the college. After much consultation, Balch dropped the pursuit of the board's response. Regardless of this letter's original intention and eventual recipients, that Balch went to the trouble to pen drafts and seek input from colleagues indicated her own outrage at the decision, one she did not calmly accept. Balch never initiated a formal investigation or charge against the trustees' action, nor did she work to bring media attention to her situation, as others in her position had done. This was partially due to her decision in May 1919 to continue to work with the Woman's International League for Peace and Freedom in a professional capacity. Mercedes Randall perpetuated Balch's claim that she calmly accepted the decision, chided herself slightly for going too far, and moved on with her life. Overlooking the subtleties in Balch's actions, however, ignores Balch's true perspective. While Randall preserves the image of Balch's "quiet, controversy-hating nature," we do not fully come to understand how skillful Balch really was at expressing her outrage. Randall, *Beyond Nationalism*, 103. EGB to Ellen F. Pendleton, 29 September 1919; see also Mary Calkins to EGB, 26 October 1919, EGBP.

30. Balch did not indicate how many years Cheever made the payments, though. EGB, interview by MMR, March 1954, EGBP.

31. The Constitution of the Women's International League for Peace in Freedom included an article regarding the international bureau, reading, "The Bureau of the League shall be established by the Executive Committee at the place where the League of Nations has its headquarters, and one or more members of the Executive Committee must always be in residence in order to conduct the business." WILPF, *Zurich Report*, 287.

32. Many international peace advocates during this period employed the term "new international order" or "new world order" to describe their vision of a postwar world. This new order was based in cooperation and interdependence. In one essay, Balch explained the "economic aspects of the new international order." She emphasized that this vision, in part, "implies the disappearance of discontent and class struggle through a growing realization of social justice in each separate country." With a broader sense of community and of shared goals, individuals in the new world order would embrace cooperation over conflict. JA to EGB, 16 October 1919, JAC; EGB, "Economic Aspects of a New International Order," in WILPF, *Fourth Congress*, 72.

33. In reality, Balch's WILPF salary was probably slightly greater than what she had received at Wellesley College. She had earned an annual salary of $2,000 during the final year for which she received payment (1916–17), and she claimed the WILPF paid her $200

per month from the WILPF. However, had the Board of Trustees reappointed her to her position, it is likely they would have increased her salary incrementally. Thus, her income from the Women's International League approximated what she would have earned from Wellesley College. JA to EGB, 16 October 1919, JAC; Wellesley College Board of Trustees, Executive Committee Meeting Minutes, 6 May 1912, WCA.

34. EGB, interview by MMR, March 1954, EGBP, http://www.westegg.com/inflation/.

35. EGB to JA, 30 September 1919 (emphasis in original); JA to EGB, 16 October 1919, JAC.

36. Balch, "Our Call," 3.

37. EGB to JA, 30 September and 13 December 1919, WILPFP.

38. The suffrage issue had plagued the American Woman's Peace Party during the war years. When the Senate ratified the Nineteenth Amendment in 1920, it seemed that these women could focus on peace, but other factors emerged to factionalize the advocates. Harriet Alonso identified four main peace groups that materialized among American women after the war: the WILPF, the Women's Peace Society, the Women's Peace Union, and Carrie Chapman Catt's National Committee on the Cause and Cure of War. Luckily, Balch's proposal that members belong to multiple organizations in order that they might retain allegiance to the WILPF seemed to work and allowed WILPF-US membership to grow during the interwar years. For more on these organizations and how they related to each other, see Alonso, *Peace as a Women's Issue*, 90–109. EGB to JA, 22 October 1919, JAC.

39. Individuals who wished to subscribe to both levels of the organization contributed "five dollars which entitle[d] them to a dollar membership in the National and four dollars for international membership fee." JA to EGB, 16 October 1919, JAC. Interestingly, the descriptions of these two forms of membership in the report of the WILPF's Third Annual Congress note that associate membership, that is membership directly with the international office, was open to both men and women. WILPF, *Third International Congress of Women, Vienna, July 10–17, 1921* (hereinafter referred to as *Vienna Report*), vi; Balch, "Our Call," 3.

40. JA to EGB, 16 October 1919, JAC. Perhaps the only campaign that rivaled famine relief for Balch's time was that of amnesty for conscientious objectors.

41. EGB to JA, 4 December 1919, JAC.

42. See Balch, "Report of Secretary-Treasurer, May 1920-July 1921," *Vienna Report*.

43. EGB to Anna Garlin Spencer, 31 December 1919, EGBP.

44. EGB to Woodrow Wilson, 9 January 1921, EGBP.

45. Balch, "Draft Autobiography."

46. Mercedes Randall argued that Balch wished to have a life of spiritual devotion, and at that time the Religious Society of Friends best met her peace politics and values. It seems plausible, also, that it was during this particular phase in her life, after the great disappointments of the war and the failure of her reappointment to Wellesley, that she felt a stronger need for a spiritual connection. There are multiple motivations for her conversion, but that she did so in 1921 is significant. It represented a decision to mark the next phase of her life, which was dominated by her work in the international peace movement, with a strong spiritual commitment. See Randall, *Improper Bostonian*, 291.

47. Balch, "Working for Peace," 14.

48. Ibid.

49. Balch, Report as Secretary-Treasurer, *Vienna Report,* 50.

50. EGB to JA, 1 November 1921, JAP. Addams, Opening Address, *Vienna Report,* 1.

51. Yella Hertzka, Address of Welcome, *Vienna Report,* 15–16.

52. EGB, Report as Secretary-Treasurer, *Vienna Report,* 50–51.

53. Catherine Marshall, "The League of Nations: Our Relation to It," *Vienna Report,* 63–64.

54. Ibid., 65: Balch, "Report of the Secretary-Treasurer, May 1920–July 1921," *Vienna Report,* 195; Second Resolution on the League of Nations, *Vienna Report,* 71.

55. Balch, "Military Use of Native Populations of Colonies," *Vienna Report,* 76.

56. *Vienna Report:* regarding Ireland, 88–94; regarding India, 95–97; regarding resolutions, 160.

57. EGB to JA, 9 November 1921, JAC.

58. Ibid. Emphasis in original.

59. JA to EGB, 16 October 1919; JA to Aletta Jacobs, 24 October 1919, JAC.

60. HC to JA, 13 November 1919, JAC.

61. JA to EGB, 27 November 1919, JAC.

62. Interestingly, in one obituary, Cheever was credited with some of the accolades that belonged to Balch. The *Boston Globe* described her as both "a founder of the Women's International League for Peace and Freedom in Geneva during World War I" and "a founder of Dennison House." Cheever acted as founder to neither of these institutions but was nevertheless integral to their work in her unending support of their actual founder, Balch. "Helen Cheever, 94, Founder of Geneva Freedom League," 5 May 1960; HC to JA, 1 February 1920, JAC.

63. EGB to JA, 19 March 1920, JAC; EGB to Friends, 8 December 1920, EGBR.

64. HC to JA, 31 March 1920, JAC.

65. Ibid.; EGB to Friends, 8 December 1920, EGBR.

66. HC to JA, 15 December 1921, JAC.

67. HC to JA, 13 September 1922, JAC.

68. EGB to JA, 17 November 1922, JAC.

69. HC to EGB, 10 March 1919 (copied by HC, 1919), EGBP.

70. EGB to AB, 9 March 1923, EGBP.

71. Ibid.

72. ABG to EGB, 1 December, n.d., EGBP. Other subjects discussed in this letter indicate that the year of authorship was most likely 1919 or 1920.

73. Regarding Boston marriages, see Faderman, *Surpassing,* 190–203; Blanche Wiesen Cook persuasively argues that historians must term such relationships "lesbian," as they were engaged in by women who chose "women to nurture and support and to create a living environment in which to work creatively and independently." Faderman disagrees, relegating the term lesbian specifically to a twentieth century framework. See Cook, "Female Support Networks and Political Activism: Lillian Wald, Crystal Eastman, Emma Goldman, Jane Addams," in Cook, *Women and Support Networks,* 20.

74. The historian Carroll Smith-Rosenberg's landmark work on nineteenth century women's friendships confirms the complexities involved in defining same-sex relationships

during this era. For the purposes of this study, it is clear enough that Balch and Cheever had a deeply loving relationship. Cheever's tremendous dedication to her friend and the amount of love and emotional and financial support she lavished on Balch suggested (as do letters from Balch's friends confirming Cheever's intensity) that Cheever's love for Balch was unrequited. Balch, "Confessions of a Professional Woman," in Smith-Rosenberg, *Disorderly Conduct, 53–76.*

75. Balch never completed this book, in which she proposed the daunting task of studying the differences and similarities between various groups of people. She gauged the interest of publishers, but when she failed to obtain a contract or significant interest, she abandoned the project to continue her work with the WILPF. As an example of the responses of publishing companies, see, H. S. Latham to EGB, 3 December 1923, EGBP.

76. JA to EGB, 20 January 1923, EGBP.

77. This is part of the subtitle to Balch, *Occupied Haiti.*

78. Ibid., v–vi; Paul H. Douglas, "The Political History of the Occupation," in Balch, *Occupied Haiti,* 20.

79. Balch, "Something of the Background," in *Occupied Haiti,* 1–2, 9; for more discussion on the American invasion of Haiti and subsequent U.S. cultural and economic dominance in that nation, see Renda, *Taking Haiti.*

80. Douglas, "Political History," in Balch, *Occupied Haiti,* 23.

81. It is believed that Franklin Delano Roosevelt, then undersecretary of the Navy, authored the new Constitution of Haiti in 1917. Interestingly, the American group found little economic incentive for American intervention in Haiti. Paul Douglas noted that there were two "sources of economic friction" between the American and Haitian governments. These concerned the National Bank of Haiti and the National Railroad Company. In both instances, the organizations wreaked economic havoc on the people of the nation, creating skyrocketing debt with little improvement in infrastructure. Despite this fact, profits for both Americans and elite Haitians did not seem remarkable. Showing that there was no great economic incentive for Americans to be involved, the committee reported, "American investments there have in general not proved a source of legitimate profits, but of loss, and there is now nothing to justify, from the selfish point of view, the continued expenditure of United States' money in administering the country." "Conclusions and Recommendations," in Balch, *Occupied Haiti,* 150; Douglas, "Political History," in Balch, *Occupied Haiti,* 25, 32, 33,

82. Balch, "Public Order," in *Occupied Haiti,* 129.

83. Balch, "Land and Living," in *Occupied Haiti,* 57, 61.

84. Balch, "Charges of Abuse in Haiti," in *Occupied Haiti,* 124, 127.

85. Charlotte Atwood, "Health and Sanitation," in Balch, *Occupied Haiti,* 86, 90, 92.

86. Zonia Baber and Emily Greene Balch, "Problems of Education," in Balch, *Occupied Haiti,* 95–96, 106–7.

87. Addie Hunton and Emily Greene Balch, "Racial Relations," in Balch, *Occupied Haiti,* 113, 114, 116–17, 120.

88. "Conclusions," in Balch, *Occupied Haiti,* 149.

89. Balch, "Social Values in Haiti," in Randall, *Beyond Nationalism,* 147.

90. Balch, "Working for Peace," 15.

Chapter 6: "The World Chose Disaster," 1930–41

1. Balch, "What of Peace Today"; Balch, "Watchman."

2. EGB, Draft of Personal History for Nobel Peace Prize, December 1945, EGBP (hereinafter cited as EGB, "Nobel History.")

3. Although the Nine Power Treaty did not incorporate any enforcement measures, its signatories, including the United States, Great Britain, France, and Italy, agreed to the principle that China's sovereignty should be protected against nations with colonial interests in its territory. EGB to Herbert Hoover, January 1932, EGBP.

4. Balch, "Memorandum on Manchuria."

5. The WILPF did convince Representative Hamilton Fish to introduce a bill forbidding the United States from providing armaments to belligerent nations. Despite its campaigns to win public opinion on the issue and its lobbying of the State Department, the American section of the WILPF failed in its efforts, and the resolution died in committee in February 1932. The following March, the newly elected President Roosevelt urged the bill's passage, but Congress refused to pass it. EGB to Herbert Hoover, January 1932, EGBP. Dorothy Detzer to Women's International League Headquarters [telegram], 12 February 1932, DDP. The American WILPF continued its campaign to end American armament sales to the region. In 1937, for example, the national office issued a press release of their public letter to President Roosevelt. In it, the leaders urged Congress to pass "a mandatory neutrality measure," and include in that a cessation of weapons sales. They highlighted that "during July, China purchased from this country $309,870 worth of war material; Japan $203,578." Women's International League for Peace and Freedom, Press Release, 17 August 1937, EGBP.

6. Balch, "Watchman."

7. See EGB, "Nobel History." It is interesting to note that in this same diary entry, Balch praised the "extraordinary legislation and psychological achievements" of President Roosevelt. EGB, Journal entry, 25 March 1933, EGBP.

8. The *New York Times* never published this letter. EGB to the Editor, 17 March 1933, EGBP.

9. EGB, "The Present Political Situation, with Special Reference to Europe," Draft, February 1935, EGBP.

10. Balch, "What of Peace Today?"

11. EGB, "Observations on a Mediated Peace in Spain," [December 1936], EGBP.

12. Ibid.

13. Ibid.

14. EGB, "A Foreign Policy for the WIL," Draft, 1935, EGBP.

15. Balch's commitment to the international body took precedence over her involvement with the national branch. For example, she opted not to attend the U.S. WILPF annual meeting in St. Louis in 1936 because the international committee demanded her attention in Europe. EGB, "The Need for Strengthening the International Work: A Report for the WILPF US Annual Meeting, 1935–1936," EGBP (emphasis in original).

16. EGB, "Foreign Policy"; WILPF International Executive Committee, "International Resolutions," Basia, January 1938, EGBP.

17. WILPF, "International Resolutions."

18. EGB, "Nobel History."

19. Ibid.

20. EGB to Isabella C. Wigglesworth, 20 April 1937, EGBP.

21. The *New York Times* reported that the amount of the Nobel Peace Prize award in 1931 totaled $40,000, which was evenly split between Addams and Dr. Murray Butler. "Nobel Peace Prize to Go to Dr. Butler and Jane Addams," December 10, 1931, http://www.westegg .com/inflation/. It should be noted that Balch's response to this letter divulged Addams's wish that, should "the WILPF be given up," the funds from her donation were to go to the Quakers. This revealed that Addams and the other leaders were fully aware of the threats posed to their organization by its internal divisions. Cor Ramondt-Hirschmann to EGB, 29 January 1932; and EGB to Cor Ramondt-Hirschmann, 11 March 1932, EGBP.

22. Kathleen Courtney, "The British Section WIL and the International WIL" undated [1932], EGBP.

23. Ibid.

24. Ibid.

25. EGB to WILPF Executive Committee, 4 March 1933, EGBP.

26. Ibid. (emphasis in original).

27. JA to Kathleen Courtney, 15 August 1932, KDCP.

28. JA to Edith Pye, 17 August 1932, KDCP.

29. EGB to Frederick Libby, 21 November 1936, EGBP.

30. Exact membership figures for the international WILPF are difficult to determine. The international leaders of the organization often failed to distinguish between international and American membership, further obscuring the data. Edith Pye to MMR, 26 June 1952, MMRP.

31. JA to EGB, 28 August 1934, EGBP.

32. Balch's papers do not suggest how she afforded a year and a half without pay. It seems most likely that, in the absence of her pension, Helen Cheever continued to support Balch financially. Family letters indicated her continued involvement in their affairs but fail to confirm the hypothesis that Cheever supported Balch until her own death.

33. See EGB to Cordell Hull, December 1934, EGBP.

34. ABS to EGB, 23 April 1935, EGBP.

35. Eleanor M. Moore to EGB, 5 June 1935, EGBP.

36. Balch, "Sketch of Jane Addams"; Balch, "From Friends," 200.

37. Balch, "Sketch of Jane Addams"

38. Balch, "What of Peace Today?"

39. Ibid.

40. Ibid.

41. Ibid.

42. EGB to Clara Ragaz, [1941], EGBP; EGB, "Nobel History."

43. Dorothy Detzer to the German ambassador, 19 December 1934, EGBP.

44. This article was published in many forms, but most likely it originated in the form of a WILPF leaflet. It was also published in multiple religious and peace magazines. Copies of different editions are located in EGBP. Mercedes Randall made the extreme claim that the widespread distribution of this particular leaflet "contributed to the liberalizing of American attitudes toward the refugee." While this cannot be substantiated, we may

assume that Balch's reputation as an immigration scholar did confer a degree of validity to her arguments. Nonetheless, the American government did not substantially alter its immigration quotas until 1965. EGB, "Refugees as Assets," 1938 (revised 1940), reprinted in Randall, *Beyond Nationalism,* 61–62.

45. EGB, "Nobel History." No scholarship currently exists analyzing the number of cases that WILPF engaged in on behalf of refugees. Often, WILPF members worked with Jewish organizations as well, and so it remains difficult to estimate its number of successes.

46. EGB to JA, 24 January 1935, EGBP, http://www.westegg.com/inflation/. Stöcker lived in the United States until her death in early 1943. See Eva Wiegelmessar to EGB, 8 May 1940, HSP; and EGB to MMR, 8 February [1943], EGBP. Edith Pye to EGB, 23 July 1940, EGBP.

47. Baer's arrival in the United States was discussed in Edith Pye to EGB, 23 July 1940, EGBP. EGB, "Nobel History."

48. Kathleen Courtney to EGB [telegram], 16 May 1939; EGB, Form letter, 16 May 1939, EGBP.

49. EGB to Ellen Starr Brinton, 6 February 1939; Ellen Starr Brinton to EGB, 29 April, 1939 (emphasis in original); Rosa Kulka to EGB, 18 May 1939 and 8 July 1940, ESBP.

50. See Irving N. Linnell to Henry Cabot Lodge Jr., 20 January 1940; and David Walsh to EGB, 11 September 1940, ESBP.

51. EGB to WILPF national sections, 13 October 1937, EGBP. When Jane Addams resigned from the position of international president of the WILPF in 1929 for health reasons, the organization set up a system in which the role of president was filled by a three-woman executive committee. This lasted until 1937, when the WILPF named Balch its next president.

52. EGB, "Nobel History."

53. Although Balch made no public declarations relating to American actions in the European war, such as the Lend-Lease program, it is likely that she strongly opposed them. She contested any action that profited one nation over another and would have disliked the United States' removing itself from a position to act as a mediator.

54. EGB to Mildred [Olmstead], 25 May 1940, EGBP.

Chapter 7: "The Things I Leave Undone," 1942–61

1. EGB, "Nobel History"; EGB to Clara Ragaz, [1941], EGBP.

2. EGB, "Nobel History."

3. EGB to Mildred [Olmstead], 19 July 1940, EGBP.

4. EGB to Clara Ragaz, [1941], EGBP (emphasis added).

5. Balch's mixed response to the Second World War undoubtedly resulted in flak within the women's international peace movement, but her conviction that the WILPF must absorb a spectrum of beliefs with regard to pacifism revealed a great deal about her character. John Herman Randall Jr., in his pamphlet on Balch, defended Balch's stance on the war, writing that her position stemmed from "the inability of even her fine-tempered and fertile mind to see how to implement that deeper and more enduring deliverance of experience, reflection and moral insight that we call 'conscience.'" Certainly, Balch's dread of fascism contributed to her tolerance of a military reaction.

Yet her reaction was, in truth, more carefully calculated. She had felt less threatened by the dangers of German militarism during the previous war and so remained committed to total opposition during that experience. Twenty years later, she worried far more intensely over the idea of a German-dominated Europe. In part, this contributed to her more comprehensive vision of peace as more than the absence of war. Randall presented Balch, albeit enveloped in unmitigated praise, as the embodiment of non-utopian pacifism, or "a realistic worker for peace." Randall's wife and fellow Balch scholar, Mercedes M. Randall, claimed in her biography that Balch herself pointed to John H. Randall's pamphlet as an accurate portrayal of her reasons for supporting (in a restricted fashion) the war. EGB, "Nobel History"; John Herman Randall Jr., *Emily Greene*, 9; see Mercedes Randall, *Improper Bostonian*, 348–49.

6. Emily Greene Balch, "Towards a Planetary Civilization," 1942, reprinted in Randall, *Beyond Nationalism*, 162–63.

7. Ibid.

8. EGB, "Nobel History."

9. John Dewey to Sir Norman Angell, 17 December 1945, MMRP.

10. "Six Americans Win Nobel Prizes, Dr. Mott and Miss Balch for Peace," *New York Times*, November 15, 1946; EGB, "Message made by EGB to be read on the day of award of Nobel Peace Prize," Draft, 10 December 1946, EGBP.

11. Quoted in Gertrud Baer, "Emily Greene Balch," *Four Lights* 6, no. 6 (1947), EGBP.

12. Ibid.

13. Balch, "Toward Human Unity"

14. Ibid.

15. EGB, Letter to the annual meeting of U.S. WILPF, 8 June 1954, EGBP.

16. Emily Greene Balch, "To the People of China," *The Christian Science Monitor* (1 March 1955): 22.

17. Emily Greene Balch, "Coexistence," *Four Lights* 14, no. 7 (January 1955).

18. Emily Greene Balch, "Harried," in Balch, *Miracle of Living*, 50.

19. ABS to MMR, 2 August 1962, MMRP.

Conclusion

1. Both quotes are based on the recollection of Hannah Hull ("Emily Greene Balch," n.d., EGBP).

2. The most insightful discussion of the integral importance of support networks to women of this generation is still Blanche Wiesen Cook's *Women and Support Networks*.

3. WILPF later published this report as a pamphlet. Emily Greene Balch, "Economic Aspects of a New International Order," in WILPF, *Report of the Fourth Congress*, 72–77.

4. EGB, "The Earth is My Home," n.d., EGBP.

5. Balch referred to this experience in an article she wrote for a Danish newspaper in 1955. See EGB, "The Era Before Us," Draft, April 1955. EGBP.

6. EGB, "Christmas, 1952," EGBP.

Bibliography

Manuscripts

Manuscript collections in which microfilm versions were utilized, either in part or in full, are denoted with an asterisk.

Alice Bache Gould Papers, Massachusetts Historical Society, Boston

Alice Bache Gould Photographs, Massachusetts Historical Society, Boston

Alumnae Bulletin, Bryn Mawr College Library, Special Collections Department, Bryn Mawr, Pennsylvania

American Union Against Militarism Records, Swarthmore College Peace Collection, Swarthmore, Pennsylvania

Anne Henrietta Martin Papers, Bancroft Library, University of California, Berkeley, California

Anti-Imperialist League Records, Swarthmore College Peace Collection, Swarthmore, Pennsylvania

Balch-Noyes Family Papers, Massachusetts Historical Society, Boston

Board of Trustees, Meeting Minutes, Wellesley College Archives, Wellesley, Massachusetts

Calendars of Wellesley College, Wellesley College Archives, Wellesley, Massachusetts

College News, Bryn Mawr College Library, Special Collections Department, Bryn Mawr, Pennsylvania

Denison House Records,* Schlesinger Library, Radcliffe Institute, Harvard University, Cambridge, Massachusetts

Dorothy Detzer Papers, Swarthmore College Peace Collection, Swarthmore, Pennsylvania

Elizabeth Glendower Evans Papers, Schlesinger Library, Radcliffe Institute, Harvard University, Cambridge, Massachusetts

Ellen Starr Brinton Papers, Swarthmore College Peace Collection, Swarthmore, Pennsylvania

Emergency Peace Federation Records, Swarthmore College Peace Collection, Swarthmore, Pennsylvania

Emily Greene Balch Papers,* Swarthmore College Peace Collection, Swarthmore, Pennsylvania

Erin-Go-Bragh Records, Schlesinger Library, Radcliffe Institute, Harvard University, Cambridge, Massachusetts

Fannie Fern Andrews Papers, Schlesinger Library, Radcliffe Institute, Harvard University, Cambridge, Massachusetts

Helene Stöcker Papers, Swarthmore College Peace Collection, Swarthmore, Pennsylvania

Jane Addams Papers,* Swarthmore College Peace Collection, Swarthmore, Pennsylvania

Kathleen D'Olier Courtney Papers, The Women's Library London Metropolitan University, England

Lella Secor Florence Papers, Swarthmore College Peace Collection, Swarthmore, Pennsylvania

Letters and Documents Collection, Special Collections Department, Bryn Mawr College Library, Bryn Mawr, Pennsylvania

Lola Maverick Lloyd Papers, Manuscripts and Archives Section, New York (City) Public Library

M. Carey Thomas Papers,* Special Collections Department, Bryn Mawr College Library, Bryn Mawr, Pennsylvania

Mary E. Dreier Papers, Schlesinger Library, Radcliffe Institute, Harvard University, Cambridge, Massachusetts

Mary K. (Mary Kingsbury) Simkhovitch Papers, Schlesinger Library, Radcliffe Institute, Harvard University, Cambridge, Massachusetts

Mercedes M. Randall Papers, Swarthmore College Peace Collection, Swarthmore, Pennsylvania

National Council for Prevention of War Records,* Swarthmore College Peace Collection, Swarthmore, Pennsylvania

People's Council of America for Democracy and Peace Records,* Swarthmore College Peace Collection, Swarthmore, Pennsylvania

People's Mandate Committee Records, Swarthmore College Peace Collection, Swarthmore, Pennsylvania

Schlesinger Library, Radcliffe Institute, Harvard University, Cambridge, Massachusetts

Women's International League for Peace and Freedom Collection,* Swarthmore College Peace Collection, Swarthmore, Pennsylvania

Periodical Sources

Boston Daily Globe
Boston Globe
New York Times
The Times (London)

Books

Abbott, Samuel W. "The Vital Statistics of Massachusetts: A Forty Years' Summary, 1856–1895" (1897). In *The Demographic History of Massachusetts,* edited by Kingsley Davis. New York: Arno Press, 1976.

Addams, Jane. *Jane Addams's Writings on Peace.* Edited by Marilyn Fischer and Judy D. Whips. Vol. 4. Bristol, England: Thoemmes Press, 2003.

———. *Peace and Bread in Time of War.* Urbana: University of Illinois Press, 2002. Original edition, New York: Macmillan, 1922.

———. *Twenty Years at Hull-House.* New York: Macmillan, 1911.

Addams, Jane, Emily G. Balch, and Alice Hamilton. *Women at The Hague: The International Congress of Women and Its Results.* Edited by Harriet Hyman Alonso. Urbana: University of Illinois Press, 2003. Original edition, New York: Macmillan, 1915.

Addams, Jane, and others. *Philanthropy and Social Progress: Seven Essays Delivered before the School of Applied Ethics at Plymouth, Mass., during the Session of 1892.* New York: Crowell, 1893.

Alonso, Harriet Hyman. *Peace as a Women's Issue: A History of the U.S. Movement for World Peace and Women's Rights.* Syracuse, N.Y.: Syracuse University Press, 1993.

Balabkins, Nicholas W. *Not by Theory Alone: The Economics of Gustav von Schmoller and Its Legacy to America.* Berlin: Duncker & Humblot, 1988.

Balch, Emily Greene. *Approaches to the Great Settlement.* Intro. by Norman Angell. New York: Huebsch/American Union Against Militarism, 1918.

———. *Miracle of Living.* New York: Island Press, 1941.

———, ed. *Occupied Haiti: Being the Report of a Committee of Six Disinterested Americans Representing Organizations Exclusively American, Who, Having Personally Studied Conditions in Haiti in 1926, Favor the Restoration of the Independence of the Negro Republic.* New York: Garland, 1972. Original edition, New York: Writers Publishing, 1927.

———. *Our Slavic Fellow Citizens.* New York: Arno Press/*New York Times,* 1969. Original edition, New York: Charities Publication Committee, 1910.

———. *Outline of Economics.* Cambridge, Mass.: Co-operative Press, 1899.

———. *Outline of Economics,* 2nd rev. ed. Cambridge, Mass.: The Co-operative Press, 1901.

———. *Public Assistance of the Poor in France.* Baltimore: Publications of the American Economic Association (8, nos. 4 and 5), 1893.

———. *A Study of Conditions of City Life with Special Reference to Boston: Bibliography.* Boston: Ellis, 1903. Reprint edition, Boston: Bliss, 1904.

Baldwin, F. Spencer, Emily G. Balch, and William L. Rutan. *The Strike of the Shoe Workers in Marlboro, Mass., November 14, 1898—May 5, 1899.* Boston: Twentieth Century Club, 1899.

Bell, Julian, ed. *We Did Not Fight: 1914–18 Experiences of War Resisters.* London: Cobden-Sanderson, 1935.

Binford, Henry C. *The First Suburbs: Residential Communities on the Boston Periphery, 1815–1860.* Chicago: University of Chicago Press, 1985.

Blaug, Mark, ed. *Gustav Schmoller (1838–1917) and Werner Sombart (1863–1941).* London: Elgar, 1992.

Brown, Victoria B. *The Education of Jane Addams.* Philadelphia: University of Pennsylvania Press, 2004.

Bruce, Brevet Lt.-Colonel George A. *The Twentieth Regiment of Massachusetts Volunteer Infantry, 1861–1865.* Boston: Houghton Mifflin, 1906.

Bussey, Gertrude, and Margaret Tims. *Pioneers for Peace: Women's International League for Peace and Freedom, 1915–1965.* Oxford: Alden, 1980.

Campbell, Helen. *Women Wage-Earners: Their Past, Their Present, and Their Future.* Boston: Roberts, 1893.

Carson, Mina. *Settlement Folk: Social Thought and the American Settlement Movement, 1885–1930.* Chicago: University of Chicago Press, 1990.

Chatfield, Charles. *The American Peace Movement: Ideals and Activism.* New York: Twayne, 1992.

———. *For Peace and Justice: Pacifism in America, 1914–1941.* Boston: Beacon, 1971.

Converse, Florence. *The Story of Wellesley.* Boston: Little, Brown, 1915.

Cook, Blanche Wiesen. *Crystal Eastman on Women and Revolution.* New York: Oxford University Press, 1978.

———. *Women and Support Networks.* New York: Out & Out, 1979.

Crunden, Robert M. *Ministers of Reform: The Progressives' Achievement in American Civilization, 1889–1920.* Urbana: University of Illinois Press, 1982.

Daniels, Doris Groshen. *Always a Sister: The Feminism of Lillian D. Wald; A Biography.* New York: Feminist Press, City University of New York, 1989.

Daniels, John. *An Outline of Economics.* Boston: Ginn, 1908.

Davis, Kingsley, ed. *The Demographic History of Massachusetts.* New York: Arno, 1976.

Degen, Marie Louise. *The History of the Woman's Peace Party.* Baltimore: Johns Hopkins University Press, 1939.

Deutsch, Sarah. *Women and the City: Gender, Space, and Power in Boston, 1870–1940.* Oxford: Oxford University Press, 2000.

Dole, Charles Fletcher. *My Eighty Years.* New York: Dutton, 1927.

Early, Frances H. *A World without War: How U.S. Feminists and Pacifists Resisted World War I.* Syracuse, N.Y.: Syracuse University Press, 1997.

Eksteins, Modris. *Rites of Spring: The Great War and the Birth of the Modern Age.* Boston: Houghton Mifflin, 1989.

Faderman, Lillian. *Surpassing the Love of Men: Romantic Friendship and Love between Women from the Renaissance to the Present.* New York: Morrow, 1981.

Foster, Carrie A. *The Women and the Warriors: The U.S. Section of the Women's International League for Peace and Freedom, 1915–1946.* Syracuse, N.Y.: Syracuse University Press, 1995.

Foster, Catherine. *Women for All Seasons: The Story of the Women's International League for Peace and Freedom.* Athens: University of Georgia Press, 1989.

Glasscock, Jean, ed. *Wellesley College 1875–1975: A Century of Women.* Wellesley, Mass.: Wellesley College, 1975.

Grubbs, Frank L. Jr. *The Struggle for Labor Loyalty: Gompers, the A.F. of L., and the Pacifists, 1917–1920.* Durham, N.C.: Duke University Press, 1968.

Haynes, George H. *Charles Sumner.* Philadelphia: Jacobs, 1909.

Heilbroner, Robert L. *The Worldly Philosophers: The Lives, Times, and Ideas of the Great Economic Thinkers*. New York: Touchstone, 1999.

Henry, Alice. *The Trade Union Woman*. New York: Franklin, 1973.

Herman, Sondra R. *Eleven against War*. California: Hoover Institution Press, 1969.

Hingham, John. *Strangers in the Land: Patterns of American Nativism, 1860–1925*. New Brunswick, N. J.: Rutgers University Press, 1955.

Holloran, Peter C. *Boston's Wayward Children: Social Services for Homeless Children, 1830–1930*. London: Associated University Presses, 1989.

Horowitz, Helen Lefkowitz. *Alma Mater: Design and Experience in the Women's Colleges from Their Nineteenth-Century Beginnings to the 1930s*. New York: Knopf, 1984.

———. *Campus Life: Undergraduate Cultures from the End of the Eighteenth Century to the Present*. Chicago: University of Chicago Press, 1987.

———. *The Power and Passion of M. Carey Thomas*. New York: Knopf, 1994.

International Congress of Women. *Report of First Congress*, The Hague, 1915. Amsterdam: International Women's Committee of Permanent Peace, 1915.

Jacobs, Aletta. *Memories: My Life as an International Leader in Health, Suffrage, and Peace*. Edited by Harriet Feinberg. Translated by Annie Wright. New York: Feminist Press, City University of New York, 1996.

Kaestle, Carl F., and Maris A Vinovskis. *Education and Social Change in Nineteenth-Century Massachusetts*. Cambridge: Cambridge University Press, 1980.

Kuczynski, Robert René. "The Fecundity of the Native and Foreign Born Population in Massachusetts." In *The Demographic History of Massachusetts*. Edited by Kingsley Davis. New York: Arno, 1976.

Kuhlman, Erika A. *Petticoats and White Feathers: Gender Conformity, Race, the Progressive Peace Movement, and the Debate over War, 1895–1919*. Westport, Conn.: Greenwood, 1997.

Knight, Louise W. *Citizen: Jane Addams and the Struggle for Democracy*. Chicago: University of Chicago Press, 2005.

———. *Jane Addams: Spirit in Action*. New York: Norton, 2010.

Lasch, Christopher. *The New Radicalism in America (1889–1963): The Intellectual as a Social Type*. New York: Norton, 1965.

Lochner, Louis P. *Always the Unexpected: A Book of Reminiscences*. New York: Macmillan, 1956.

———. *The Neutral Conference for Continuous Mediation*. Stockholm: Neutral Conference for Continuous Mediation, 1916.

Lurie, Edward. *Louis Agassiz: A Life in Science*. Chicago: University of Chicago Press, 1960.

MacMillan, Margaret. *Paris 1919: Six Months that Changed the World*. New York: Random House, 2001.

Meigs, Cornelia. *What Makes a College? A History of Bryn Mawr*. New York: Macmillan, 1956.

Nutter, Kathleen. *The Necessity of Organization: Mary Kenney O'Sullivan and Trade Unionism for Women, 1892–1912*. New York: Garland, 2000.

Palmieri, Patricia Ann. *In Adamless Eden: The Community of Women Faculty at Wellesley*. New Haven, Conn.: Yale University Press, 1995.

Patterson, David S. *The Search for Negotiated Peace: Women's Activism and Citizen Diplomacy in World War I*. New York: Routledge, 2008.

Randall, Mercedes M. *Beyond Nationalism: The Social Thought of Emily Greene Balch*. New York: Twayne, 1972.

———. *Improper Bostonian: Emily Greene Balch, Nobel Peace Laureate, 1946*. New York: Twayne, 1964.

Renda, Mary A. *Taking Haiti: Military Occupation and the Culture of U.S. Imperialism, 1915–1940*. Chapel Hill: University of North Carolina Press, 2001.

Riis, Jacob. *How the Other Half Lives*. New York: Scribner's, 1890.

Rodgers, Daniel T. *Atlantic Crossings: Social Politics in a Progressive Age*. Cambridge, Mass.: Belknap Press/Harvard University Press, 1998.

Ross, Dorothy. *The Origins of American Social Science*. Cambridge: Cambridge University Press, 1991.

Rupp, Leila. *Worlds of Women: The Making of an International Women's Movement*. Princeton, N.J.: Princeton University Press, 1997.

Schott, Linda K. *Reconstructing Women's Thoughts: The Women's International League for Peace and Freedom Before World War II*. Palo Alto, Cal.: Stanford University Press, 1997.

Scudder, Vida Dutton. *On Journey*. New York: Dutton, 1937.

———. *Socialism and Character*. Boston: Houghton Mifflin, 1912.

Seymour, Charles. *The Intimate Papers of Colonel House: Arranged as a Narrative*. Boston: Houghton Mifflin, 1926.

Simkhovitch, Mary Kingsbury. *Neighborhood: My Story of Greenwich House*. New York: Norton, 1938.

Sklar, Kathryn Kish. *Florence Kelley & the Nation's Work: The Rise of Women's Political Culture, 1830–1900*. New Haven, Conn.: Yale University Press, 1995.

Smith-Rosenberg, Carroll. *Disorderly Conduct: Visions of Gender in Victorian America*. New York: Oxford University Press, 1985.

Snowden, Mrs. Philip [Ethel]. *A Political Pilgrim in Europe*. New York: Doran, 1920.

Solomon, Barbara Miller. *In the Company of Educated Women: A History of Women and Higher Education in America*. New Haven, Conn.: Yale University Press, 1985.

Steinson, Barbara J. *American Women's Activism in World War I*. New York: Garland, 1982.

Stowe, William W. *Going Abroad: European Travel in Nineteenth Century American Culture*. Princeton, N.J.: Princeton University Press, 1994.

Swanwick, H. M. *I Have Been Young*. London: Gollancz, 1935.

Thwing, Charles Franklin. *The American and the German University: One Hundred Years of History*. New York: Macmillan, 1928.

von Hoffman, Alexander. *Local Attachments: The Making of an American Urban Neighborhood, 1850–1920*. Baltimore: Johns Hopkins University Press, 1994.

Warner, Sam Bass Jr. *Province of Reason*. Cambridge, Mass.: Belknap Press/Harvard University Press, 1984.

———. *Streetcar Suburbs*. Cambridge, Mass.: Harvard University Press and MIT Press, 1962.

Wells, H. G. *The Future in America: A Search after Realities*. London: Granville, 1987.

Who Was Who in America Historical Volume 1607–1896, rev. ed. United States: Marquis, 1967.

Women's International League for Peace and Freedom (WILPF). *Report of the Fifth Congress of the Women's International League for Peace and Freedom: Dublin, July 8 to 15, 1926.* Geneva: WILPF, 1927.

———. *Report of the Fourth Congress of the Women's International League for Peace and Freedom: Washington, May 1 to 7, 1924.* Geneva: WILPF, 1925.

———. *Report of the International Congress of Women: Zurich, May 12 to 17, 1919.* Geneva: WILPF, 1920.

———. *Report of the Third International Congress of Women: Vienna, July 10–17, 1921.* Geneva: WILPF, 1922.

Woods, Robert A., ed. *The City Wilderness: A Settlement Study by Residents and Associates of the South End House.* Boston: Houghton Mifflin, 1898. Reprint edition, New York: Arno, 1970.

Woods, Robert A., and Albert J. Kennedy, eds. *Handbook of Settlements.* New York: Arno, 1970. Original edition, New York: Sage, 1911.

Articles

Balch, Emily Greene. "An Artist of Life." *Christian Science Monitor,* December 3, 1951.

———. "A Sketch of Jane Addams' Work for Peace." *Pax International* 10 (May-June 1935).

———. "College Settlements and the Opportunity to Gain Social Intelligence." *Wellesley College News,* February 1915.

———. "The Economic Role of the Housewife." *Home Progress,* September 1914.

———. "The Education and Efficiency of Women." *Annals of the Academy of Political Science* 1 (1910).

———. "From Friends in the International League." *Unity* 115, no. 10 (1935).

———. "International Socialist Workers' and Trade Union Congress." *Lincoln House Review* 2, no. 1 (November 1896).

———. "Memorandum on Manchuria." EGBP (1932).

———. "Our Call." *Bulletin of the WILPF.* Geneva: Women's International League for Peace and Freedom, February 1922.

———. "The Stockholm Conference." *New Republic,* September 9, 1916.

———. "The Time to Make Peace." *Survey* 35 (October 2, 1915).

———. "To the People of China." *Christian Science Monitor,* March 1, 1955.

———. "Watchman, What of the Night?" Unpublished manuscript. EGBP (June 1936).

———. "What of Peace Today?" Draft of Wellesley College Armistice Day Address. EGBP (1935).

———. "'What's Hecuba to Me or I to Hecuba'; or, Thoughts on the Text of Mr. Wells' Impressions of Wellesley College." *Wellesley Magazine* 15 (January 1, 1907).

———. "Working for Peace." *Bryn Mawr Alumnae Bulletin* 13, no. 5 (May 1933).

Ballantyne, Edith. "WILPF History: Past, Present, Future." *Peace and Freedom* March 22, 2004.

Conway, Jill. "Perspectives on the History of Women's Education in the United States." *History of Education Quarterly* 14, no. 1 (Spring 1974).

Dulles, Foster Rhea. "A Historical View of Americans Abroad." *Annals of the American Academy of Political and Social Science* 368 (November 1966).

Edwards, Clem. "International Socialist Congress." *Economic Journal* 6, no. 23 (September 1896).

Foley, Caroline A. "Review of *Public Assistance of the Poor in France* by Emily Greene Balch." *Economic Journal* 3, no. 12 (December 1893).

Green, David I. "Review of *Public Assistance of the Poor in France* by Emily Greene Balch." *Annals of the American Academy of Political and Social Science*, 5 (July 1894).

Horowitz, Ruth Sapin. "Coming of Age at Wellesley." *Menorah Journal*, 38, no. 2.

Johnson, R. A. "'Russians at the Gates of India'? Planning the Defence of India, 1885–1900." *Journal of Military History* 67, no. 3 (July 2003).

Kelsey, Carl. "Reviewed Work: *Our Slavic Fellow Citizens.*" *Annals of the American Academy of Political and Social Science* 37, no. 1 (January 1911).

Lloyd, Robin. "Emily Greene Balch and Haiti." *Peace and Freedom,* March 22, 2004.

McKenzie, F. A. "Reviewed Work: *Our Slavic Fellow Citizens.*" *American Journal of Sociology,* July 1911.

Scudder, Vida D. "The Challenge of College Settlements." *Wellesley College News,* December 1945.

Semmel, Bernard. "Sir William Ashley as 'Socialist of the Chair.'" *Economica,* New Series, vol. 24, no. 96 (November 1957).

Stolarik, M. Mark. "From Field to Factory: The Historiography of Slovak Immigration to the United States." *International Migration Review* 10, no. 1 (Spring 1976).

Miscellaneous

Balch, Emily Greene. Autobiographical notes. EGBP (undated).

———. "Confessions of a Professional Woman." Unpublished manuscript. EGBP (undated).

———. "Draft Autobiography." Unpublished manuscript. EGBP.

———. "Observations on a Mediated Peace in Spain." Draft manuscript. EGBP ([December, 1936]).

———. *Report of the Envoys' Interview with Sazonov.* Women's International League for Peace and Freedom. WILPFP: June 16, 1915.

———. "Toward Human Unity, or Beyond Nationalism." Reprinted in *From Megaphones to Microphones: Speeches of American Women, 1920–1960,* ed. Sandra J. Sarkela, Susan Mallon Ross, and Margaret A. Lowe, 243–49. Connecticut: Praeger, 2003.

Balch, Francis V. "An Oration delivered before the Class of 1859, June 24, 1859." Boston: Mudge, 1860.

Giddings, Franklin H. "Americanism in War and in Peace." First Lecture on the Carroll Davidson Wright Memorial Lectureship, May 1, 1917. Worcester, Mass.: Clark University Press, 1917.

Randall, John Herman Jr. *Emily Greene Balch of New England, Citizen of the World.* Pamphlet. Philadelphia: Women's International League for Peace and Freedom, 1946.

Index

KRISTEN E. GWINN is a visiting scholar in the history
department at Northwestern University. She has contributed
to the *Encyclopedia of Activism and Social Justice* and was
an editorial fellow for *The Eleanor Roosevelt Papers:
The Human Rights Years, 1945–1948.*

The University of Illinois Press
is a founding member of the
Association of American University Presses.

———————————————————

Composed in 10.5/13 Minion Pro
with Minion Pro display
by Celia Shapland
at the University of Illinois Press
Manufactured by Thomson-Shore, Inc.

University of Illinois Press
1325 South Oak Street
Champaign, IL 61820-6903
www.press.uillinois.edu